Kenya's Running Women

Kenya's Running Women

A History

Michelle M. Sikes

MICHIGAN STATE UNIVERSITY PRESS | *East Lansing*

Michigan State University Press
East Lansing, Michigan 48823-5245

Library of Congress Cataloging-in-Publication Data
Names: Sikes, Michelle, author.
Title: Kenya's running women : a history / Michelle M. Sikes.
Description: East Lansing : Michigan State University Press, 2023. |
Series: African history and culture | Includes bibliographical references and index.
Identifiers: LCCN 2023001810 | ISBN 9781611864809 (cloth) | ISBN 9781611864816 (paperback) |
ISBN 9781609177492 | ISBN 9781628955149
Subjects: LCSH: Women runners—Kenya—History.
Classification: LCC GV1061.23.K4 S55 2023 | DDC 796.42082—dc23/eng/20230117
LC record available at https://lccn.loc.gov/2023001810

Cover design by Shaun Allshouse, www.shaunallshouse.com
Cover art is A Kenyan marathon runner training in the city of Iten.
Photo from kovop, with permission from Shutterstock.

Visit Michigan State University Press at *www.msupress.org*

Contents

Acknowledgments

This book owes its existence to the love and support I have received from a community that stretches from Oxford, England, to Iten, Kenya, to State College, Pennsylvania. I am particularly grateful to the women who graciously shared their time, experiences, and insights. They provided a level of detail without which this book could not have been written. I am also indebted to the many who provided guidance, encouragement, and hospitality in Kenya as well as access to documents and archives. Thank you to my friend and guide, Godfrey Kiprotich, for his humor and endless support, who was introduced to me by Tom Ratcliffe whose friendship and insights were invaluable. To Ray and Doreen Meynink, for their hospitality in Nairobi and Ben Maiyo, for essential help with transportation. To Bruce and Sue Tulloh, whose counsel shaped my running experience in Kenya. Thank you to Anniel Njoka for meticulously compiling articles from *The Nation* and to Winnie Jebet for translating the Kalenjin language. To the librarians at the Kenya National Archives in Nairobi, the Rift Valley Provincial Archives in Nakuru, and the Bodleian Library of Commonwealth and African Studies at Rhodes House Library in Oxford, thank you for unfailing patience and creative research suggestions.

Thank you to the entire Michigan State University Press team and particularly Peter Alegi, Caitlin Tyler-Richards, and Anastasia Wraight. I will always be grateful for their editorial brilliance and advocacy of this project. I am also grateful to the anonymous reviewers whose excellent feedback greatly strengthened the manuscript.

I would like to thank the Rhodes Trust, Beit Fund, and Lincoln College, Oxford, as well as the Center for the Study of Sports in Society, the Department of Kinesiology, and the African Studies Program at Penn State for essential financial support. Spending one semester as a Penn State Humanities Institute Faculty Scholar in Residence afforded me time to revise this book. My gratitude extends to John Christman, Director of the Institute, and Associate Director Lauren Kooistra who nurtured a collegial and intellectually enriching environment.

I greatly benefited from sharing this work with colleagues at meetings of the African Studies Association, the African Studies Association of the United Kingdom, the Association for the Study of the Middle East and Africa, the British Society of Sport History, the North American Society for Sport History, and Sports Africa Network. I also appreciate all those involved with workshops and seminars at which I presented early drafts: the Economic and Social History seminar at Oxford, the African and Gender History Research Seminar at the University of Reading convened by Heike Schmidt, the African History graduate workshop at Oxford led by the late Jan-Georg Deutsch, the Historical Studies departmental research seminar at the University of Cape Town, the Center for the Study of Sport in Society research seminar at Penn State convened by Mark Dyreson, and the Penn State Humanities Institute seminar series.

This book could not have been completed without the support that I have received at Penn State. Heartfelt thanks to my heads of department, Bill Dewey, Sinfree Makoni, Cheryl Sterling, and Nancy Williams, for their unfailing encouragement. In the Department of Kinesiology, my colleagues in the History and Philosophy of Sport, Mark Dyreson, Javi Lopez Frias, and Jaime Schultz, helped to shape many of the themes explored in this book. I cherish their intellectual support and friendship. In the Kinesiology Department, particular thanks to Sadhna Agrawal, Lacy Alexander, Sara Banker, Jonna Belanger, Melissa Bopp, John Challis, David Conroy, Mary Jane De Souza, Jon Dingwell, Danielle Downs, Katie Dry, Michele Duffey, Bob Eckhardt, Lori Gravish Hurtack, Larry Kenney, Mark Latash, Devon McChesney, Beth Oberdick, Jim Pawelczyk, Steve Piazza, David Proctor, Jonas Rubenson, Bob Sainburg, Tarkeshwar Singh, and Mary Waechter. In the African Studies Program, I am grateful to Clemente Abrokwaa, Gabeba Baderoon, Busi Makoni, Richard Mbih, Kidane Mengisteab, Abderrahim Ouarghidi, Bronwen Powell, Edwin Sabuhoro,

Segun Soetan, and Lauren Taylor. I have been fortunate to work with outstanding undergraduate and graduate students, including Zach Bigalke, Aaron Bonsu, Ann Cook, Mike Delayo, Jake Fredericks, Cam Mallett, Eden Mekonen, Rachel Park, and Taliah Powers. Special thanks to Jake, who digitized a trove of materials, for his meticulous research assistance.

I am grateful to my colleagues in the British Society of Sport History and the North American Society for Sport History. I appreciate the generous insights and helpful critiques from the following collaborators and journal and book editors: Cat Ariail, John Bale, Heather Dichter, Mark Dyreson, Robert Edelman, Russell Field, Janice Forsyth, Grant Jarvie, Rob Lake, Matt Llewellyn, Malcolm MacLean, Christine O'Bonsawin, Christian Ostermann, Murray Phillips, Toby Rider, Greg Ryan, Fiona Skillen, Jaime Schultz, Dave Wiggins, and Christopher Young. Thank you to the Sports Africa Network, especially Gerard Akindes, Simon Akindes, Anima Adjepong, Peter Alegi, Susann Baller, Chris Bolsmann, Matt Carotenuto, Derek Catsam, Todd Cleveland, Itamar Dubinsky, Mari Haugaa Engh, Tyler Fleming, Sean Jacobs, Tarminder Kaur, Matt Kirwin, Lorna Kimaiyo, Bose Maposa, Dawson McCall, John Nauright, Claire Nicolas, Papa Owusu-Kwarteng, Martha Saavedra, and Chepchirchir Tirop. This book emerged in dialogue with these scholars and many others whose research inspires me, including John Aerni-Flessner, Nina Berman, Laura Fair, Kara Moskowitz, and Paul Ocobock. Thank you to Brett Shadle, who offered thoughtful feedback, and to David Anderson, who read an early draft of this book and provided invaluable advice.

Thank you to the friends who kept me accountable during regular writing sessions throughout the pandemic and beyond: Adam Berg, Abigail Celis, Colleen English, Chris Heaney, Andy Linden, Jackie Maher, Lindsay Parks Pieper, and Dain TePoel. Their comradery, generous advice, and conversation sustained me and enlivened work on this project. To other friends who have enriched my life immeasurably: Jen Agans, Sunny Bai, Alexander Betts, Caitlin Chrisman, Alicia Decker, Ed Goodman, Anne Heffernan, Anthony Hotson, Emily Kerr, Rouven Kunstmann, Emma Lochery, Cassandra Mark-Thiesen, Moritz Mihatsch, Khumisho Moguerane, Caitlin Mullarkey, Oliver Murphy, Wiebke Nissen, Michelle and Greg Osborn, Daniel Pascoe, Ashley Schroeder, Tanya Sen, Jillian Snyder, Jill Stupiansky, Anna Sullivan, and Kathleen Vongsathorn.

To my first academic mentors Nic Cheeseman, Jan-Georg Deutsch, and Deb Oxley, whose teaching, writing and research, not to mention warmth and humanity, travel with me each day. Finally, I thank my brother, Roger, who believed I would finish. Among this wonderful group, I must single out three people: my husband, Liam Goldsworthy, and Bob and Bonnie Sikes. Thank you. Liam, Mom, and Dad, I love you, and this is for you.

Introduction

"From obscurity, she emerged as a heroine," declared the Kenyan *Daily Nation* in July 1996 after Pauline Konga won silver in the 5000 meters event at the Atlanta Olympics, becoming the first Kenyan woman to win an Olympic medal. Konga had qualified for the team by winning the Kenyan Olympic Trials and running 15:00.4 at altitude.[1] That time placed her fifteenth in the world at the 5000-meters distance, making her a longshot to win a medal. "Nobody gave Konga a chance of making it to the final," noted the *Daily Nation*. Yet in that race she asserted herself, moving to the front after five laps and leading the field until she was overtaken in the final lap by world 10,000 meters record-holder Wang Junxia of China. The Kenyan press applauded her "determined" front running, noting that she approached each lap with "eyes wide open . . . while Junxia gritted her teeth to keep up the pace."[2] Mary Chege, head of the Kenya Amateur Athletics Association women's subcommittee, congratulated Kenya's "wonder girl" for her historic achievement, stating that Konga's historic silver medal had "opened a new chapter for Kenyan women athletes."[3] Since her Olympic breakthrough, the world has become accustomed to seeing Kenyan women amass medals at major championships, sweep marathons, and set world records.

Kenya's Running Women explores the roots of Konga's "wonder girl" performance, a history that stretches back several decades. The book assembles accounts of individuals from the pioneer generation of internationally competitive female runners who in the 1960s began to challenge the many barriers before them and successfully engage in a pursuit monopolized by men. It examines the difficulties they encountered and the strategies they devised to participate and ultimately excel on the world stage, thus building the foundation used by later generations of Kenyan women who have established dominance in long-distance running.

Konga's silver was one of 113 Olympic medals won by Kenyans through 2020 since Wilson Kiprugut took the bronze medal in the 800 meters at the Tokyo games of 1964. They and their Ethiopian arch-rivals regularly dominate international cross-country competitions and the world's most prestigious marathons. Athletes born in East Africa recorded eighteen of the twenty fastest women's marathon times and all of the men's top-twenty marathon times in 2021.[4] "Considering that running, and in particular long-distance running, is the most universal, accessible, and widely practiced sport in the world, it is remarkable that one tiny corner of the planet can dominate it so thoroughly," observes Adharanand Finn, author of *Running with the Kenyans: Discovering the Secrets of the Fastest People on Earth.*[5]

Training camps in Kenya's Rift Valley highlands attract runners and researchers from around the world, seeking to emulate and understand the success of Kenyan athletes (there is no magic, according to Kipchoge Keino, legendary winner of two gold and two silver medals at the 1968 and 1972 Olympics, just high altitude, nearly perfect year-round climate, and hard work). Among the notable popular and scholarly books that look at East African runners' extraordinary success are John Bale and Joe Sang's *Kenyan Running: Movement Culture, Geography and Global Change*, Ed Ceasar's *Two Hours: The Quest to Run the Impossible Marathon*, Michael Crawley's *Out of Thin Air: Running Wisdom and Magic from Above the Clouds in Ethiopia*, Finn's *Running with the Kenyans*, Tim Judah's *Bikila: Ethiopia's Barefoot Olympian*, Paul Rambali's *Barefoot Runner: The Life of Marathon Champion Abebe Bikila*, and Toby Tanser's *Train Hard, Win Easy: The Kenyan Way* as well as his *More Fire*, along with Dave Prokop's edited collection *The African Running Revolution* and Yannis Pitsiladis and colleagues' widely ranging anthology, *East African Running: Towards a Cross-Disciplinary Perspective.*[6]

Despite the many popular and scholarly efforts to unravel the recipe for Kenyan runners' exceptional record, few have paid attention to female runners. Instead, the experience of male athletes has come to serve as the normative reference point.[7] Sport geographers Bale and Sang went so far as to claim in *Kenyan Running* that "women athletes have not been mentioned simply because they were not significantly involved."[8] The editors of *East African Running* fall into a similar trap, and note in their introduction, "There is little [in this book] that deals with issues of gender."[9] The accomplishments of Kenya's running women in the twentieth century were considerable, however, and included participation at all Olympic, Commonwealth, and All Africa Games to which Kenya sent a team from 1965 onward and even an Olympic medal.

This book is dedicated entirely to Kenya's running women. To my knowledge, it is the first academic monograph to focus on the history of any women's sport in Africa. By taking a woman-centered approach to Kenyan running history, it also seeks to provide a more complete examination of how gender informed Kenyan track and field than its predecessors. This is accomplished in three ways. First, the book retrieves the gendered experience of Kenyan athletics from the periphery of African history and sport history. Second, it shares the perspective of the ground-breaking women themselves. Through interviews these women explain why and how they pursued athletics despite the difficulties they faced. Finally, the book looks at how evolving ideas about female athleticism at the international level spawned changes within local communities and the nation.

A central contention of the book is that sport history should not be relegated to the margins and that it is in fact an important component of a nation's story. In 2006, anthropologist Bea Vidacs surmised that Africanists had given the topic of sport little serious attention because it appears "trivial, light, without consequence and not on a par with the grave problems the continent faces from poverty and corruption . . . in short, underdevelopment."[10] Yet people often see sport as a way out of poverty. Many find in it a source of hope and inspiration, which has been highlighted in research on basketball and boxing in American communities, baseball in the Dominican Republic, football (soccer) in Brazil, Liberia, and Cameroon, and basketball in Senegal and Trinidad and Tobago.[11] To Olympic gold medalist Meseret Defar, "Ethiopia is not just about famine and drought—I want the world to see strong women clutching the Ethiopian flag in stadiums all over the world."[12]

Studying sport in African history should also be of interest to scholars because of its scale and significant presence in people's lives. Steve Bloomfield, author of *Africa United: How Football Explains* Africa, observes, "Everywhere I've travelled—from the beaches of Freetown to the streets of Mogadishu—people have been playing football. They don't even need a proper football; a bundle of plastic bags and rags tied together into a roughly spherical shape is enough."[13] In Kenya, people crowded around televisions and radios on back-to-back days in 2019 to witness Eliud Kipchoge and Brigid Kosgei record the fastest men's and women's marathons ever run. For legions of fans and Olympic Games hopefuls, running represents a passion and a source of pride. Girls and boys engage in races and avidly follow the fortunes of the best runners in the Diamond League athletics circuit, the Olympic Games, the major world marathons, and other international events. Running has become so integral a part of Kenyan culture that when Mombasa hosted the World Cross-Country Championships in 2007, the governing body Athletics Kenya promoted the event with the slogan "Cross Country Comes Home." According to one report, "Tens and tens of thousands of people, many of them packed body to body between a barbwire fence, others hanging out of trees, many not able to see any of the racing at all except for a torso here and there, packed the Mombasa golf course in excruciating heat and humidity to witness 'cross country come home' to its birthplace of Kenya."[14]

Applying cultural anthropologist Karin Barber's argument that the arts merit serious scholarly attention because "they loudly proclaim their own importance in the lives of large numbers of African people," we find that sport, too, illuminates important aspects of the societies in which they take root and "communicate all kinds of meanings."[15] For historians Emmanuel Akyeampong and Charles Ambler, taking seriously sport and leisure "offers an opportunity to capture the historical texture of everyday life."[16] Analysis of the social dimensions and history of African sport and games thus becomes an investigation into the workings of societies as a whole.

This specific history of Kenyan women runners adds to our understanding about Kenya as a nation by joining a long history of Kenyan women reshaping the parameters of acceptable female conduct. It also adds to studies of sportswomen around the world who fought for access to the full range of athletic opportunities enjoyed by men. Finally, by examining the lives of the sports-oriented early achievers who hailed from a range of geographies and communities, this study moves beyond what historian Paul Ocobock describes as the "ethnicization of Kenya's past," which "has produced a history of Kenya as a sum of its ethnic parts, rather than a history of the whole."[17] He calls for scholars to create "a shared history of Kenya."[18] Studying gender and sport offers an effective means to achieve that goal.

Beyond reconstructing Kenyan women runners' rise to international stardom, this book argues that sport became a vehicle for expanding the boundaries of acceptable female behavior. Kenyan women were dynamic actors in the history of track and field who traveled the world, served their country, won athletic international accolades, and demonstrated a wider vision of what women could achieve than many people advocated at the time. *Kenya's Running Women* charts how the sport of running was established in Kenya, how athletes gained power, and how women were able to tap into that power. Concentrating on the extraordinary stories of Kenya's early international running women brings nuance to our understanding of the history of Kenya's phenomenal running program. It also shows how ideas about gender and sport have been co-constructed, understood and changed over time. In making this argument, the book makes a case that women should be incorporated into the history of African sport, as well as sport history into the study of Africa.[19]

A Brief Introduction to Sport in Africa

From track and field to rugby to soccer, many of today's most popular sports originated in Britain in the nineteenth century while imperialists steeped in these pastimes were fanning across the African continent.[20] These sports were core components of British school and military training and became a bridge for interaction between European and African men, as historians including James Mangan, Michael Gennaro, and André Odendaal have documented.[21] Missionaries informed by "muscular Christianity"—a Victorian-era term for energetic, masculine, Christian activism—mobilized sport to inculcate values of fair play, discipline, and teamwork and to teach proper comportment.[22] Sport historian Markku Hokkanen observes that in colonial Malawi, missionaries believed that sport would "civilize" the peoples they sought to evangelize.[23] Educators in the Gold Coast (Ghana), Tanganyika (Tanzania), and South Africa similarly sought to inculcate the British games ethos in their African students, attempting to inscribe gendered values around sport and masculinity.[24] Colonial administrators shared these values and supported their advancement, as historian Laura Fair demonstrates in the context of Zanzibar and this text will show for Kenya.[25]

Initially, scholars portrayed the arrival and development of colonial sport in Africa as simply an extension of Western sport culture. However, works such as Peter Alegi's *Laduma! Soccer, Politics and Society in South Africa* and Nuno Domingos's *Football and Colonialism: Body and Popular Culture in Urban Mozambique* undermine these Western-centered interpretations by emphasizing how local people both embraced and resisted these new sporting initiatives.[26] Following in their steps, this book demonstrates that the historically masculine character of Kenyan running emerged through the compatibility of colonial and existing local gendered cultures of running. The first chapter describes the colonial officers, teachers, military leaders, and clergy who shaped the culture of Kenyan running according to principles and codes of behavior that largely excluded women. It then reveals how this template was compatible with pre-existing divisions in society where men traveled long distances in pursuit of cattle, among other endurance-based activities, to support their families. A focus on the exclusion of women shows the masculine character of track and field in colonial Kenya was not only an extension of Western sport culture but also emerged as the product of both imperial and Indigenous cultures of running.

The explosive success of male Kenyan athletes that began in the 1960s brought worldwide attention to the newly independent nation. Olympic champions became symbols of national pride, their achievements providing a vehicle for their nation to assert full membership and a measure of gravitas in the international community. Elsewhere, many other African leaders employed their peoples' most popular pastime, football, to garner international validation and promote national identity, as scholars such as Paul Darby and Hikabwa Chipande have demonstrated.[27] Historian of sport Mark Dyreson explains, "More than any other modern institution with the exception of war, sport provides the necessary conditions for the patriotic bonds that bind citizen to citizen."[28]

Stadiums came to serve a similar role at this time. In Kenya, new constructions included Uhuru (independence) Stadium, a venue built in Nairobi that could seat forty thousand people.[29] Also during this era of decolonization, Accra and Lusaka both named new, impressively large sporting venues "Independence Stadium."[30] The 5 July Stadium in Algiers, Algeria, and the 28 September Stadium in Conakry, Guinea, memorialized each nation's respective date of independence. Arenas have been dedicated to the politicians who led their nations to independence, such as Félix Houphouët-Boigny Stadium in Abidjan, Ivory Coast. As historian Katrin Bromber observes, Emperor Haile Selassie of Ethiopia laid the foundation stone for the stadium in Addis Ababa that would take his name and remains the capital's most important sports venue.[31] These stadiums conveyed an image of state power and became "almost sacred ground for the creation and performance of national identities," according to historian Peter Alegi.[32]

The growth and popularity of African sport made it a platform with a "peculiar ability . . . to unite as well as divide," in the words of historian Phyllis Martin.[33] Football clubs across the continent fostered ethnic divisions, such as in Ghana, where the game has long been politicized, with the heated rivalry between the two biggest clubs, Accra Hearts of Oak and the Kumasi Asante Kotoko, reflecting divisions by ethnicity, geography, and party affiliation that burst into open conflict in the early 1960s and resulted in riots, property damage, and even lives lost.[34] "Football can be a mobilizing force for all those involved—players, spectators, supporters, and organizers—and this can go far beyond any direct control by political authorities," emphasize scholars of African sport Susann Baller and Martha Saavedra.[35] Teams in Kenya's Premier League similarly served as politically charged symbols within the country's fraught ethnic geography. Matches that pitted ethnic rivals drew large crowds, such as when the AFC Leopards played Gor Mahia, teams rooted in, respectively, Luhya and Luo ethnic identities, as football expert Wycliffe W. Simiyu Njororai shows in his work on the enduring rivalry between two of the oldest and most successful clubs in Kenya.[36] Through the play and performance of team sports fandom, communities inscribed their culture, observe Kenyan sport scholars Solomon Waliaula and Joseph Basil Okong'o.[37]

Decisions by individual athletes also affected national unity. Liberian international football star George Weah buoyed fellow citizens amid civil war when he became the first player from the continent to be named the Fédération Internationale de Football Association (FIFA) World Player of the Year.[38] Similarly, white South African Mark Fish became a symbol of reconciliation when he excelled during his nation's transition to democratic rule in the early 1990s. Sport scholars Chris Bolsmann and Andrew Parker argue that his exceptional athleticism and "racial cross-over qualities" won Fish immense popularity, wealth, and fame, fanned by the embrace of sport for racial harmony by the government and President Nelson Mandela himself.[39]

Adding to this growing body of work on sport in newly-independent African nations, the second chapter focuses on the hitherto unexamined case of Diana Monks, a white, Kenyan-born sprinter who won her nation's first medal in women's track and field at a major international meet when she claimed a silver at the 1965 All Africa Games. Two years later, the lengthy suspension levied on Monks for her failure to participate at an important track and field competition spawned debate among journalists, government officials, citizens, and athletes on topics of national loyalty, race relations, athletes' rights, and the advancement of women in sport. Monks's ban stood in stark contrast to the punishments, or lack thereof, that male athletes guilty of similar offenses received. Her case exemplifies how expectations about loyalty to the newly formed nation played out in the realm of sport. As many scholars of gender and women in African history have demonstrated previously, Monks's gender reveals additional dynamics and limitations regarding a government's expectations of its citizens.[40]

The next two chapters turn attention to the small group of internationally competitive female Kenyan runners who emerged between the late 1960s and mid-1980s. The book refers to these years as the "fragile period" in Kenya, when the vast majority of accomplished girls exited the sport prematurely and only a handful of women competed at the international level. Chapter 3 shows how during this time, female athletes became increasingly involved but continued to lag behind men in both opportunity and accomplishment. Girls were competing but failing to continue with sport into adulthood, while male runners flourished and became sources of national pride. Those who persisted in sport as wives and mothers often faced considerable familial and community hostility. Chapter 4 explores the international sports scene, showing that while Kenyan men took full advantage of invitations to compete abroad as well as athletic scholarships available in the United States, women were limited to domestic competitions, thereby curbing their opportunities to compete at a high level.

Women athletes elsewhere on the continent were similarly underserved. As sport scholars including Cynthia Pelak, Mari Haugaa Engh, and Jennifer Hargreaves describe, when South African women began competing in soccer, their participation was trivialized or devalued, and their matches were often a sidebar to the marquee events played by professional male teams.[41] Racial inequalities also created enormous disparities, limiting access to training facilities, coaching, and resources. In post-apartheid South Africa, national leaders prioritized racial integration ahead of building gender equality. Many scholars have argued for the promotion of women to sport leadership positions but historically few have held such roles, as Denise Jones shows for South Africa, Chuka Onwumechili for Nigeria, and Claire Nicolas for the Ivory Coast.[42]

Childbirth, childcare, and cultural norms imposed other constraints. Focusing on the East African context, anthropologist Hannah Borenstein shows that many Ethiopian female runners find the competing demands of childbirth and competitive running largely incompatible.[43] Renowned Kenyan track and field athlete and scholar Jepkorir Rose Chepyator-Thomson navigated similar issues in the 1970s. In a chapter on African women's sport, she speaks to the challenges she faced as a mother attempting to compete against younger, childless women.[44] Scholars Prisca Massao and Kari Fasting observe that Tanzanian women's continued participation in sport after marriage depended on familial and spousal support, and that "most women cease their sporting career either on marriage or giving birth" and wives who continued confront "conflict stemming from both the sports structure and their families."[45]

At the global level, the International Olympic Committee (IOC) for much of the twentieth century restricted women to sprints and middle-distance track events based on the belief that women's bodies were not strong enough to endure long-distance races. The rollout of distance events for women at the Olympics and other major competitions was incremental and slow, limiting opportunities for them to excel in the endurance events where Kenyan men enjoyed the most success.[46] It was not until the 1980s that the program of men's and women's Olympic track events almost reached parity. These new events created competitive opportunities that previous generations of women never had, an expansion that coincided with the reluctant embrace by the international track and field governing body of fully professional sport.[47]

As chapters 3 and 4 detail, despite the obstacles that Kenyan sportswomen faced during this "fragile period," a small group achieved international success in track and field. Female athletes typically gained exposure to the sport through formal schooling. Some gained entry as soldiers, police officers, and employees of other traditionally male government institutions that encouraged athletic development. Choosing to delay marriage or refuse it outright facilitated their ascent as runners. These women left home, secured waged employment, and established alternative lifestyles demonstrating that women could flourish within masculine domains. The professionalization of running that began in the 1980s and intensified in the 1990s created unprecedented opportunities for women runners, allowing the best among them to create new spaces for themselves and negotiate new roles as community patrons.

Chapter 5 concentrates on that first group of female Kenyan runners who established themselves as professional athletes. The wealth they earned empowered the most successful among them to replicate behaviors typical of men, thereby achieving civic virtue through the sharing of that wealth with families and community.[48] Similar to earlier scholarship that looked at how some Kenyan women adopted prototypically male behavior through an established practice whereby they became "female husbands" after marrying a wife and were widely regarded socially as males, the pioneers of women's professional running in Kenya demonstrated similar adaptability.[49] Some returned home from the international circuit to share prize money with local communities. In a society where men of means were expected to provide for those in their care, successful female runners who supported their communities earned respect for their adherence to an older moral economy whereby the prosperous gained status from such actions.[50] These women paid homage to the mores of their communities while meaningfully challenging the gender constraints that they faced. Professional sport and the roles they played in the local economy offered a way for these women to expand how people perceived respectable female conduct. The lives of running women reveal the structure of gender relations in postcolonial Kenya and show how sport became a vehicle for expanding the boundaries of acceptable female behavior.

In making these arguments, this book contributes to a long legacy of historians of Kenya exploring how women navigate various forms of authority to find new avenues of power. In the *Politics of the Womb*, historian Lynn Thomas uses reproduction and the female body to explore colonial engagement with gender relations and the long-standing custom of female initiation.[51] Her analysis, in conjunction with Luise White's work on prostitution, Kenda Mutongi's observations of widowhood in Maragoli, and Tabitha Kanogo's analysis of the female experience during the colonial period frame Kenyan history through the politics of reproduction and the tactics women used to maintain agency.[52] These scholars show how women found ways to access male-dominated spaces, often by exploiting gendered margins and applying older cultural norms in new ways. At independence, although the new regime "signified little political or economic change" for women, as historian Kara Moskowitz emphasizes, noting the "patriarchal structure of early independent Kenya" that limited women's personal autonomy and access to land ownership and control of family finances, some women, including Kenya's first female member of parliament, and the first woman to serve as Mayor of Kisumu, Grace Onyango, nevertheless ascended to positions of political authority.[53] Historian Kathleen Sheldon stresses the value that studying such women's lives adds to our understanding of African history, declaring that "the inclusion of topics such as marriage, motherhood, women's work, and women as religious and political leaders establishes the reality that knowledge of women's history is essential to making sense of African history more broadly."[54] Critical to that endeavor is inclusion of women's sport.

Methodology and Sources

My interest in the history of Kenya's running women began with my own experiences as a runner. I first competed in track and field in middle school in a suburb just outside Cleveland, Ohio. In high school, I qualified for two Footlocker National Cross-country Championships, a highly selective competition for US high school runners. Winning multiple state championships and becoming a high school All-American in cross-country and track opened the door to an athletics scholarship from Wake Forest University in Winston-Salem, North Carolina, where I competed under the supervision of Coach Annie Bennett, at the time one of very few women to direct both the men's and women's cross-country and track and field programs at a Division I university. This athletics scholarship fully funded my undergraduate degree and afforded the opportunity to travel to competitions across the United States and compete against the top collegiate runners in the nation, which included athletes born and raised in Kenya. Winning an NCAA Division I national championship in the 5000 meters in a meet record time, earning all-American honors in track and cross-country, and qualifying for the US Olympic Trials contributed to a sponsorship by Nike to compete professionally while undertaking graduate work in history.

My continued interest in the sport of track and field, and curiosity about the history of women's running in a nation renowned for its distance runners, led me to undertake this study. I began by pursuing evidence of women's running in British archives, ethnographies written during the colonial period, and microfilmed newspapers of the Kenyan press. I then consulted archives in Nairobi before interviewing the trailblazers of Kenyan women's running—while also training at Lornah Kiplagat's High Altitude Training Center in the village of Iten in the Rift Valley highlands, a renowned hub of distance running, for several months. The network of relationships that I had formed through competition was essential for the research undertaken for this project, providing a measure of credibility as well as a bond derived from shared experience. I was one of three women to represent the United States in the 5000 meters at the 2007 World Athletics Championships held in Osaka, Japan, and also raced in the Diamond League (then known as the Golden League), the world's most competitive circuit of track and field meets. These experiences were helpful in building camaraderie with women who shared an understanding of competing and training at a high level. Sharing the video of the 2007 NCAA Division I 5000 meters championship race featuring my narrow victory over future Kenyan Olympian Sally Kipyego, who grew up in the Eldoret area, provoked warm and animated conversation.

In addition to personal interest, a major impetus for this project was to retrieve the gendered experience of Kenyan runners from the margins of African and sport history. The British colonial administration created an extensive and detailed trail of progress reports and correspondence, many of which can now be found in archives across Kenya and the United Kingdom. The Kenya National Archives in Nairobi, the Rift Valley Province archives in Nakuru, District archives in Iten and Eldoret, and Rhodes House Library in Oxford are the primary source locations of official documents consulted for this book. However, within these historical records there is no cohesive archive pertaining to African women in sport.

The challenge for the historian interested in women's sport is thus to ferret insights from documents that were intended for other purposes. To take one example, early ethnographers detailed the social, cultural, and political arrangements they observed, thereby providing a glimpse of people's physical activity and movement cultures at the onset of the colonial period. Colonial administrator Jack H. Driberg, who lived in British East Africa from 1912 to 1925, noted that people "generally conceded that women have a power of endurance equaling, if not exceeding, that of men," but their responsibilities precluded "going far afield for long periods, whereas men are subject to no such constraints."[55] Activities organized by gender informed broader movement cultures, and such texts allow us to observe the local conditions that helped to shape later forms of sport, including track and field. None of these documents were written with sport or women's physical activity in mind. Focusing on women—even when they are absent—expands our understanding of sport in Kenya and African history more generally.

The major daily English-language Kenyan newspapers, *The Standard* and *The Nation*, were extensively consulted; however, often their coverage of women runners focused on their absence from competition. Interviews with leading female athletes regularly invoked questions of why Kenya's sportswomen were not "keeping pace" with the men. The *Weekly Review* magazine that covered the major political and economic issues of the day and the East Africa edition of *Drum* occasionally discussed women runners, underscoring the importance of sport to the state. While men's sport predominated the pages of the *Sports Review, Sports Gazette,* and *Sportsworld*—Kenyan-based publications dedicated to athletics—they also occasionally shed some light on female athletes' experiences. Kenyan women's general interest magazines, such as *True Love, Trust,* and *Viva*, were surprisingly valuable chroniclers of women in sport. These periodicals regularly published essays on the achievements of Kenyan female runners.[56]

Because Kenyan women's running is not a well-documented history, the oral testimonies of athletes, coaches, agents, and journalists provided essential contributions to this book. Interviews with Kenya's early running women shed light on their experiences which have been neglected in traditional documentary sources. Their testimonies helped me to better understand the central place that female athletes have occupied in making Kenyan sport history. Although I was a cultural "outsider," my history with running ultimately rendered me a fellow track and field "insider" and created a level of trust. Godfrey Kiprotich was a critical connection made through running and indispensable to these discussions. A resident in the Eldoret area and a former world-class runner, his knowledge and extensive connections among the runners, together with a reservoir of goodwill from the wider community, opened many opportunities for personal interviews. I first became acquainted with Godfrey at races in the United States prior to traveling to Kenya for this project. This connection and many others were established through my manager, Tom Ratcliffe, whose company, KIMbia Athletics, has represented Kenyan runners for more than thirty years.

I greatly admire the accomplishments of Kenya's female athletes, and I am truly grateful to the many people who shared a part of their history with me. *Kenya's Running Women* brings overdue focus on and credit to these pioneer female runners who were late arrivals to athletics. One of the primary goals of this book is to add the experiences of Kenya's first internationally competitive running women to the historical record, and to make the case for the importance of studying their engagement with athletics for histories of sport and African history more broadly. By fusing local case studies with international sporting history over the course of the twentieth century, this book shows how these early achievers and their successors used running as a vehicle for expanding the boundaries of acceptable female behavior.

CHAPTER ONE

The Gendered Development of Athletics in Colonial Kenya

Warriors, Raiders, and Gentleman Amateurs

By the middle of the twentieth century, an organized structure of women's track and field (athletics) competitions in Kenya did not yet exist. Only after all-male Kenyan teams debuted at the 1954 Empire and Commonwealth Games and at the 1956 Olympic games did the Kenya Amateur Athletic Association (KAAA) finally add discussion of women's competitions to its agenda. Sport administrators then organized the first women's provincial track and field championships in 1958. At the Rift Valley Provincial Championships held that year in Kapsabet, women from Baringo District achieved what one district officer termed a "Feminine Hat Trick," which meant finishing first and second in every event.[1] They would advance no further, however, as the first colony-wide Women's Athletics Championship was not held until the following year.

By contrast, six Baringo men emerged from the 1958 Rift Valley Provincial Championships to represent the province at the national championships. Four were selected to join the Kenyan team competing at the East African Championships against neighboring Uganda and Tanganyika (Tanzania). Of these men, Bartonjo Rotich joined nine other Kenyan track and field athletes who competed at the 1958 Empire and Commonwealth Games held in Cardiff, Wales, where he won one of the first medals for Kenya at a major international games.[2] In the waning years of the colonial period, just before the first conference convened in London to establish the constitution that would guide Kenyans to independence, a sense of urgency regarding women's track and field finally appeared in 1960, when KAAA secretary Archie Evans, writing to all provincial associations, declared the governing body "anxious that the women's championships in its second year should be supported and hoped that many athletes from the various provinces would be encouraged to attend the meeting."[3] By independence in 1963, women had yet to compete in a track and field competition outside of Kenya.

An exclusive male culture of track and field had been consolidated under British rule. Nineteenth-century ideas about athletics and masculinity in which men monopolized the increasingly organized world of sport remained intact for much of the colonial period in Kenya. Educators encouraged playing sport because of its professed ability to discipline and to civilize boys and young men. Colonial officers and administrators also enthusiastically promoted athletics and introduced a running culture among men in Kenya congruent with experiences shared in Britain. They shaped policies and institutions reflective of a gender regime apparent at the highest levels of international sport resistant to women's involvement as competitors or decision-makers. Athletics in colonial Kenya divided men by race in the absence of women.

Nevertheless, British colonial influence was not the only cause of unequal access to power and resources in sport. Scholar Dorothy Hodgson has argued that gender relations in East Africa emerged from a "historically particular constellation of interactions" involving both British norms and previously existing ideas and practices.[4] Her insight is germane to the form that track and field ultimately assumed in Kenya. The male-dominated character of Kenyan athletics was not simply imposed. The masculine character of Kenyan running emerged by way of the fusion and general compatibility of British colonial institutions with existing local practices. Both sets of movement cultures shaped the gendered character of Kenyan track and field in its formative years.

Gentlemen Amateurs and the "Games Revolution"

In addition to the electric telegraph, railways, and steamships, many of today's most popular sports were introduced to the world by nineteenth-century Britain. Historian Richard Holt notes that "while modern sport was not precisely invented during the years from the 1850s to 1880s, this was the period in which sport began to differ from earlier, traditional forms in important respects."[5] A burgeoning British middle class drove the popularity that games and sport increasingly enjoyed. Higher income levels and more time for leisure enabled greater participation in recreational activities and new sports. Games previously played in a local or impromptu manner came under the auspices of national and international governing bodies with participants following a single set of official rules.[6] Team games played by men, notably soccer (football) and rugby, rose to prominence.[7] In 1880 the final of the Football Association Cup tournament attracted six thousand fans. Not twenty years later, in 1899, a crowd of almost seventy-four thousand gathered to watch that same event.[8] During the same period, upper-class pursuits such as golf, rowing, and tennis grew by number of participants and spectators to attain the status of sport.[9] Participation in such sports demarcated as the preserve of the privileged revealed one's position in the Victorian social hierarchy. As historian Eric Hobsbawm notes, "the new invention of sport" demonstrated membership in a certain social class.[10]

Nineteenth-century British track and field concretized these class differences. The origin of the sport can be traced to competitions first held between Oxford and Cambridge universities in 1864 and to the founding of the all-men's Amateur Athletic Club (AAC) for Oxbridge students in 1866. Track and field clubs proliferated, and organized competitions pegged running, jumping, and throwing events to specific parameters amid a wider push for classification and systematization. By the end of the century, the sport had been institutionalized under the official umbrella of amateur athletics.[11] Britain's Amateur Athletic Association (AAA) and its "fervently anti-professional" upper-middle-class leaders attempted to shield the sport from participation by working-class competitors.[12] If an athlete accepted financial remuneration for competing, a lifetime ban could result.[13] This policy emulated the practices of the Oxbridge AAC, which barred both manual laborers and monetary compensation in all events. Historian John Lowerson explains that this arrangement arose from the suspicion that working-class men's "muscularity" would give them an edge.[14]

The nation that birthed the sport of athletics did not produce the first women's national track and field association. That honor went to other European nations in which women's athletics clubs were established and international competitions for women held beginning in the 1910s. A small group of female British track and field athletes first participated in formal international events starting with the 1921 and 1922 Women's Olympiad in Monte Carlo and in Brussels, respectively, and they competed at the inaugural Women's Olympic Games of 1922 in Paris.[15] The British Women's Amateur Athletics Association (WAAA) was established in 1922, but it took until 1926 for a resistant AAA to recognize the WAAA as exclusively in charge of women's track and field, and until 1932 to agree that permits for all women's events should be issued solely by the WAAA. The White City Stadium in London, the main venue for the most important men's university meets, did not include women's competitions until 1934, largely due to opposition from the AAA.[16]

Opposition to participation by British women in track and field continued throughout much of the first half of the twentieth century. Attitudes differed between those involved at the club level, where many of the developments leading to the eventual emergence of British women's athletics were located, and those who governed national and international athletics, such as the AAA and the IOC.[17] University sports days acquainted women in higher education with track and field, starting with Manchester University's organization of women's intervarsity events in 1921. The program included the 100 yards, 120-yard hurdles, half-mile, mile, high jump, and long jump.[18] However, as late as 1938, just 2 percent of nineteen-year-old female Britons were enrolled full-time in universities, limiting the possible exposure to track and field that women could attain by way of collegiate sport.[19] The London School Athletic Association (LSAA) organized boys' athletics competitions from 1900, while participation for girls there began in 1921. Boys enjoyed a full program, but girls were initially restricted to 100-yard races and relays because of concerns about the risk of injury and that they may overextend themselves. Despite increasing evidence that competitive running was not harmful for female athletes, entrenched resistance to girls' athletics in British education remained resilient. As late as 1951, the Schools Athletic Association (SAA) recommended that races for girls not exceed 150 meters.[20]

This was the milieu in which many of the future leaders of track and field in colonial Kenya were raised. The self-conscious "manliness" associated with competitive sport in boys' schools was particularly pronounced in team games such as cricket and rugby that became prominent in the curricula of the prestigious boarding schools including Eton, Harrow, and Marlborough that produced many colonial administrators. Guided by principles most famously expressed in the 1851 publication *Tom Brown's School Days*, an early distillation of the moral significance of competitive sport in boys' education, leading educationalists extolled the inherent virtue of athletics and saw it as a useful tool in education to build moral and upright Christian gentlemen.[21] Noting the often-repeated claim that the Battle of Waterloo had been won on the playing-fields of Eton, Hobsbawm describes how from the mid-nineteenth century, these elite public schools elaborated the "games-dominated Tory imperialism which was to remain characteristic of them."[22] For sport historian James Mangan, "the public schoolboy learnt *inter alia* the basic tools of imperial command: courage, endurance, control and self-control and principally did so on the sports field."[23]

The fervor of the imperial endeavor and the rise of the British public school system contributed to a sense of morality that imbued the nineteenth-century games revolution. Muscular Christianity emerged as a doctrine in which the values of the games revolution joined with the civilizing mission of Christianity and colonial education to become a valuable tool for the furtherance of empire.[24] The British regarded sport and empire as mutually reinforcing, gendered structures with a higher moral purpose. To the region that would become known as Kenya, by then assured of their civilizing authority, a legion of colonial administrators and missionaries brought with them the belief that sport forged a strong moral character in young men.

Segregated Sport in Colonial Kenya

One of the most famous Muscular Christians in Kenya was Church of Scotland Mission (CSM) leader Dr. John Arthur. Football represented the "stylized epitome of a moral order and the metaphoric essence of a cultured civilization," he observed in 1909. The "Great Football Match" that year between two CSM teams involved twenty-two Kikuyu boys. In his report about the game, Arthur noted the rise of "the playing-fields of sport, in which manliness, courage and unselfishness shall add their quota to the formation of Christian character."[25] While winning was welcomed, the primary function of the match was to impart the positive qualities of discipline, respect, and honor to Kikuyu boys. The emergence of loosely organized track and field competitions began at least as early as 1906, also under the influence of Christian missions. In his study of the antecedents to Kenyan men's distance running success, sport geographer John Bale describes these early events as "more like junior school sports with events like obstacle and sack racing."[26] Historian of Kenya Tom Cunningham similarly emphasizes the informality of mission sport in the early part of the twentieth century in his examination of the CSM's attempt to use games to "uplift" the peoples of central Kenya.[27]

The "civilizing mission" and the strategies used for its achievements were, however, secondary to the ultimate goal that the colony be self-sustaining and that enough wealth be extracted to justify the venture. This effort can be traced to the onset of the colonial period in Kenya, when in the wake of the collapse of the Imperial British East African Company in the late nineteenth century, Britain declared a protectorate over the territory between Uganda and the coast.[28] The ambitious decision to construct a railway from Mombasa to Uganda exacerbated the challenge of attaining financial solvency.[29] Reducing a three-month journey to only three days, the "Lunatic Line" finally finished in 1901 cost Britain dearly.[30] The government was forced to generate sufficient income to repay this large debt while still visibly ruling in the interests of colonized Kenyan peoples.[31]

Their solution to the burdensome debt obligation was to encourage Europeans to immigrate to Kenya to establish a "White Man's Colony" in which settlers gained private control of the most fertile land. The promise of land and cheap labor attracted nearly three thousand white settlers to Kenya by 1905, most living in the fertile and temperate highlands.[32] Westernized cash-crop agriculture was expected to achieve economic growth and self-sufficiency and clashed with the colonial state's declared duty to protect and benefit local populations. In 1923 the British government affirmed the principle that African interests must be paramount but even then, the Devonshire declaration was hedged with conditions that in practice left room for settler supremacy. When these dual mandates conflicted, the interests of the white settlers generally took priority.[33] Nor were British taxpayers expected to pay for the cost of colonial infrastructure, which was as much as possible to be borne by colonized peoples. Requiring cash payments of taxes in conjunction with banning Indigenous people from exporting profitable crops such as coffee over time essentially forced the local population into the monetized economy and the employ of white settlers for whom labor was a constant necessity. Institutionalized price-fixing, unfair competition, and job reservations prevented African enterprises from emerging as an economic threat. These settlers made sustained efforts to insulate and defend their interests within a colonial power structure that denied African access to the most productive lands, provisioned education along racial lines, and maintained a color bar that transcended every dimension of Kenyan social, political, and economic life.[34]

Sport was no exception. White settlers established exclusive sports clubs throughout the colony that provided a vibrant social life across a range of activities. As one woman recalled about the significance of the Mombasa Sports Club to the

European community, "For those of us who were brought up in Mombasa, the Sports Club was the recognized gathering place from childhood to marriage, parenthood and beyond. When we were young and unattached, there was squash and tennis to play, cricket, rugby and soccer to watch, dances and general merrymaking."[35] Each community typically built a club house, golf course, swimming pool, and tennis and squash courts. The excellent facilities associated with these clubs were available to Europeans only. Clubs were also masculine spaces to which women gained access through their husbands but were denied membership in their own right.[36] Workers from South Asia who arrived at the turn of the century similarly brought their own sporting cultures. As a prosperous business class evolved among them, they established clubs and facilities, chiefly for field hockey, cricket, tennis, and badminton, membership of which was generally restricted to people of that community and sometimes to those of the same caste or religion. The army, police forces, and mission schools encouraged Western sport among African men.[37]

Formal track and field meets began to be held in the 1920s that were absent women and set European and Asian athletes apart from African competitors. In 1924, director of education James Orr formed the Arab and African Sports Association (A&ASA).[38] The A&ASA's leadership was drawn from male members of the colonial elite, including Governor of Kenya Sir Robert Coryndon and his deputy Sir Edward Denham, who served as A&ASA President. Their mandate was to "foster, encourage and control all Arab and African sports organisations and athletics meetings in the colony."[39] Prominent leaders from the settler community as well as the police, army, schools, and churches organized national "Olympic" meetings in which Arab and African athletes competed among themselves.[40] Track and field competitions evolved into a pyramidal system of local, district, provincial, and colony championships based on the British model. District and Community Development Officers promoted the sport through the strength of their ties at the local level while the Colony Sports Officer concentrated on the territorial level, training athletes for colony competitions and later for Olympic and Commonwealth Games. Christian missions continued to promote track and field events during sports days. Competition between schools was encouraged, and government and mission schools added athletics to their curricula to teach students discipline and the virtue of playing fairly and by rules that closely adhered to the ethos of Muscular Christianity. Institutions such as the police, the prisons, and the military, known as the King's African Rifles (KAR), supported the involvement of African servicemen in track and field.[41]

The mutual satisfaction derived from participation in sport proved helpful for maintaining a sense of mutual purpose between colonizer and colonized. As historian Sydney Hall observes about communication between African peoples and British administrators in Kenya in the early decades of the twentieth century, "sports and games served as a language that everyone understood."[42] That shared understanding, however, rested on Indigenous sensibilities that gave rise to distinctly gendered movement cultures prior to the arrival of British sport evangelists that nonetheless operated harmoniously with the historically masculine orientation of Western athletics. As the next section shows, the cultural elements that shaped the introduction of Western forms of running in Kenya did so in the absence of women.

The focus of this section falls on the Kalenjin peoples whose runners have enjoyed disproportionate success at the international level. A 2014 study that tabulated male track runners' results in events from the 800 meters upwards at all major global athletics championships in the fifty years between 1964 and 2013 as well as the annual top twenty-five world marathon performances since 1990 found that the extraordinary success of Kenyan distance runners had been largely driven by the Kalenjin.[43] One of more than forty identifiable ethnic groups in Kenya and accounting for 12 percent of the total Kenyan population, male Kalenjin runners have won more accolades from international athletics than have athletes from the rest of the country combined. Kalenjin men led Kenya to eighteen straight world cross-country team championships beginning in 1986 onwards, a streak broken by Ethiopia only in 2004.[44] Sport scholar John Manners calculates that for eight of the twelve world titles they won between 1986 and 1997, noting "If only the Kalenjin runners had competed, they would still have taken the team title. I contend that this record marks the greatest geographical concentration of achievement in the annals of sport."[45]

Understanding the historic running cultures of Kalenjin peoples in the early twentieth century relies on reports by ethnographers and colonial administrators stationed in the Rift Valley, where the Kalenjin constitute the principal population and from which one can assume some continuity with earlier times.[46] These static accounts exemplify what anthropologist Jane Guyer calls the "jural model"—a sterile portrayal of peoples' lives with little mention of the ambiguity, contingencies, and conflict inevitably present.[47] Such accounts generally offer little explicit discussion of the games, contests, and play that existed, focusing instead on the documentation of customs, rituals, politics, and kinship structures of Rift Valley communities.[48] These reports can nevertheless shed light on local "movement cultures of running," a phrase coined by sport geographers John Bale and Joe Sang to refer to the configurations of basic bodily movements that make up the repertoire of track and field.[49] The movement cultures of running observed by early colonists were entirely gendered activities.

Movement Cultures of Running

Early ethnographers, administrators, and missionaries praised the stamina of men who covered long distances across the Rift Valley with seemingly little effort. Anthropologist Ian Orchardson who from 1910 spent nineteen years living among the Kipsigis, the most populous of the Kalenjin peoples, observed that men might travel for days or weeks at a time in search of water and pasture for their cattle and that "the men's endurance on the march and ability to go for long periods without food and without complaint [were] remarkable."[50] "It does not take a Nandi long to travel twenty miles," remarked George W. B. Huntingford, an ethnographer and school headmaster who lived in the Rift Valley highlands from 1921 to 1940.[51] Writing in the 1930s about the Tugen, another Kalenjin subgroup, Baringo District Officer R.O. Hennings confirmed, "The young men of Masop, in the High Country, spend many days of their lives on long foot journeys, across the grasslands and the hills, to see their family cattle."[52]

Most of the peoples known today as the Kalenjin lived within one-hundred miles of Eldoret at the time of their first contact with British colonialism, practiced similar customs, and spoke broadly the same language albeit in different dialects. Upon marriage, women left their birth home and integrated into their husband's community. Families lived in homesteads consisting of the husband with one or more wives, each of whom presided over her household and children. A constellation of families combined to help each other, forming a *kokwet* overseen by a council of elders. No chiefs existed in these communities until they were initiated by the British according to the imperatives of indirect rule. Power and influence were stratified by age, wealth, and gender, such that older women and men, especially those with large herds and families, were accorded more rights and greater respect.[53]

Kalenjin children played a variety of games in the early years of the twentieth century. Historians Benjamin Kipkorir and Joseph Ssennyonga describe traditional Marakwet games played prior to the introduction of Western forms of athletics, noting that running was "a game or sport for boys which at times involves girls."[54]

Boys were taught to graze cattle in fields far from home, use weapons, and other classically male activities. Girls learned about cooking, cultivating, and gathering crops, caring for younger siblings and other domestic duties. Initiation rituals that marked the transition to adulthood for boys emphasized physical fitness. Historian Paul Ocobock describes the ritual succeeding initiation among the Kipsigis, whereby boys were secluded with elder instructors who taught them the code of adult male behavior, including preparation for physical combat.[55] Kipkorir similarly observes about his own society that Marakwet boys took part in rigorous physical exercise and supervised fighting during the educational portion of their initiation.[56] In his account of Keiyo initiation, D. K. Kiprono notes that "incessant war with other tribes required a fighting force of tremendous fitness. During initiation, each man's capacity for endurance was tested to its limit. They could now be trusted with the ultimate test of war, in which they might have to march for days without food before coming suddenly upon the enemy."[57]

Along with martial matters, cattle were integral to many of the male-dominated movement cultures of running that preceded and extended into the colonial period. Representations of wealth, given as gifts or loans, or even returned as punishment for crimes, cattle were of great importance to many communities and remain so today. Highly valued by all members of a household, for men they were necessary assets for their full participation in the social and political life of the community and were a prerequisite for marriage, as a father received stock from a suitor to solidify bonds between families and to compensate for the loss of his daughter's labor. "Livestock reproduced, and thus were uniquely suited to bridewealth," notes historian Luise White.[58]

Raiding cattle held by neighboring communities offered men the means to acquire wealth, and that enterprise demanded physical fitness. Elders selected warriors based on dependability, past raiding successes, strategic thinking, and speed. Scouts traveled stealthily on reconnaissance missions into neighboring groups' territories. Once cattle were captured, the fastest men drove them home. Raids could cover hundreds of kilometers and often, the original owners would follow in pursuit.[59] The persistence of cattle raiding throughout the early twentieth century greatly concerned the colonial administration. Officers came to regard the practice of stealing cattle from neighboring groups as endemic and considered the Kalenjin peoples to be among the most frequent offenders. Manners describes a campaign in the 1930s designed to curtail the practice, in which the colonial administration employed a slogan that translated means "Show your valour in sport and games, not in war."[60] One Rift Valley Provincial Commissioner noted, "Stock theft is the traditional sport of the young men of many tribes," to which historian David Anderson adds, "If cattle theft by Africans in colonial Kenya was thought of as a 'young man's sport' by European settlers and administrators, then the young men of the Kalenjin in Kenya's Western Highlands were undoubtedly the sport's most enthusiastic participants."[61]

Powerful incentives drew men to the enterprise, including the high regard in which people held successful raiders. "No warrior was worthy of his name unless he had distinguished himself in one of these raids," notes Nandi historian Samuel K. arap Ngeny.[62] Posted to Keiyo in the Rift Valley in 1922, District Commissioner J. A. Massam observed that "warriors were always on the alert to repel raiding parties foraging for stock; and if things were quiet, they were ever ready to make forays themselves whenever opportunity seemed to offer plenty of plunder with little fighting."[63] Huntingford commented that "the life they normally lead requires men to be fit in order to survive it."[64]

By adulthood, utilitarian functions that involved long-distance endurance activities were almost exclusively the province of men. Historian Albert T. Matson, who was stationed in colonial Kenya as a health inspector for almost twenty years after the Second World War, observed about the Nandi:

> The division of labour between men and women left the able-bodied men free to devote most of their time to military activities and training exercises. Military aptitude, endurance and discipline were developed by games and herding duties in early boyhood and by long journeys to salt licks, *kaptich* grazing areas and on raiding expeditions before initiation into warriorhood. The warriors were expected to maintain their physical fitness, including abstinence from beer and tobacco.[65]

Tasks within households divided according to gender and age, which encouraged mutual autonomy and interdependence between and among relations. Boys herded cattle, a task that included twice daily trips to often distant water sources, while young men roamed the country raiding cattle, hunting, and protecting the community, all tasks requiring running and physical fitness. Men cleared land for cultivation, cut trees, built fences, started fires, and worked iron. Women, too, performed work that was physically intense but largely confined to the homestead. They prepared food, collected water, brewed beer, milked cattle, tended to smaller livestock, and cared for children with the assistance of daughters. Women also helped each other in these daily tasks and collaborated in rotating labor groups. Colonial administrator Jack H. Driberg, who lived in British East Africa from 1912 to 1925, noted that their responsibilities "were more or less sedentary" and precluded "going far afield for any length of time for long periods, whereas men are subject to no such constraints."[66]

The existence of "female husbands" in communities of the Rift Valley illustrates both the firm demarcation between male and female domains and how certain individuals transcended these divides. Gendered practices associated with male or female social roles could obscure even anatomical differences. Also known as woman-woman marriage, these unions involved a woman, generally older, sometimes widowed, and without children, fulfilling male social roles after giving bridewealth for and marrying another woman. An agreed upon consort would impregnate her wife and children born of these unions belonged to the female husband's lineage. Orchardson describes how female husbands among the Kipsigis undertook the same ceremonies when marrying a wife as if the female husband were a man, ritualistically transforming a woman into a husband and consequently a social male. Such unions for an older woman without sons afforded protection, support as she aged, and heirs to inherit her accumulated wealth.[67] From her research on the Nandi in the 1960s and early 1970s, anthropologist Myrtle S. Langley describes the incidence of female husbands in that community as fairly common, noting "I know of no area in Nandi which I visited without hearing of an example in the neighborhood."[68]

Anthropologist Regina Oboler has examined the extent to which the female husband fulfilled expected male social roles, addressing the question "Is the Female Husband a Man?" in the Nandi context. A woman who took a wife in that community was in theory expected to abandon all women's work and cease attending female initiation, while behaving in all social contexts "exactly as would any ordinary man." As one Nandi female husband stated, "No, I don't (carry things on my head). That is a woman's duty and nothing to do with me. I became a man and I am a man and that is all. Why should I assume women's work anymore?"[69] Oboler found that the position of a female husband as a man was more ambiguous in practice even though her informants, male and female alike, consistently insisted that a woman who married a wife became a man. The success of the institution depended on its acceptance by the wider community and on their collective perception of the female husband attaining all the stature and prerequisites of social males. Oboler concluded that this general perception resolved contradictions with strictly defined boundaries between male and female roles.[70]

The institution of woman-woman marriage demonstrates that social categories of gender were very important within Rift Valley societies. By inverting her gender and behaving as if she were male within this socially sanctioned arrangement, a woman could access male domains without disrupting firmly demarcated female and male spheres. Though numerically few women followed this path, the existence of "husbands" of both sexes displays how gendered social roles of husband and wife, male and female, were highly distinct within Rift Valley societies—and the fluidity of gender for individuals in certain circumstances. Together, these complex, gendered mechanisms worked to ensure the survival of households and communities.

When it came to labors and behaviors related to running, the ethnographic record presents men but not women engaging in regular endurance-based activities. These gendered patterns of movement were organic to the social and economic organization of communities before the first Europeans reached the Rift Valley in the nineteenth century. Although the arrival of the British succeeded in altering some tasks previously ordered along those lines, gender and age continued to determine the kinds of labor one would undertake, and running and tasks of endurance were two with male designation.

Kenyan Athletics Follows the British Model— Women Need Not Apply

By the mid-century mark, women had yet to enter formal athletic competitions in Kenya, while men's provincial teams from across the colony descended on Nairobi to contest sixteen events at the 1950 Kenya African Championships, including eight running events from the 100 yards to six miles, three relay races, and five field events. Top athletes at that meet qualified for the East African championships and remained in Nairobi to continue training at the Jeanes School, where food and board were paid for by the A&ASA. Organizers suggested adding four more men's events the following year—the discus, shot put, 440-yards hurdles, and the marathon. No suggestion was made of adding any women's events.[71] In presidential addresses, race results, newspaper reports, and other official correspondence about track and field of this era, women were not mentioned.

Colonial officials in Kenya were instead concerned to benchmark their efforts against the British track and field world from which they came. They repeatedly asked meet organizers to keep accurate records of times and distances in athletic competitions, particularly with regard to official colony records. "The cooperation of everyone is asked for in connection with records because with two years of steady improvement in African athletics, it is essential that we have a complete list of official records for accurate comparison with those of other countries," requested Colony Sport Officer Archie Evans in a 1950 circular to all districts, provinces, schools, and institutions.[72] Every effort was made to comply with AAA rules regarding tracks and equipment as well as rules related to amateurism. The A&ASA recommended against cash prizes, advising that winners instead receive cups, shields, medals, and certificates.

Pressure grew for the establishment of a single track and field governing body. On March 16, 1951, the Kenya Amateur Athletic Association (KAAA) was established at a meeting attended by representatives of all "races" of Kenyan society. Its goal was "to encourage, foster, develop and control athletics amongst all races in the colony."[73] Founding the KAAA was a historic event that, according to Bale and Sang, "constituted the beginnings of the globalisation of Kenyan athletics."[74] For track and field athletes from the colony to compete at the Olympic games, Kenyan sport leaders were required to have established both a national athletics association as well as a National Olympics Committee recognized by the IOC. The formation of the Kenya Olympic Association (KOA) in February 1954 under the chairmanship of Reginald S. Alexander followed by formal recognition by the IOC in June 1955, fulfilled the latter requirement.[75] Kenya made its Olympic debut at the games of 1956, and was one of only four African countries represented at Melbourne. It sent a team composed of twenty-six men—eight African track and field athletes, two white shooters, and sixteen Asian field hockey players—and one white female swimmer, Peggy Northrup.[76]

Colony Sport Officer Archie Evans was a driving force behind the formation of the KAAA and many of its subsequent successes. He first served as secretary of the A&ASA and later in the same capacity for the KAAA. Evans was a skilled administrator who kept meticulous records of provincial, national, and inter-territorial championships, authored several articles on track and field published in the Kenyan press, and worked with sport bodies beyond the continent. He also advanced the effort to build tracks around the colony that met international standards and held responsibility for the training of athletes for colony competitions and ultimately for events beyond Kenya.

White men steeped in the heritage of male-dominated sport and the moral authority implicitly bequeathed to it held other prominent positions in the mid-twentieth-century governing bodies of sport in Kenya. The chair of the A&ASA of this era was Thomas Askwith, who became a founding and executive member of the KAAA and encouraged Kenyan participation in the Commonwealth and Olympic games. Born in 1911 in Surrey, Askwith matriculated at Peterhouse, Cambridge, where he excelled at rowing, twice winning the annual boat race against Oxford, and also represented Britain at two Olympic Games. In 1935 Askwith was sent to Kenya as a district commissioner, where he rose through the ranks of the colonial administration ultimately serving as commissioner for community development.[77]

Askwith, who excelled at athletics and academics, personified the ideal colonial official of that day. Athletic success factored into the screening and recruitment of Britain's colonial administrators and selection into the ranks of district officers favored sportsmen. The position required significant time spent outdoors and the general assessment, in the words of historian Anthony Kirk-Green, was that rural administration consisted of "saddle and safari, not files and fine prose."[78] According to sport geographers John Bale and Joe Sang, from 1890 to 1959, of the 216 British officers stationed in Kenya and for whom data is available, roughly three-quarters attended public schools and matriculated at either Oxford or Cambridge.[79] As a Cambridge graduate and two-time Olympian, Askwith became an influential member of the white male nucleus that steered track and field in colonial Kenya. Consistent with the tenor and value system of his day, Askwith never meaningfully visited the subject of women's sport.

During the Mau Mau uprising of the 1950s, when the peoples of Central Kenya divided over calls for land and freedom, Askwith was responsible for the government's rehabilitation program that sought to use sport and recreation to maintain control within detention centers. He believed that the rebellion had emerged in part because the colonial administration failed to identify productive ways for young men to expend their energies, demonstrate courage and skill, and gain respect for authority. Historian Paul Ocobock describes Askwith's philosophy as one of replacing "dancing, hunting and warfare" with "schooling, scouting, and sport."[80] Askwith's ideas were well received at a detention center for boys known as Wamumu. This all-male youth camp of some 1,800 detainees, boys who had been Mau Mau combatants, spies, and couriers, as well as orphans and vagrants, underwent a program of rehabilitation in accordance with Askwith's vision. Many renounced their allegiance to the rebel movement, some converted to Christianity, and all found their lives organized in the same manner as those in the British public school system. They lived in houses with assigned colors, wore uniforms, and took classes after which they were allowed to play sports. "Football, boxing and track and field, masculine activities socializing millions of British young men, were wildly popular at Wamumu," observes Ocobock.[81] In the struggle to win the "hearts and minds" of those in rebellion, youth sport, efforts to increase literacy, and skills training were all intended to inculcate colonial ideals about discipline, authority, and productivity in boys.

Female Mau Mau adherents were active participants in the resistance, but detention camps were overwhelmingly male. The rehabilitation program at Wamumu had no facility for girls. One official attempted to develop an equivalent camp for girls, but the treasury refused to fund it and denied the need for it. Girls were either sent back to their families or incarcerated at one of two female-only camps where they commenced hard labor alongside adult women. "Rehabilitation was a gendered project designed specifically for men," Ocobock notes.[82]

Other prominent expatriates in business and politics promoted track and field for African men. Among the most notable was Derek Q. Erskine, son of MP Sir James Erskine and graduate of Eton College and the Royal Military Academy Sandhurst, who arrived in Kenya in 1927 at the age of twenty-two as a commissioned officer in the King's Dragoon Guards. He went on to lead successful companies and serve as a member of Kenya's National Assembly (later the Legislative Council), including a three-year stint as chief whip of the Kenya African National Union (KANU). His knighthood in 1964 was awarded for "his bold stand for racial equality and his leading role in the achievement of sport."[83]

A powerful member of the governing class, Erskine was a key figure in the formation of the Kenya Olympic Association, and he served as president of the KAAA for thirteen years. He purchased the land in Nairobi where the thirty-five-thousand-seat Nyayo National Stadium was built, used his own funds to send an all-male Kenyan track and field team to compete in Madagascar in 1952, oversaw the organization of the Kenyan men's track and field teams that traveled to Vancouver and Cardiff for the 1954 and 1958 British Empire and Commonwealth Games, and chaired the Commonwealth Games Association.[84]

The exuberance for Kenyan track and field that Erskine and his peers manifested throughout the first half of the twentieth century was expended entirely on behalf of male Kenyan athletes. In a reply to a question following his presidential address, the minutes of the 1953 Annual General Meeting of the KAAA record Erskine's words to the effect that:

> It was the intention to assist the Ladies as much as possible and there was every hope of including some ladies events in the near future, but he thought that everybody would agree that the retiring Committee had its hands full with preparations for the Vth British Commonwealth and Empire Games.[85]

For the KAAA leadership team, preparing African men to race abroad at the British Empire and Commonwealth Games in Vancouver, Canada, was more pressing than the development of women's athletics. As it had been since the founding of organized track and field in Kenya, the management of the sport in the 1950s remained an extension into the world of athletics by the political and economic elite of the colony. Adhering to the Victorian games model, track and field was a component of the public school code that many had experienced as students and that Askwith and others sought to inculcate among boys at Wamumu. Ardently devoted to sport and eager to garner international prestige for Kenyan athletics, Erskine's efforts and those of most of his colleagues remained rooted in an uncritical acceptance of the gendered cultural context of western sport.

Changing Times

The schools, and not the governing body of the sport, led the way in promoting track and field for girls and women in Kenya in the final decade of the colonial era. Advances in educational opportunities beginning in the 1950s increased the number of girls in formal schooling, which greatly accelerated their engagement with sport including track and field. The Nyanza Training Centres and Secondary Schools Athletic Association began hosting annual championships in 1952 and included female athletes at least as early as 1954.[86] Four years later, more than 350 male and female competitors participated at the championship event held at Siriba College that brought together four men's training center teams, six boys' secondary schools, and five women's training centers. Siriba College coach Edwin Evans, brother of Colony Sport Officer Archie Evans, afterwards shared that the KAAA had discussed "the question of women's athletics" at a recent meeting and remarked that "it is possible that in the near future a Women's Colony Championships will be held."[87]

Finally, in 1959, the KAAA organized the first individual Women's Colony Athletics Championships. This landmark event in Kenyan women's sporting history took place in Nyeri in Central Province alongside the Men's Decathlon Championships but separate from the rest of the men's events held at a different place and time. Women athletes could compete in as many events as they wished, no limit was placed on the number of entries, and the competition was open to female athletes of all races.[88] The team from Nyanza dominated, winning six of ten events with athletes selected from the Women's Training Centres annual meet as a basis supplemented by girls chosen from the Nyanza Intermediate Schools annual competition.[89]

As the results indicate, the annual Nyanza District Intermediate Schools track and field championships offered an important forum for female athletic development. The best athletes were selected to represent their district in the Provincial Intermediate Schools competition, where girls' records continued to improve each year amid growing numbers of participants.[90] By 1961 about six hundred competitors including boys and girls took part in the ninth annual Nyanza Province Students' Games.[91] The following year a flood of entries for the tenth edition of those games compelled organizers to split the event into two meets, one for secondary school boys and the other for girls' secondary schools and men's and women's training colleges. For the first time, there were also sufficient entries from girls and women to justify dividing their events into two sections, with athletes from the women's training colleges and girls' secondary schools competing separately. "With more than 150 women students taking part, the event was probably the largest of its kind for women in East Africa," declared the *East African Standard*.[92]

From the town of Nakuru came another outpouring of interest by female residents. "Les Girls Waited for This Change," headlined a brief article in the *East African Standard* on September 28, 1961. Earlier that week, the Nakuru Municipal Council had sought participation by women or girls who might be interested in competing at the Women's Colony Championships. "They got the shock of their lives," reported the Kenyan daily, when no fewer than 128 schoolgirls requested consideration for the competition. The overwhelming response quieted widespread skepticism about female interest in sport, and the article concluded with the observation that "if Nakuru is anything to go by, women all over the Colony have been awaiting a chance to make their name in athletics."[93]

Girls and women in the Nakuru area had witnessed the excitement and pageantry generated by the most competitive men's track and field events, including the first (of two) Olympic trials of 1960 held at the recently reconstructed Nakuru Stadium. That facility included a new track, football field, and grandstand.[94] They had also watched the 1961 East African Championships held in that venue three weeks prior to the call for female athletes to compete at the colony championships. *East African Standard* columnist James Dow deemed the East African Championships at Nakuru "a success in all respects," noting "above all, it was a crowd-puller."[95] More than three thousand people paid to watch the region's finest male athletes set ten new inter-territorial records.[96] That interest extended to participation by girls and women when presented the opportunity to do so.

The 1961 Kenya Women's Individual Athletic Championships, the third of its kind, was held at Nakuru Stadium on a soggy track. The meet produced new records in six of its ten events.[97] The Rift Valley Province Sports Association secretary noted that "much interest has been shown by the women folks in athletics," and that "three of our girls won first places at the Women's Championships, two of them breaking Kenya records."[98] A total of nearly eighty athletes competed that year, setting Kenyan records in several events which the *East African Standard* detailed in a report titled "Standards Highest Yet: Six Records Go at Women's A.A.A. Meeting."[99]

The women's 1962 track and field season brought more records as well as cancelation of what would have been the fourth Women's Colony Championships. Following the Rift Valley Provincial Championships, *East African Standard* columnist Charles Disney, reporting on the women's results, noted that "in general, Rift Valley performances appear to be decidedly better, in the main, than those put up in other parts of Kenya."[100] Outstanding sprinters at the Coast appeared poised to challenge that claim. At the Coast Provincial Championships held in Mombasa, "it was the women competitors who took pride of place and set the Kenya-best times," celebrated the *East African Standard*. Mombasa schoolteacher Meldrita Laurent, the reigning colony champion in the 100-yard and 220-yard dashes, earned the trophy for best individual performance after she won the 220-yards and the high jump, broke the colony record for the 100-yards dash, and helped to break the colony 4x110-yard relay record.[101]

Despite promising performances at the various provincial championships, officials canceled the 1962 Women's Athletics Championships planned for Kisumu due to lack of entries. The decision to call off the meet came after the competition had already been postponed by a week in hopes that entry numbers would increase, an indication of the still emergent state of the sport among women. Acknowledging that "promising performances have already been put up," and also that "Kenya girls in general are relatively new to athletics," the *East African Standard* blamed the low turnout on the lack of uniformity in girls' school holidays. Nearly all the entries for the women's competitions typically came through the schools or teacher training colleges. Athletes from Nairobi and district schools, almost all of which were on holiday, were among the absentees. An ongoing teachers' strike in Nyanza Province further reduced the number of entries. "As schools are almost the entire source for women's athletes, only with the co-operation of the Department of Education can a time suitable be arranged. And until school term times and holidays become uniform throughout the country, such an arrangement presents almost insuperable difficulties," declared the *Standard*.[102] This cancelation underscored the importance of schools for the development of female Kenyan runners. It also exposed the contrast with their male counterparts who that year were able to compete at national and inter-territorial championships and even the 1962 British Empire and Commonwealth Games in Perth, Australia.

The Women's Athletics Championships returned in 1963 when, for the first time, their meet was combined with the full program of men's events. The women's results were scored separately, with the men competing for the Erskine Shield and the women vying for a new team award.[103] Over two days, some five thousand spectators in Kisumu witnessed the setting of four men's and three women's records on the recently resurfaced track. Newly appointed minister for home affairs, Jaramogi Oginga Odinga, served as the guest of honor.[104] Rift Valley women triumphed to become the first holders of the Kenya Muslim Sports Association Shield, which celebrated the year of independence.[105] Following the 1963 national championships, the Kenyan men's team once again dominated the East African Championships. The win marked their fourteenth consecutive victory at the regional title meet, which still did not include women.[106] The East African Amateur Athletic Board declared that the following year, the event would include women for the first time.[107]

Conclusion

Women from the Rift Valley, the region that has made Kenya famous for distance running, first competed beyond the local level at the inaugural Rift Valley Provincial Women's Championships of 1958. The first colony-wide Women's Individual Athletics Championships took place the following year, where the longest of three race distances was 220 yards. Independence brought new opportunities for female athletes, although as one *Daily Nation* journalist acknowledged in 1965, "So far the potential of women's athletics has barely been tapped: It is there, just as it is with the men. It only awaits discovery and development."[108]

Spawned by the games revolution of the late nineteenth century, British sports culture was the model imported to colonial Kenya, a masculine culture of athletics that re-created the social exclusion and hierarchy that characterized British athletics, though race rather than class stratified male runners. The officials who administered track and field in Kenya promoted a model that reflected their common belief in the intrinsic morality and masculinity of sport. This vision was institutionalized in the 1920s and remained intact until the final years preceding independence. A desire on the part of many for recognition in international athletics finally dislodged racial barriers, allowing for a merit-based level playing field for all Kenyan men.

This gendered form of athletics was perpetuated even in extreme instances such as armed uprisings. British officials promoted sport within detention camps for young men established during the Mau Mau uprising. The rebellion in Kenya's Central Province was a bitter struggle against the colonial administration that divided rebel and loyalist kin. Young men suspected of being under the influence of Mau Mau were detained and put through a process of "rehabilitation" that involved work, discipline, and competition. Sports such as football and track and field played an important role and were embraced by detainees. No equivalent intervention took place among young women.

Few transformations emerged in the gendered composition of Kenyan athletics throughout the colonial period. While Kenyan sportsmen were building reputations as athletes at home and abroad, competitive opportunities for women in colonial Kenya remained exceedingly rare, though in the final decade of British rule some Kenyan schools created opportunities for female participation. The men at the highest levels of the sport maintained the continuity of athletics as a masculine domain while making end-of-empire concessions that resulted in greater racial inclusivity, an instance of what historian Martin Francis calls the "reconfiguration of masculine hierarchies on the margins of empires during its death throes."[109]

Colonial influence was not the only cause of unequal access to track and field participation, however. Endurance running was an exclusively male activity in Kenyan communities prior to the introduction of Western forms of athletics. Running cultures among men had no counterpart for women prior to and during the formative years of colonial rule. Scholars of gender in other East African contexts have observed that many gendered practices during the colonial era emerged through a combination of both imperial norms and previously existing ideas and practices. Track and field was no exception. Existing movement cultures found compatibility with British forms of sport and fused to shape the gendered character of Kenyan running. African and European men preserved older cultures while jointly building the foundations of international sporting success.

CHAPTER TWO

Nation, Race, Gender, and Athletes' Rights in the Early Independence Era

The Case of Diana Monks

A t the 1967 Kenyan national championships held at Nairobi's Jumhuri Park Stadium, four women stood out as potential qualifiers for the upcoming Mexico City Olympic Games: Lydia Stephens of Nairobi, who won national titles in the 100-yards and the 220-yards sprints; Tecla Chemabwai of the Rift Valley, who won the 440-yards dash; and Elizabeth Chesire, also from the Rift Valley, who claimed the 880-yards run. The fourth and most outstanding athlete of the meet was Diana Monks, a white, Kenyan-born university student, who won the 80-meters hurdles, high jump, and long jump, setting a Kenyan and East African record in the latter.[1] Two years earlier Monks had earned a silver medal in the 80-meters hurdles at the inaugural African Games, becoming the first woman to ascend the podium for Kenya at a major international track and field competition.[2] Only three of these athletes would make history as the first women to represent Kenya in track and field at the Olympic Games.

Monks found herself at the center of controversy when she failed to compete at the 1967 East African Championships one week after her triple triumph at the national championships. Her absence at the regional championship meet would ultimately cost her the chance to qualify for the 1968 Kenyan Olympic team. The president, secretary, and publicity officer of the Kenya Amateur Athletics Association (KAAA) and the secretary of the Nairobi Amateur Athletic Association (NAAA) closed ranks with the minister in charge of sport and the Mayor of Nairobi, all of whom agreed that missing the East African Championships without communicating her whereabouts warranted a two-year suspension from track and field. Monks's defenders included her father, fellow athletes, the leaders of the Games Union at her university, observers who addressed the issue in letters published in the press, and the editors of the *East African Standard*. These constituencies were outmatched by the country's most powerful sporting authorities, who singled out a white female athlete with what some commentators described as particular viciousness. High-ranking officials and politicians argued that Monks, by depriving the Kenyan national team of her participation at the East African Championships, committed an "abuse to the nation" and that such disloyalty necessitated a suspension that would set an example to other athletes. Monks appealed the sanction but never publicly commented on the matter herself.

This controversy in track and field unfolded as ten million Kenyans with ethnic, religious, and linguistic differences were engaged in a complicated effort to create a viable and cohesive nation. Colonial rule officially ended in 1963 when the British relinquished control to Jomo Kenyatta and his Kenya African National Union (KANU) party. Kenyatta had returned to Kenya in 1947 after having spent sixteen years in Britain, where he studied at the London School of Economics, co-sponsored a Pan African Congress with future Ghanaian president Kwame Nkrumah, and authored *Facing Mount Kenya,* in which he elucidated and defended the cultural practices of the Kikuyu, his ethnic community that predominated the region around Nairobi in Central Kenya. During the Mau Mau uprising of the 1950s, which pitted Kikuyu loyal to the British against their marginalized, rebel kin, the colonial administration suspected that Kenyatta masterminded the conflict and detained him for nine years. Upon his release in 1961, Kenyatta, by then a heroic symbol of resistance, accepted leadership of KANU, the most popular and ambitious nationalist party of that day, which won the first democratic national elections. He subsequently became Kenya's first prime minister and, following a constitutional change, its first president.[3]

The newly created nation retained many aspects of the colonial era, and it remained to be seen whether Kenyatta could forge national unity from a society riven by politicized ethnic cleavages and entrenched racial divisions. White settlers in Kenya had long held enormous economic and political clout and fought tenaciously to protect their interests. Inequalities persisted wherein that small but economically powerful minority held most of the managerial, professional, and technical posts, lived in affluent homes close to hospitals, schools, churches, and clubs, and together with a somewhat larger Asian minority, predominated in business and trade in the new Kenya, particularly in urban areas.[4]

To dismantle this colonial-era hierarchy, the new political elite introduced a plan to "Kenyanize" the economy by replacing noncitizens with citizens in the civil service and other sectors of the workforce. Although commonly referred to as "Africanization," the scheme was not officially cast in racial terms. It was instead couched in the language of citizenship, which stressed the advancement and equality of all Kenyans, regardless of race, ahead of those who refused to become Kenyan nationals.[5] The constitution at independence made provision for all who wished to obtain Kenyan citizenship, though it required giving up any other form of national identity. Any Kenyan-born resident with one parent born in Kenya automatically qualified.[6] All others were allowed to naturalize by applying for citizenship within two years, yet relatively few responded. Of the 180,000 Asian residents in Kenya in 1963, only twenty thousand applied for citizenship by the deadline of December 1965, joining about fifty thousand others who qualified automatically. The low response by Europeans was even more stark—fewer than two thousand out of sixty thousand applied.[7] By 1969, that number had not yet reached four thousand.[8] Most of those with British ancestry who remained in the country chose to retain their British citizenship, and most Asians also decided to keep or obtain a British passport, an option the British government made available to them at independence.[9] Many officials and public commentators saw the lackluster response as a failure to commit to the new Kenyan nation.

As the country strove to "Kenyanize" the workforce, the KAAA followed the same template in its aggressive stance toward Diana Monks in athletics. When she was suspended by the KAAA in 1967, a ban that initially included all sports, cries of foul play, racism, and dictatorialism were met with the stern retorts of those in power and their defenders who leveraged the moment to declare citizenship a criterion for participation in domestic track and field meets. Monks's failure to attend the East African Championships was seen as disrespectful by Kenyan sport administrators, who, despite their public encouragement of women's athletics, were sufficiently embarrassed by her decisions to move ahead with a ban against arguably the strongest female track and field athlete in Kenya at the time.

The story of Monks and her treatment by governmental and sport authorities highlights issues of athletes' rights as well as of race, gender, citizenship, and loyalty to the nation that were undercurrents in the dispute and society more broadly.[10] The sudden discontinuance of the athletic ascent of Diana Monks was a setback that momentarily interrupted the progression in international track and field of Kenyan women for whom the early independence years brought historic debuts as they began to compete at the All Africa, Commonwealth, and Olympic Games. The united compact of governmental and athletic administrators, all of whom were male, agreed that suspending Monks was necessary to impose discipline among athletes, even if it required making an example of one of the country's top female athletes. At a moment when African leaders were asserting their inheritance of political and economic power, sport administrators were tightening their control of athletics in the name of defending the honor of the Kenyan nation.

The 1967 East African Championships

At the end of a lengthy article describing the achievements at the 1967 Kenya national championships by Commonwealth Games six-mile champion Naftali Temu, 3000-meters world-record-holder Kipchoge Keino, and the army's record-breaking 4x440-yards men's relay team, the *East African Standard* acknowledged: "The women also had a good weekend with records going in the long jump, 4x110 yards relay, 100 yards, and shot put with Diana Monks taking three titles including a Kenya record in the long jump." The report also highlighted African short-distance runner Lydia Stephens who "proved beyond doubt that she is Kenya's top woman sprinter" when she broke a Kenya record in the 100-yards dash before winning the national title in the 220 yards.[11]

The track and field season culminated one week later with the 1967 East African Championships, an event held annually among teams from Kenya, Uganda, and Tanzania, which that year took place at Kisumu Municipal Stadium. The KAAA announced it would send the maximum contingent of two women per event for each of the eleven events on the women's program. Among the standouts invited to compete were Stephens, whom officials asked to represent Kenya in the 100 yards, the 220 yards, and the long jump, Chemabwai in the 220 and the 440 yards, and Chesire in the 880-yards event. Monks was selected in the 80-meters hurdles and the long jump, but the press noted that she was unavailable to compete in Kisumu.[12]

Monks was by then well known for her athletic achievements. Her first commendation in the press came in 1962 for setting a new school record in the intermediate high jump as a student at the predominately white Kenya Girls' High School.[13] In 1964 she was selected from hundreds of young athletes as one of three girls and four boys to receive the inaugural Nation-Taifa award for outstanding performances in sport, presented that year by Wilson Kiprugut Chuma, the first Kenyan Olympic medalist, during a televised Voice of Kenya program.[14] In 1965, Monks won three national titles in the high jump, long jump, and 80-meters hurdles after qualifying as one of two women and eighteen men selected to represent the Nairobi Amateur Athletic Association at the national championships in Mombasa. Her performance at the national championships earned her a berth on the Kenyan team bound for the inaugural All African Games in Brazzaville, Congo, at which more than 2500 athletes participated from twenty-nine African nations.[15] This event served as "a powerful symbol of African independence, the first truly African Games, organized and contested entirely by Africans," observes sport historian Terry Gitersos.[16] That continental festival of 1965 was also a historic occasion for Kenyan sport, marking the first time that two women, Monks and thrower Anna Vivian Chepkorir, competed in track and field for a Kenyan national team at an event beyond East Africa. Chepkorir was a Kipsigis schoolteacher from the Rift Valley who first earned national acclaim in 1964 when she broke the Kenyan record for the javelin.[17]

Before they left for the continental meet, the forty-three-person Kenyan contingent visited President Jomo Kenyatta at his invitation. He described the Kenyan flag as a symbol of victory and declared his certainty that they would return from Brazzaville with medals. "Kenya's reputation is in your hands and if you are defeated, then Kenya has been defeated. We are looking forward to your victorious homecoming," he proclaimed.[18] The *Daily Nation* published a photo of the president flanked by the two women athletes, captioned "the President forms a happy group with Anna Vivian, who will compete in the field events, and Diana Monks, sprinter and hurdler."[19]

Monks made the final in all three of her events at the All Africa Games in Brazzaville. After missing the bronze in the long jump by only one inch, she made history when she won silver in the 80-meters hurdles to finish one-tenth of a second behind Ghanaian star Rose Hart in a personal best time.[20] That same day, Chepkorir finished fourth in the javelin.[21] Kenya finished third in the overall team medal count behind the United Arab Republic and Nigeria. Laden with twenty-two gold, silver, and bronze medals, the athletes on their return home paid a second visit to Kenyatta who commended them for putting "Kenya on the world sporting map." Tom Mboya, a leading Kenyan politician, prominent trade unionist, pan-Africanist and Kenyatta's minister for economic planning and development, also cabled praise from London.[22] The *Daily Nation* published another photo of Kenyatta congratulating Monks for becoming the first woman to win a medal for Kenya at a major international games.[23] She received national attention when the Nation/Taifa newspapers honored her with the 1965 young Sportswoman of the Year award and declared in a press release that "Diana Monks of University College, Nairobi, needs no introduction for she represented Kenya with distinction at the All-Africa Games in Brazzaville, winning the silver medal in the 80 metres hurdles."[24]

The following year, the British Empire and Commonwealth Games held in Kingston, Jamaica, marked the most important event in the Kenyan track and field calendar. Kenyan Commonwealth Games teams had been entirely comprised of men since making their debut at the quadrennial multi-sport festival in Vancouver twelve years before. That changed when Monks and Stephens were selected to join a large contingent of male athletes and one female swimmer, Kay Donoghue, and compete in Kingston.[25] Although neither Monks nor Stephens returned with a medal, their presence at the 1966 British Empire and Commonwealth games marked another important beginning for Kenyan women in international track and field.[26]

As the 1967 track and field season reached its peak in September with the East African Championships in Kisumu, the *East African Standard* published a detailed report ahead of the competition, anticipating the victories of Kenya's best male athletes, many of whom were already giants in the track and field world. Their predictions included Keino recording the "fastest sub-four mile to be run in Africa" and Daniel Rudisha outshining his rivals in the quarter-mile along with Wilson Kiprugut winning the half-mile, Ben Kogo the 3000-meters steeplechase, and Paul Cherop the three miles. The final sentence of the extensive write-up reserved hope for a positive outcome for the women: "The women's [track] events could be more thrilling [than the field events] with Lydia Stevens [*sic*], T. Chemabwai, D. Sigara, Chesire, A. Wanja and M. Chepkemoi expected to have tussles with their Ugandan opponents."[27] The report listed by name all the female athletes selected for the team and made no mention of Diana Monks.

Many distinguished local and national luminaries attended the East African track and field championship competition in Kisumu. Jaramogi Oginga Odinga, Kenya's first vice president, ardent African nationalist and by then one of the most outspoken critics of Kenyatta's government, watched the meet held in the region of Kenya where his political support was strongest.[28] He was joined in the

VIP section by the Mayor of Kisumu Grace Onyango, the most prominent female politician of the era, Nyanza Provincial Commissioner Charles Murgor and other high-profile guests.[29] The Minister for Co-operatives and Social Services Ronald G. Ngala praised the high standard of sportsmanship displayed by the three East African teams, which he emphasized would generate prestige for the continent, stating "the cooperation in sports between the three countries could make the whole of Africa take the lead in the sports world," and declaring that women especially "have a very important role to play in the field of sports." Ngala assured his listeners that the government fully backed women's athletics and urged Kenyan women "to try to intensify their efforts in athletics and sports."[30]

These dignitaries were treated to the fastest mile ever recorded on African soil when Keino led the race from start to finish on a soft track following a deluge the previous day to set a new Kenyan national and Commonwealth mile record of 3:53.1.[31] Keino then won the three-miles event an hour later in yet another record-breaking time.[32] Rudisha won the quarter-mile in the fastest time ever over that distance by an African athlete while Wilson Kiprugut became the first African runner to break 1:47.0 in the half-mile with an effort that "looked like a mere canter," according to the *East African Standard*.[33] Kenyan men won every track event and in most cases claimed second place as well, finishing with 136 points to Uganda's forty six and Tanzania's ten.[34]

Kenyan women took first place overall ahead of runner-up Uganda and third-place Tanzania. Stephens won the 100-yards dash and took second in the 220 yards one-tenth of a second behind Chemabwai, both of whom broke the former Kenyan national and East African record for the event. Chemabwai, running in spikes for the first time, also claimed victory in the 440-yards event.[35] In the absence of Monks, Kenya failed to win both events that she had dominated at the national meet the previous week. Ugandan athletes won these titles with performances inferior to those achieved by Monks shortly preceding these championships.[36]

The final meet of the 1967 season took place two weeks later between an invitational KAAA team and a Kenya Schools Athletic Association delegation comprised of the top junior athletes in the country. It was held in Kabete outside Nairobi at the Kenya Institution of Administration, formerly known as the Jeanes School.[37] "Never before has there been such rivalry between athletes in Kenya," declared the *East African Standard*, which expected a record crowd to see "what could be as fine a meeting as the recent Kenya and East African championships."[38] International stars Keino, Kiprugut, Kogo, and Temu once again headlined the KAAA men's side while many of Kenya's most promising male athletes represented the schools team, including future Olympian Robert Ouko in the half-mile, East African championship sprinter Julius Sang of the Rift Valley, and Paul Cherop, who set a new Kenyan junior record finishing second to Keino at the East African Championships in Kisumu.[39]

"Women athletes will also provide thrills with the main rivalry coming from Tegla Chemabwai and Lydia Stevens [sic]," the press declared.[40] Precocious and accomplished primary school student Chemabwai was entered in the 220- and the 440-yards events for the KAAA team that also featured Elizabeth Chesire in the 880 yards and Stephens in the short sprints.[41] Chemabwai and Stephens were matched up against President Jomo Kenyatta's daughter, Jane, competing for the Kenya Schools' team in the 220 yards and as a member of the schools' 4x110-yards relay team.[42] The Ugandan Amateur Athletics Association also sent a small team to run as guests. The press expected Ugandan Jane Bawaya to try to avenge her loss to Stephens in the 100 yards and noted an "interesting" match-up between Diana Monks and Rosemary Namusisi of Uganda in the 80-meters hurdles.[43]

The next day, the press reported that Monks was a "notable absence" from the 80-meters hurdles, long jump, and high jump at the Schools/KAAA competition. The KAAA executive committee had suspended her from competing in any track and field meet in Kenya or East Africa for two years because she had failed to represent the country, when selected, at the East African Championships.[44] Monks at the time held the Kenya national, Kenya open, KAAA, and East African records for the 80-meters hurdles and long jump and had recently won national titles in three events. She was selected to compete for Kenya at the East African Championships in Kisumu but failed to show up because, according to the press, "she was in Mombasa."[45] Although journalists were aware that she would not attend the meet and had reported as much, track and field officials were caught off guard when she did not appear. The suspension period started the day of the KAAA/schools meeting on September 22, 1967.[46]

Arrival of Lydia Stephens

One month after the 1967 KAAA/Kenya Schools showdown in which she set a Kenya record in the 100 yards, won the 220 yards ahead of Chemabwai, and contributed to the record-setting 4x110-yards relay team in the absence of Diana Monks, the

East African Standard ran a lengthy article on Lydia Stephens.[47] "Kenya's place in international athletics has already been won by Kipchoge Keino, Ben Kogo, Naftali Temu and Wilson Kiprugut. Now an up-and-coming athlete promises to achieve the same fame in the women's sphere," declared journalist Hezekiah Wepukhulu, who closely monitored the Kenyan track and field scene. Calling her the "undisputed fastest woman sprinter in East Africa," he predicted Stephens to be "on the brink of making the Olympic team." She herself dreamed of becoming one of the first women to represent Kenya at the Olympic Games. Stephens declared her intention to concentrate on the 100-yards event and to do her utmost to attain the Olympic qualifying mark before the deadline of September 25, 1968.[48] "I am now convinced more than ever before that I can run the 100 yards under 11 seconds," she said. "One encouraging thing about my performances is that I have been improving with every race I have run this year."[49] She had recently matriculated for a BA degree at University College (now known as the University of Nairobi), where she sought to continue with sport, telling Wepukhulu: "I shall be afforded facilities for my training at the University College, and I expect to improve on my performances."[50]

Stephens first attracted international attention in 1966 when she and Diana Monks were selected as the first women to run for Kenya at the British Empire and Commonwealth Games in Kingston. Then a student at Alliance Girls' High School, Stephens regularly competed for the school hockey team and emerged as one of the most accomplished netball players in Kenya, representing the country at its first international netball tournament in 1966. Her track and field training consisted of practices at the former Jeanes School in Nairobi twice a week for two hours. She recalled being put on a "special diet" to gain strength prior to the Kingston meet and appreciated competing against the best runners in the Commonwealth, noting in a 2021 interview: "It was a good opportunity for us. At least we were exposed. We came to know what it's all about, you know, being in international sports." From Kingston, the Kenyan team proceeded to Edinburgh, Scotland, for the Highland Games. "It was cold and wet and miserable," she remembered. "But that was also a good opportunity for us." Stephens also recalled meeting Jomo Kenyatta. "The opportunity of meeting our first president and shaking his hand—that I can't forget. I remember him looking at me straight in the eyes and that was at State House. That was good. That was something."[51]

Born into a sports-minded family in Mombasa, Stephens had won prizes in track and field throughout her youth.[52] Her mother was a talented athlete who supported her daughters' interest in sport. "My mother was a very good runner. She always used to come to the Mombasa Stadium to see me run. Always, since I was in school," Stephens recalled. "We used to compete my sisters and I, the three of us." Awards at the annual school sports day motivated her. "We were given little gifts. Girls always got little dolls. Boys always got tennis balls. And I had quite a number of them." After entering intermediate school in Kilifi District, Stephens began to win races and compete in the long jump and the high jump at the district level. She narrates: "We did very well in our school. We won most of the races." From Kilifi Girls' School, she moved to Taita to Murray High School. "[This was] where now things started getting even better for me . . . we now were running for Taita district in the provincial championships, and we won most of the events. But unfortunately, we never went beyond the provincial championships. We were never selected to go for the national championship. It was always . . . we were always left out. You know in those days there was a lot of discrimination."[53]

Stephens describes how the racial segregation that pervaded sport during the colonial era continued to blight track and field in the first decade of independence. Most Coastal schools of the 1960s remained divided along racial lines. Sport failed to transcend the discrimination that accompanied these educational divides to the extent that she recalls the only women selected to represent the Coast team at the national championships were those from European and Goan schools. "So you would find that despite winning, selections were made from the whites, those browns, and we were left out. Always."[54] The failure to choose Stephens to compete at the national championships in 1965 cost her the chance to earn a berth on the Kenyan team at the inaugural All Africa Games, a team for which Monks qualified as one of two female Kenyan representatives.

According to Stephens, racial inequalities also extended to the spaces that the track and field athletes occupied while waiting to compete:

Even the seating arrangement, in fact the way we used to go into the stadium, it's not like today just walking in. We used to have a kind of a parade. You would have a band playing and then you would walk in. The first team would be white. And they would sit in the shade, the VIP stand, which was in the shade. The next team was from the Goan school. Goans are half Asian, half Europeans. So, the next ones would be the Goans. If there was any little room left in the shade, they would sit there. And then the third would be the Asian. The fourth was us. We would always sit in the sun. Mombasa's sun is hot.[55]

Track and field at the school level reflected sport in Kenya and society more generally as it emerged from the institutionalized racism of colonial rule. Governing bodies that organized competitions for African men had long been run by white male sports administrators, solidifying a structure of racial hierarchy in the advancement of Western sport. After independence African men replaced their white counterparts at the helm of track and field, but de facto racial segregation continued to burden sports in Kenya in many ways. Golf courses, swimming pools, and tennis and squash courts remained far more available to the wealthier white communities while the Indian community continued to engage in hockey, cricket, tennis, and badminton through established separate facilitates and leagues. African athletes predominately contested boxing, football (soccer), and track and field, though a strong Goan contingent led by Olympian and two-time Commonwealth Games gold medalist sprinter Seraphino Antao brought athletics glory to the newly independent nation.[56] Diana Monks stood out as the only white track and field athlete of international caliber of this era.

Stephens's breakthrough came when she left the Coast to attend Alliance Girls' High School, one of the most prestigious boarding schools in Kenya. The location of the school outside Nairobi meant that she could compete for Kiambu District in Central Province. "That was the first time I ever had the opportunity to run at provincial level and that was 1966," Stephens recalled. She also remembered Monks, who attended a rival girls' school, as "always the best in 100 and 200 yards." The two were close in age and regularly encountered each other at Nairobi schools' competitions before traveling to Jamaica for the Commonwealth Games. Referring to Monks, she describes: "Of course we had also been competing at our school because we used to have the school championships, so we had always been competing, and I won the races."[57] In both the interview that Stephens gave to the *East African Standard* in October 1967 and in the conversation retracing her career in 2021, the controversy over Monks's suspension did not come up. That event, however, rocked the Kenyan track and field world of the late 1960s.

Suspension and Dissention

"Top Sportswoman Banned from University Team," announced the *East African Standard* on October 26, 1967, reporting the news that Diana Monks could not compete in any sport in Kenya, or anywhere in East Africa, for the next two years for failure to attend the 1967 East African Championships. Monks, the first female medalist for Kenya at a major international track and field meet and one of Kenya's best athletes in multiple sports—the press billed her as "Nairobi's top all-round sportswoman"—was now not only unwelcome at athletics meets but also ineligible to represent Kenya in any sport.[58] This latest ruling had already cost Monks her berth on the Kenya Women's Hockey Association (KWHA) national team, which had played against Uganda at the annual hockey international in Kampala the previous weekend. It also appeared set to deny Monks a place on her University College team at the East African University Games later that year. The KAAA's ruling extended to all sports, explained KAAA public relations officer William Yeda: "In amateur sport a person suspended by one association is automatically suspended from taking part in any other sport. Miss Monks, therefore, cannot play for Kenya at hockey or even compete in the University Games."[59]

Her father, E. T. Monks, sought to correct an impression that the *Standard* article may have left on readers, declaring in a public response: "It is not correct that Diana Monks was suspended for not attending the Kisumu meeting to which she was asked and had agreed to attend. She was not asked to attend nor had any entry form been issued for completion." He then itemized the actions that the KAAA and the Nairobi Amateur Athletic Association (NAAA) failed to take prior to the championship meet. Neither organization either verbally or in writing notified her of the date of the meet, invited her to compete, informed her that she had been selected for the team, or asked if she would be available to compete. Nor had they provided an entry form listing the events in which she wanted to participate or shared information about transportation and accommodation arrangements. He added that a press release about the Kenyan team chosen to compete in Kisumu constituted the "first and only information" that she received about the East African Championships. That release appeared on the Wednesday before the Saturday meet, by which time Monks had already left for Mombasa and was unable to return in time. "As a result of this she was suspended for two years," added her father, noting that the KAAA had failed to allow her to present her version of events before rendering its decision.[60]

The elder Monks asked what precedent existed for "such a sweeping pronouncement" and "what authority he [Yeda] has to enable him to apply such a harsh censure amounting to vindictiveness." Monks described his daughter as an amateur athlete who competed out of enjoyment of sports and devoted considerable time to training, stating that Yeda, the Kenya Sport Officer, was "one of the few associated with sport who is paid for his services." Monks concluded that if Yeda was "in a position of authority to dictate such terms to our amateur sports lovers then I can only say that it is quite wrong for so much power to be vested in one man."[61]

Abdul V. Hirani, the president of the Games Union at University College where Monks was a student, also weighed in to support her participation at the annual University Games. Declaring in a public message that his union was not affiliated with the KAAA and therefore outside its jurisdiction, he described the University Games as an "internal event" in which the three colleges that comprised the University of East Africa convened annually to compete in games and sports, which further contradicted the notion that she should be banned by an association that had nothing to do with those institutions, two of which were outside of Kenya. He suggested that Yeda owed Monks a public apology.[62]

Yeda's response two days later was blistering. In a letter to *the East African Standard*, he communicated the KAAA's strong condemnation of "the attitude adopted by Mr. Monks and his daughter, Diana, and the president of the Games Union," warning that his organization "will not tolerate any such future threats to its affiliated bodies or, indeed, members." He pronounced that the KAAA "does not run her affairs through the Press," an ironic statement given that that was precisely the means he was using to communicate his displeasure with Monks. Yeda then addressed the Games Union president's contention that Monks should be able to compete for her university team by quoting from the British Amateur Athletic Association constitution, which set forth that any person who knowingly competed against a suspended athlete also forfeited their own right to compete.[63] Yeda next rebutted the points raised by Diana Monks's father, asserting that all athletes named to the Kenyan team had been verbally informed of their selection and that the first- and second-place finishers in each event at the national championships were told to "remain behind." He responded to the elder Monks's other itemized complaints with a single question: "How did the athletes selected by the Kenya A.A.A. happen to know that they were selected and how did they get to Kisumu, and was there accommodations for them in Kisumu or not?"

After labeling Monks's failure to compete at the East African Championships "an abuse to the nation," he announced that because of her truancy, all noncitizens were to be barred from participation in future meets organized by the KAAA.[64] Visiting overseas athletes too would be excluded from KAAA meets, a ruling that flouted a widely accepted custom wherein international athletes were allowed to compete as guests in the domestic competitions of other nations.[65] The KAAA had invited athletes from Britain, Hungary, and Ethiopia to compete at the 1967 Kenyan national championships, which the highest-ranking minister in charge of sport, Ronald Ngala, praised at the time as "giving our athletes the top class competition needed in preparation for the Olympic Games to be held in Mexico next year." Ngala also commended the KAAA for creating closer links with other countries by having welcomed competitors from Canada, New Zealand, and East Germany to the Kenyan national championships the previous year.[66]

This new policy echoed the larger drive in Kenya to end the prerogatives that minority members of the colonial order and their heirs continued to enjoy. The push for Kenyanization in the workforce and civil service was an effort to overcome the country's racial stratification by prioritizing equality and full participatory rights among Kenyan Africans and those who adopted Kenyan citizenship. Africans quickly came to occupy most of the top government positions while private industry and technical fields proved resistant to such changes. By 1967 more than 90 percent of the highest government posts were occupied by African citizens while less than a quarter of professional positions had been claimed by that population, and the percentage of public-sector jobs held by Africans was vastly larger than the percentage of jobs held by them in the private sector.[67] Under pressure from members of that constituency who perceived little apparent change in the economy, the government introduced legislation that banned noncitizens from transacting in many common consumer products, limited the areas in which they could engage in trade, and required them to obtain a work permit that was only granted if a citizen was not available to fill the position.[68] These policies adversely affected the livelihood of many Asians who dominated the merchant sector of the economy, precipitating a wave of emigration in the late 1960s and early 1970s.[69] Track and field, too, was now reserved for Kenyan nationals.

On the same day that Yeda issued his scathing response, the *East African Standard* printed an editorial entitled "Authoritarian Athletics," declaring that Monks's suspension "looks like condemnation without a hearing" and issuing threats of its own. The paper noted that Yeda was paid to promote sport in Kenya but doing so depended on the goodwill of the many people who cared about Kenyan track and field, including journalists who "feel misgivings over this incident." If such constituencies were antagonized, the editorialists claimed, it would not bode well, for track and field existed only through voluntary support given by amateur athletes, financial support from commercial entities, and free publicity in the press. The editorial contended that the ministry in charge of sport should review the entire episode, including Yeda's most recent statement, because the controversy could damage Kenya's international reputation.[70]

A flood of letters responded, all of which found fault with the KAAA's decision. According to the *East African Standard*, "Several letters have been published out of a large postbag and it is noticeable that not one has supported [Yeda's] attitude."[71] One commentator congratulated the paper on its "outspoken" editorial and proposed a boycott of all KAAA meets, including suspension of any financial contributions, until Monks received a fair hearing and the KAAA rescinded its ban on non-Kenyan athletes.[72] Another respondent called Yeda's attempt to ban non-Kenyan nationals from KAAA meets "dictatorial" and argued that this "ridiculous" statement could not go unchallenged. The commentator questioned why Monks, or any other KAAA member, was not entitled to due process of law, what facts led to the harsh penalty, and why Yeda had failed to state whether Monks was known to have missed any other meet.[73] Horace Owiti, the outgoing president of the University College Students' Union, expressed concern that people beyond the university sought to become involved in "our domestic affairs," noting that because the Makerere, Dar es Salaam, and Nairobi Colleges formed one university, their internal activities must be considered domestic, and thus no one had the right to "dictate to our private activities unless he can constitutionally indicate his authority."[74]

Fellow athlete Philip Ndoo, who would go on to represent Kenya at the 1970 Commonwealth Games and 1972 Olympics before forging a long career as a journalist, deplored the heavy punishment levied on Monks without the opportunity to defend herself as "more than saddening." He also criticized Yeda for responding with a single question to the elder Monks's concerns that his daughter was never properly informed of the arrangements as "the worst thing for a high official like Mr. Yeda to do." Addressing that query of how other athletes named to the team came to know that they were selected, he lamented, "What a pity that Mr. Yeda fails to find out such a simple answer!" Speaking from his personal experience, he opined that for Monks to claim that she was uninformed only indicated that she had not heard the public address. "The verbal announcement that the first and second places athletes in each event at the Kenya Championships were to remain behind did not reach her ears." He found it "unjust and inconsiderate" for the KAAA to render such a harsh verdict based on the potentially false assumption that Monks was aware of the announcement, rather than providing evidence that she was guilty of refusal to represent Kenya.[75]

Ndoo ended by acknowledging that a white woman was at the center of the conflict. "This harsh verdict over Miss Monks by Mr. Yeda and his colleagues cannot escape suspicion of racism," he submitted. He noted a precedent, namely that an outstanding male African runner had failed to turn up at the recent KAAA versus Kenya Schools' competition, which was "a great disappointment to the sporting public who had paid to see the best quarter-miler in Africa."[76] Ndoo did not name him explicitly, but followers of Kenyan sport would have known that Daniel Rudisha was then the undisputed fastest African 440-yards runner in the history of event. Officials did not inform the public as to where he was and why he had not turned up at the meet, Ndoo observed, nor did the KAAA suspend the truant runner for "abusing" the nation and athletics in Kenya.[77] Although Ndoo did not cite it, KAAA officials had also overlooked Rudisha's absence earlier that year when he failed to arrive at the Nairobi airport alongside the rest of the seven-man Kenyan all-star team selected to compete in Tananarive (now Antananarivo), Madagascar.[78] Rudisha's dereliction of duty to a Kenyan national team five months before Monks missed the 1967 East African Championships went unmentioned in the Kenyan press at the time. Team manager Aish Jeneby in his internal KAAA report about the Madagascar tour simply noted the absence in parentheses next to his name in the list of athletes invited to represent Kenya: "D. Rudisha (did not report in Nairobi)."[79]

Other commentators highlighted the possible racial dynamics of Monks's suspension and related plans to reserve KAAA-organized meets for Kenyan citizens. The *East African Standard* renewed its focus on the issue with a second editorial entitled "Racialism in Athletics." Focusing on the KAAA's intention to exclude non-Kenyans from its events, the press reminded readers that this ban, according to Yeda, arose from Monks's failure to compete at the East African Championships. The paper considered it doubtful that Monks could even be considered a non-Kenyan, making the accompanying general ban against noncitizens even more unwarranted. Monks was born in Kenya to British parents, and sport officials had previously regarded her as enough of a Kenyan national to win a medal for the country abroad. As she was not yet twenty-one, the age at which she could choose to pursue either Kenyan or British citizenship, she should be considered Kenyan, the *East African Standard* contended, especially since Monks had already attempted to apply for Kenyan citizenship but had been rejected because she was a minor.[80] Regardless of the status of Monks's citizenship, the paper queried, what did a dispute over her absenteeism at the East African Championships have to do with the community of non-Kenyan track and field athletes "other than being included out of a discriminatory attitude unworthy of the *harambee* [meaning "all pull together"] spirit of the country"?[81]

The controversy coincided with wider continental debates of sport and race. Conflict was brewing over the participation of apartheid South Africa at the upcoming Mexico City Olympic Games that would culminate in a global stand-off in which some forty nations, including Kenya, threatened to boycott the Olympics if South Africa took part.[82] Kenyan politicians four years before the Monks controversy had played a leading role in the anti-apartheid sport struggle, most notably by refusing to allow an all-white South African Olympic delegation to enter the country to attend the pivotal 1963 International Olympic Committee (IOC) annual meeting planned for Nairobi at which South Africa's Olympic participation was to be decided. When Kenyan leaders refused to yield to pressure to grant the South African Olympic delegates entry, the president of the IOC, Avery Brundage, shifted the session from Nairobi to Baden-Baden, West Germany, at the last minute.[83] The *East African Standard* likened the KAAA's decision to ban Monks from sport not to Kenyan leaders' principled stand against white South African delegates but rather to the sweeping discrimination that plagued South African sport and society that threatened to make the southern African nation a pariah. "If Kenya persists in applying a narrow doctrine of racial and political prejudice in sport," the press warned, "the country will find itself outlawed from these international events."[84]

KAAA secretary Aish Jeneby, to temper the outcry, issued a public response clarifying that Yeda's proclamation "in future no non-Kenyans will be allowed to compete in athletic meetings organized by the Kenya A.A.A" had omitted the important caveat "except those invited by the K.A.A.A."[85] Jeneby explained that Kenyan citizens, guest athletes from overseas, and "any other athlete," by which he meant competitors living in the country without Kenyan citizenship, would be welcome as long as they were invited by the KAAA.[86] His more moderate version of the new policy referred to the minutes of the KAAA meeting at which this decision was made, which indeed indicate that Yeda had overstepped by announcing a blanket ban of all noncitizen track and field athletes. These documents show that the KAAA executive agreed unanimously that because Monks "had let the country down," she should be suspended for two years and that "in future no NON-CITIZENS will be allowed to compete in the National meetings in Kenya except those invited by the K.A.A.A."[87] This ruling, compared with Yeda's sweeping disbarment of all non-Kenyan nationals, preserved the possibility of latitude for all competitors to take part but also concentrated power in the hands of officials who now possessed greater control over athletes' competitive lives.

Jeneby, who had been involved in Kenyan sport since 1954, the year after he graduated from the Coast Teacher Training College, Mombasa, and held a degree in education from Loughborough College completed in 1960, explained at length in his public letter how track and field athletes in Kenya advanced from one level of competition to the next.[88] A competitor who won an event at a district championship automatically gained selection for the provincial championships, where athletes were supposed to remain under the supervision of the provincial team manager. All athletes finishing in the top two in each event at the national championships were automatically selected to compete at the East African Championships. The day after the national meet ended, provincial managers received the final list of athletes selected to advance and then returned home with those who failed to qualify. Selected athletes were to remain at the location of the national championships to train for six days before traveling together to the East African Championships. Jeneby, as KAAA secretary, was supposed to notify the press, provinces, and managers of the athletes chosen to compete, and it was the provincial associations' duty to inform the athletes' employers that their absence from work was required.[89]

Jeneby claimed that he had executed all his responsibilities. At the 1967 national championships held at Jamhuri Park, he announced in both English and Swahili that all athletes placing first or second in their events should report to Kenyatta College the following morning, and that after the national meet all managers should convene to finalize the roster. Managers were to inform their athletes who had been selected. Jeneby described how on September 4, he sent the names of the selected athletes to all provinces, officials, and the press, and the *East African Standard* printed the list on September 5.[90] He failed to mention, however, that above the list of names of selected athletes published in the *Standard* was a subheading titled "Not available" under which it stated that Monks "has been included in the team for the 80 metres hurdles and long jump events, but she indicated at the weekend that she would not be available to compete in Kisumu."[91] Perhaps Monks, or someone close to her, shared her travel plans to let everyone know through the press that she could not attend East African Championships. If so, that effort to communicate her whereabouts went unmentioned by the numerous KAAA and government officials who condemned her absence.

For There to Be an Athletics Association, There Must Be Athletes

The Games Union of University College, Nairobi, led by a nine-person executive committee elected by the captains of twenty-one affiliate clubs, continued to fight on Monks's behalf.[92] This body issued a second statement calling for Yeda's resignation along with a full investigation into the affairs of the KAAA. A Games Union spokesperson noted that Yeda had quoted rules from the British AAA constitution, and not those of the KAAA, which the union determined had not been updated since the 1950s, prior to Kenya gaining independence. "These rules stated by Mr. Yeda are, therefore, totally irrelevant to the issue in question and it would be interesting to know why Mr. Yeda has decided to use these irrelevant rules," he asserted. The union also discovered that the 1950s KAAA bylaws permitted affiliate organizations whose membership was defined by race. "The constitution states 'affiliation to the association is open to colony-wide associations of a racial nature,'" noted the union representative, who declared his organization unwilling to be associated with an entity whose constitution condoned such practices.[93]

The union also reiterated that the KAAA had no right to interfere with athletes seeking to compete in university events. Yeda had quoted selectively from the British AAA constitution, the union contended, by failing to mention its policies on "Domestic Autonomy." "Under this heading, we came to the conclusion that the University Games is an internal event completely outside the jurisdiction of the Kenya A.A.A." The union likened these games to a competition among three houses of a school, from which it followed that if Monks could not compete for Nairobi College in Kampala, then she should also be barred from intramural sport within the college, an intervention at a level that stretched credulity. The union declared that it wanted Monks to represent the college at the University Games in field hockey, not track and field, and that it was beyond the scope of the KAAA's powers to prevent her from doing so. In a final parry, it argued that the new policy barring non-Kenyan nationals from athletics could not be upheld because such a change required an amendment to the constitution, which, according to the KAAA's own bylaws, could only be accepted at an extraordinary general meeting.[94]

Among the large feedback from the public that the *East African Standard* received, one letter stood out from another fellow athlete who took up Monks's cause. J. Ambrose Awuoro Apunda declared, "With all my heart I support the statement issued by the Games Union of the University College, Nairobi, and all the correspondence in your newspaper condemning the suspension of Miss Diana Monks, one of the most outstanding female athletes in Kenya." Apunda shared the challenges that he had faced in learning about the logistics of the meet as a member of the team that competed in the 1967 East African Championships: "I know of one other athlete as well as myself who was notified just a day before the team's departure for Kisumu," noting that he then had to make arrangements with his employer within that brief period and, as other athletes experienced difficulties regarding the logistics of the meet, Monks should be given the benefit of the doubt and her suspension withdrawn.[95]

He then emphasized the importance of athletes and the need to treat them well. "For there to be an Athletics Association there must be athletes, and if athletes are to participate in amateur championships respect and good treatment must be accorded them. In short, the world of sport, or rather athletics, belongs to athletes as well as the executives."[96] His demand met a global moment in which American track and field athletes half a world away were similarly campaigning for better treatment from sport administrators in the United States.[97] After Keino's middle-distance rival Jim Ryun set a world record in the 880-yards events, the Amateur Athletic Union (AAU), the national governing body of the sport, refused to ask the international governing body to ratify the performance because Ryun had competed at a college meet.[98] In January 1968, twelve of the best US men's track and field athletes, including Ryun, responded to AAU threats to suspend athletes who competed in a scheduled college competition by voluntarily collectively disqualifying themselves if the AAU sanctioned any one of them. The "Daring Dozen," so dubbed by *Track and Field News*, declared, "We feel each individual athlete should have the choice to compete when and where he desires."[99] That demand for greater control for athletes concerning their competitive opportunities was echoed in Kenya by Apunda, who argued that it was Monks's choice whether to compete and that she need not seek permission for doing otherwise. "The definition of an amateur athlete embraces the fact that the athlete participates at his or her own wish. Hence, if Diana failed to appear at the East African championships on grounds that she was not notified of the arrangements, she is in the right."[100]

He also connected the racial dynamics of the case to other international contexts, including its resonance with South African apartheid that encroached on sport in various ways. White athletes in that country enjoyed superior facilities and selection to teams that represented South Africa at home and abroad. Racially circumscribed associations divided athletes, black spectators were banned from certain venues while segregation reigned in most others, and in almost all circumstances, black and white athletes could not compete against each other. Echoing the *East African Standard*, Apunda argued that singling out Monks on racial grounds would not only hurt the KAAA's reputation for fairness, it would "also make the South Africans sing with joy when they see Kenyans following almost the same path as theirs."[101]

Turning to the attempt to ban non-Kenyan nationals from domestic meets, Apunda pointed to the United States as an example to emulate, noting their athletes' outstanding progress in track and field by both black and white athletes. "When we come to the question of athletics, we should step outside the field of colour, race and nationality," advised Apunda, and instead focus on allowing all athletes to excel in the sport. If the association only allowed Kenyan nationals to participate in domestic meets, he posed a question: "Who would lose—the K.A.A.A. or individual athletes?" His answer extended not only to the noncitizens in question but also to their competitors. "As a sportsman of understanding, I cannot tolerate exempting a better expatriate athlete from athletics just because he is not a Kenyan," further contending that such a ruling would cost fans who enjoyed watching Kenyans and non-Kenyans competing together.[102]

In addition to race, nation, citizenship, and athletes' rights, Apunda paid attention to gender, criticizing the KAAA for suspending one of the country's best woman athletes without clear cause as doing so could prove a deterrent just as Kenyan women were beginning to compete at the international level. "To worsen the affair," he asserted, "Diana is a female and the first to represent Kenya abroad." He considered it a "calamity" to suspend her from sports at a point when "we are advocating that women take part in sports." Minister Ngala himself at the 1967 East African Championships in Kisumu had encouraged more women to participate in sport and committed the government to supporting their involvement. Apunda ended by imploring that "I think I am right in my views in my capacity as an athlete. It costs time and energy to produce an athlete as fine as Diana, and in view of the fact that yours is an amateur association, Mr. Yeda, I call upon your officials to rescind Diana's suspension."[103]

Yeda's Powerful Allies

Ronald Ngala, the former leader of the Kenya African Democratic Union (KADU), which had once rivalled Kenyatta's ruling party, and recently appointed minister for Cooperatives and Social Services, whose purview included sport, entered the debate to defend the KAAA's decision to ban Monks for two years. In a lengthy press release, he offered full support for her suspension, declaring:

> The suspension of Diana Monks is in accordance with the regulations and rules governing amateur sport . . . the Ministry has examined carefully the circumstances leading to the suspension of Miss Monks and the Ministry is satisfied that the reasons justified this suspension, the details leading to the suspension having been given by the president of the K.A.A.A. We are, therefore, in compete support of the action taken by the K.A.A.A. in their endeavour to maintain a high standard of discipline in amateur sport.[104]

Contrary to campaigners such as Apunda, who defended the right of athletes to choose when and where to compete, Ngala supported the principle that administrators should maintain control. Though acknowledging that the administration of sport should be separate from government, he reserved final decision-making powers for his ministry. "It must be made clear that no incident, no matter how small it may be, will go unnoticed by the Government and when facts leading to such incidents come to light, the Government will not hesitate in taking the necessary steps as it may deem fit for the benefit of amateur sport in Kenya."[105] The year before, the government had established a new governing body for sport, the Kenya National Sports Council (KNSC), a move that historian Kara Moskowitz notes "initiated the nationalization of sport," as "for politicians, the stakes were high, and sport represented an important arena where the fight for full decolonization was waged."[106] Not only did government officials control the purse strings, doling out annual subsidies to Kenyan sports associations, but also they oversaw athletes' movements through their authority over entry and exit visas. By intervening in Monks's suspension, Ngala, as a minister who formed part of Kenyatta's inner circle, was showing his willingness to apply the full weight of governmental authority to sport, thereby superseding the authority of sport associations and further constraining the agency of the athletes themselves.

The minister repudiated the suggestion that race played any role in the matter. "Racialism" had nothing to do Monks's suspension, Ngala asserted, noting that "non-Kenyans" had historically been included in Kenyan national teams, though "each competition is governed by its own rules," an ambiguous claim that hinted that those precedents no longer applied. By rejecting the salience of race in the matter, Ngala followed the approach taken by his government that was sending a message of inclusion to minority groups who adopted Kenyan citizenship. In sport, too, Ngala contended that racism played no role, but that national unity certainly did. Participation by top athletes in Kenyan national teams, particularly those competing at home in front of powerful politicians such as himself, was paramount. His government placed utmost value on loyalty from its athletes, and by missing the championship meet, Monks had failed her country, thus: "It is the Government's intention to ensure that a high standard of discipline is set and it is for these reasons that the Ministry fully supports the action taken by the K.A.A.A. in suspending Miss Monks."[107] The minister did offer some solace to Monks when he clarified that her suspension only applied to KAAA-organized track and field events: "This decision is binding on those athletic associations affiliated to the Kenya Amateur Athletics Association and not binding on other forms of sport, e.g. hockey or university students' associations, which are not affiliated to the Kenya A.A.A." He also affirmed that Monks could lodge an appeal with the KAAA if she wished.[108] Beyond that, as a third *East African Standard* editorial on the matter observed, Monks also had recourse to appeal to the Kenya Olympic Association and to the International Amateur Athletic Federation.[109]

The episode reached the front page of the Kenyan press upon news breaking that Monks's father was indeed considering appealing the suspension on her behalf. He planned to examine the KAAA's constitution to determine if officials had followed correct procedures. "If I find that there are loopholes, I will certainly appeal to the Kenya A.A.A. and maybe even to the Kenya Olympic and Commonwealth Games Association," he told the *East African Standard*, which noted another area of ambiguity regarding the relationship between the KAAA and its Nairobi affiliate, of which Monks was a member. The KAAA had voted to suspend Monks at one of its council meetings, but it was the NAAA, and not the national body, that communicated that decision to her. Her father stated that "the letter of suspension came from the N.A.A.A., Diana appealed against the suspension to the N.A.A.A., whose secretary, Mr. A.A. Cockar, wrote back to say that the Kenya A.A.A. would not reconsider her case."[110]

While the Monks considered their options, other powerful members of the government were falling in line behind the position taken by Ngala whose response, as the highest-ranking Kenyan official with responsibility for sport, set the tone. The Mayor of Nairobi, Isaac Lugonzo, serving simultaneously as chairman of the KNSC, announced that the latter organization, too, fully supported the decision made by the KAAA. "We have considered the facts put before us regarding the Diana Monks issue and we feel that the Kenya Amateur Athletic Association were well within their powers in taking disciplinary action." Lugonzo echoed Ngala's position that Monks was welcome to participate in other sports beyond track and field and to submit an appeal with the KAAA. He also wished to dispel the notion that race had anything to do with her suspension, asserting: "We do not believe in racialism and the Kenya A.A.A. considered Miss Monks's case on its merit and we are not happy in seeing racialism being brought into this case."[111] "Racialism had nothing to do with the suspension of one of the country's top women athletes, Diana Monks," affirmed KAAA president Musembi Mbathi in his subsequent public statement on the matter. He framed the issue as a matter of honor for his association. An athlete had transgressed the rules that demanded his association hold her to account. To pardon Monks simply to demonstrate its nonracial bona fides would bring the KAAA into disrepute. "My guess is that my association is expected to condone irresponsible action to prove to the world how non-racial we are. This is utter rubbish; my association is not prepared to stoop this low."[112]

The sixth and final statement from a high-ranking sport official came from A. A. Cockar, the secretary of the Nairobi AAA. He too declared support for Monks's banning, stressing that shortly before the Kisumu meet, Monks left for a holiday in Mombasa aware that she would have been selected for championship team as one of the country's best woman athletes: "Would an international athlete of Miss Monks' standard take a holiday knowing that an important athletics meeting like the East African championships was going to take place in less than a week's time?"[113] Cockar also took exception to Monks's failure to communicate her whereabouts to the Nairobi AAA directly. "Had she informed my association the story would have been different," he claimed. He inferred that Monks "did not have any intention whatsoever of representing her country," and speculated that she had not foreseen any consequences for missing the championship event. Such temerity merited harsh punishment. "My association thinks that by suspending Miss Monks the Kenya A.A.A. has set an example and that other athletes, if they repeat such a foolish incident, risk the same action being taken against them."[114]

Honor Carries with It an Obligation

Against this drumbeat of solidarity from the most powerful men involved in sport in Kenya came more voices from below whose letters were published in the press. An individual self-identified as "Concerned" postmarked a letter declaring it "very disturbing to see the way sport in Kenya is messed about by a few individuals" and arguing that suspending athletes, especially younger competitors who might become champions in the future, was counterproductive and that they should instead be offered as much encouragement as possible.[115] "Concerned" also criticized the KAAA for verbally informing athletes about details related to the championship meet, calling it "ridiculous" that written invitations were not sent to each person. The commentator wondered if Yeda himself had communicated personally with every athlete and if it might be possible that out of the forty or fifty athletes selected for the team, someone forgot to inform one or two? The letter writer ended with the proposal that Yeda resign from his position in the KAAA to allow someone "more constructive" to take his place.[116]

One member of the public stood out for supporting the punishment levied on Monks. Jacob Wangatia argued that Monks's father's response showed "incredible disdain" and "fallacy." Monks had damaged "the national interest" by costing Kenya points in a competition against its regional rivals. "Had she participated the results would have been different," he claimed. The week before the East African Championships, Monks had indeed produced superior results compared to the Ugandans, who won the two events in which the KAAA sought her involvement. Wangatia then claimed that her failure to participate in the Kisumu meet made a mockery of the outlay of administrative support for sport, not to mention of Kenyan national pride. "The country and the K.A.A.A. has shown pride in her and accordingly she has been given every opportunity to develop her talent and record her maximum efforts in amateur sport this year." Ultimately, Wangatia attributed Kenyan athletic success to the country's sport administrators and to state provision of resources and competitive opportunities that allowed athletes such as Monks to perform at their best. The effort by athletes to excel in sport was secondary to the investment and support of the government. "It is because the State has made facilities available that Miss Monks emerged as one of the leading sports stars of today and it is high time our students were discouraged from writing rude letters against the country's administrators who are the masterminds behind their own progress and attainments."[117]

Wangatia, like other commentators, pointed to sport in the United States as a way to frame Monks's suspension, but he chose to compare her case to that of world heavyweight boxing champion Muhammad Ali, who had been drafted into the US military but refused induction on grounds that, to quote Ali, he would not fight "brown people in Vietnam while so-called Negro people in Louisville are treated like dogs and denied simple human rights."[118] He was arrested, prosecuted, and received the maximum sentence of five years in a federal prison and a $10,000 fine. Wangatia omitted these details and portrayed the champion boxer's draft refusal not as a principled stand against racism and imperialism but as a selfish undermining of his government, opining that "this man tried to suppress the interests of the State by considering his own position. He was obsessed by his crown and forgot that it was the State which opened the road for him to such boxing status."[119] By implication, Monks too had placed her own interests over those of the nation. Therefore, she was deserving of the ban she received.

Unlike Ali, no broader social or geopolitical dynamics prevented Monks from competing at the East African Championships, and her choice to visit Mombasa rather than compete drew particular criticism. KAAA president Mbathi stated that his association imposed a two-year suspension on Monks "because she gave a very lame excuse for her failure to show up."[120] He characterized the university student as a savvy veteran of track and field as she had previously represented Kenya at major international games. "It has been alleged that Diana was not aware of her selection in the national team, but she is not a newcomer to competitive athletics. She has represented Kenya in international competitions before," Mbathi asserted. The procedure for choosing the East African Championship team had not changed from previous years. "Furthermore, she was approached regarding her participation at Kisumu," he affirmed, also highlighting the "numerous" public address announcements about the upcoming championship meet. "I must say that there is not much hope for her if she did not realise that she had been selected for the national team after all this," he declared.[121] Mbathi then warmed to the patriotic theme first broached by Yeda when he called Monks's absence an "abuse to the nation." A track and field athlete selected to compete for the national team brought glory to the individual and to the new Kenya, he claimed, but that "honour carries with it an obligation to the association and the nation as well." Mbathi believed that after his association chose an athlete for the national team, "it is automatically expected that the athlete will make the team unless there are extenuating circumstances beyond the athlete's control." Failure to appear because she went on vacation constituted an "abuse" in track and field that KAAA rules were designed to check. "Diana's reason for not participating at the meeting at Kisumu was that she had to go to the Coast for her holidays. This is the reason she gave to an official of the N.A.A.A. when he went to see her at her father's shop," Mbathi explained.

He lastly echoed Cockar's complaints about her failure to communicate with his organization directly. "Surely Diana should have had the courtesy to notify at least an official of my association if she had decided not to fulfil her obligation," Mbathi averred, omitting the fact that two press reports about the meet stated her planned absence in the week prior to the championships. Monks herself offered no public defense or explanation of why she chose to go on a holiday rather than compete at the championship meet, or why she informed the press of whereabouts and not the KAAA or the Nairobi AAA. Although Kenyan papers made her absence public ahead of the meet, Monks had failed to make KAAA officials personally aware that she would be unable to participate, which embarrassed them in front of an assemblage of dignitaries in Kisumu when Ugandan athletes won her events. Mbathi's executive council thus agreed unanimously that Monks's absence from the national team without a satisfactory excuse and her failure to communicate her whereabouts to officials "constituted misbehaviour and unfair practice" that warranted a two-year suspension. Mbathi concluded: "It must be appreciated that an athlete who qualifies to represent his or her nation must be prepared to abide by the rules and regulations governing amateur athletics. He or she must also be prepared to accept the joy and glory as well as the demands, the sacrifices and obligations which go with them."[122]

Conclusion

On December 12, 1967, the four-year anniversary of Kenyan independence, the press broke the news that the KAAA executive council had rejected Monks's appeal. KAAA president Mbathi issued a statement affirming that the two-year penalty would be upheld because Monks "failed to turn up at Kisumu for the East African Championships, without genuine excuse or reason, in accordance with the rules and regulations governing amateur athletics in Kenya." This verdict differed from the original decision only in the added justification that Monks had not provided a satisfactory reason for missing the competition. Skipping the meet for a holiday at the Coast "in spite of her awareness of the Kisumu meeting" violated the patriotism, discipline, and loyalty that administrators demanded of athletes. "Amateur athletics will be doomed if leniency is exercised on deliberate actions like Diana's," pronounced Mbathi. The KAAA executive council agreed unanimously that her suspension must be served in full.[123]

Although her rejected appeal kept her from KAAA-organized events, Monks was able to compete in other sports and she continued to play field hockey at a high level, including a stint on the Kenyan national team in 1969.[124] She also competed in track and field at the University Games in Kampala in 1967, a victory for the Nairobi College Games Union.[125] But Monks never returned to competitions organized by the KAAA. At the Olympic Games in Mexico City in 1968, the Kenyan track and field team included women for the first time. Tecla Chemabwai, Lydia Stephens, and Elizabeth Chesire comprised that stellar contingent. But for her two-year suspension, Monks would likely have been among them.

It had become apparent that not all athletes were held to the same standard as Monks regarding attendance at important domestic meets. Daniel Rudisha's absences from both the 1967 KAAA/Schools meet and the Kenyan tour of Madagascar exemplified this double standard. In the year following her suspension, reporting on a major invitational meet in May 1968, the *East African Standard* declared "Top Runners Again Absent" when Kipchoge Keino and Rudisha along with rising stars Ben Jipcho, David Mungai, and Kimaru Songok were unexplained no-shows.[126] At the 1968 national championships in early August, steeplechaser Benjamin Kogo, whose times ranked third in the world the previous year, did not compete and Keino initially watched as a spectator, only deciding to race the three-miles event on the final day as a guest.[127] None of these men received sanction of any kind.

Diana Monks missed a major international meet at a time when pressure on noncitizens was building across Kenyan society while the government was constitutionally required to guarantee equal treatment of all Kenyan nationals, regardless of race. As this episode shows, "Kenyanization" involved more than the replacement of noncitizens with citizens in economic and political spheres. The early independence years witnessed a larger social transformation wherein Africans endeavored to harness, capitalize on, and make amendments to the cultural institutions they had inherited from Britain.[128] Sport was among them, and Kenyan sport administrators, embracing the language used by Kenyatta's government, emphasized the equality of citizens in track and field even as they embarked on a course of action that punished Monks for similar infractions committed by the male athletes on whom no retribution was levied. The episode spawned debate among journalists, government officials, citizens, and athletes on topics of national loyalty, race relations, athletes' rights, and the advancement of women in sport. Despite interventions on her behalf, Monks received a two-year suspension, and Kenyan administrators responded to Monks's infraction by making the future participation of all noncitizens conditional on their approval.

During the latter half of the 1960s, Kenyan sportswomen were ascendent and accomplished even by international standards of excellence. The infrastructure for women's track and field had developed sufficiently to allow a small group of female athletes to qualify for major international events for the first time. Simultaneously, government and sport officials sought to control athletes' mobility and competitive choices, making an example of Monks, whom they claimed reneged on her obligations to the nation. They argued that her two-year ban was necessary to protect the honor of the KAAA, and Kenya itself, but such conduct was in fact a show of power that sought to establish the command of administrators over athletes.

CHAPTER THREE

Precocious Achievement and the Long Run to Inclusion

Marriage, Motherhood, and the Military

When are we going to see some fresh talent at these meetings?" a reporter for the *Daily Nation* asked after the women's 400-meters event had to be canceled at a major track and field meet held in Nairobi's Jamhuri Park in June 1972, three weeks before the Kenyan Olympic Trials, when no competitors came forward. The same event for the men required two heats. The reporter questioned, "Why was Tecla Chemabwai, Kenya's Munich qualifier in this event, in the stadium yet not competing, and Ester Makayo who lives in Nairobi just not there?"[1]

The 400-meters event was the most dramatic example of the dearth of women competing that day. The paucity of women at the Jamhuri meet was typical of the time and starkly contrasted with burgeoning numbers of boys, men, and teenage girls participating in track and field. Fifteen-year-old Cherono Maiyo of Kapsabet in the Rift Valley stole the show. In the 1500 meters that day, Maiyo turned a comfortable early lead into an eleven second win over rival teenager Elizabeth Chelimo. Less than an hour later she claimed her second victory, this time in the 800 meters by thirteen seconds. Self-trained by way of a regimen that consisted of a daily two mile run to school and back, she had already achieved the Olympic time standard for the 1500 meters which placed her among the very best in the British Commonwealth at that distance. A reporter for the *Daily Nation* wrote, "It is staggering to think of the potential of this young girl."[2] A commentator exclaimed a year earlier when Maiyo and Chelimo jointly broke the African record for the 1500 meters, "At last they have made it! Kenya women for long overshadowed by their world famous men came into the scene yesterday."[3] But their numbers, few at the start of the postcolonial years, remained discouragingly low until the retreat of amateur athletics at the end of the century.

Between Kenya's independence in 1963 and the Los Angeles Olympics in 1984, only ten Kenyan women competed in track and field at the four Summer Olympic Games to which Kenya sent a team. During this same period, seventy-three Kenyan men competed at the games, steadily increasing their numbers at the world's most prestigious sporting venue while women remained locked in a twenty-year pattern of comparative underperformance. In these early post-independence years, while men were creating worldwide awareness of their new nation, Kenyan women contended with a host of obstacles. Many recorded extraordinary times as girls but for a number of reasons dropped out of competition altogether before they reached adulthood. Schools were the main avenue into track and field for the vast majority of male and female competitors, yet relatively few girls advanced to secondary school. Family and societal gendered expectations about childcare, education, and domestic labor impeded many young women, often causing them to abandon promising sport careers. Staid cultural views regarding appropriate female behavior were difficult to overcome.

Nevertheless, a handful of talented runners earned an international standing in sport, attained educational qualifications and employment opportunities beyond the norm for women of this era and became citizens of the world. Almost all were exposed to sport at school with at least one parent supporting their athletic ambitions. Competing at the highest levels of track and field by any woman often included the unconventional choice to delay marriage or refuse it outright. These women left home, secured waged employment, and established alternative lifestyles demonstrating that women could construct their own identities within masculine domains. This vanguard contingent of female runners challenged expectations and established the foundation used by later generations of women who forged careers as professional runners.

A Fragile Project, 1964–1984

After the first major meet of the 1973 Kenyan domestic track and field season, the *Daily Nation* reported that two-time Olympian Tecla Chemabwai had won the long jump "against no competition."[4] In December that year at the Kenyan trials for the 1974 Christchurch Commonwealth Games, the highlight was thirteen-year-old Rose Tata's qualifying time of 2:10 in the 800 meters. It was "all the more impressive for there were only two competitors in this race."[5] Tata's excellent time and Chemabwai's victory were noteworthy, as were the sparse number of female competitors in these events. Two years later, the *Daily Nation* reported that a major meet lost "the majority of our top local girls" when six athletes from Chepterit Girls' High School instead competed at the schools' cross-country championships in Eldoret, leaving the women's division at the track and field meet with "little to watch."[6]

The Kenyan media throughout the 1970s and 1980s regularly bemoaned the dearth of women in track and field and remained preoccupied with the fact that Kenya's female athletes were not "keeping pace" with the men.[7] Describing the 1972 national championships, the *Daily Nation* announced, "Six More for Munich: Women Fail to Shine." Kenyan men at that meet had broken four national records and achieved six additional qualifying times for the Munich Olympic Games. The men's 800-meters event was "expectedly, another great race with an incredibly high-class field going to the start," part of "an afternoon of excitement" that culminated in Ben Jipcho winning the 3000-meters steeplechase "in a fabulous Kenya best-ever time of 8 minutes 28.6 seconds." Enthusiasm waned for the women as the Kenyan daily observed in words that typify this fragile period: "Again, the fact has been underlined that the women are going to require a great deal more attention over the next few years if their performances are to compare favourably with those of the men."[8]

Renowned distance runner and *Daily Nation* journalist Philip Ndoo, who had publicly opposed the suspension of the All Africa Games silver medalist Diana Monks in 1967, regularly expressed his concerns about the gender gap in Kenyan athletics in the pages of the daily press. In 1970 he questioned why the "home of middle distance runners like Kip Keino" did not feature women running to the same standard.[9] Sixteen years later, Ndoo as sports editor of the *Daily Nation* decried "Kenya has as many talented women in athletics as the men, but for various reasons, Kenyan women have lagged far behind in performance, especially on the international scene."[10] Later that year, he lamented, "Kenya is littered with numerous women athletes who have shown great potential at the tender ages, only to fade away when they should be maturing."[11]

By the time that Ndoo issued the latter complaints in 1986, only two Kenyan women had won track and field medals at Commonwealth Games competitions, and no medal had ever been won by a Kenyan woman at the Olympic Games. Fifteen-year-old Sabina Chebichi was the first to claim a medal when she won bronze in the 800-meters event at the 1974 Christchurch Commonwealth Games in New Zealand, a competition at which Kenyan track and field men won six gold, two silver, and five bronze medals. Four years later at the Edmonton Commonwealth Games in Canada, Tecla Chemabwai claimed the sole medal for Kenyan women, a silver in the 800 meters, while Kenyan men in track and field won five golds, three silver, and two bronzes.[12] It would take until the arrival of professional track and field for headlines to begin signaling a new era in Kenyan women's distance running, with the *Daily Nation* reporting that the upcoming 1992 Barcelona Olympic Games were "Women's Best Chance Since Mexican Debut."[13]

Direct comparison between numbers of men and women who competed at the four Olympic Games to which Kenya sent a team from 1964 to 1984 does not accurately assess the gap between them, however, as Kenyan men competed in long-distance running events from which women of all nations were barred. Yet even considering only the events for which both sexes could qualify, their numbers were grossly unequal during this period. A total of fifty-three Kenyan men competed in the same set of events available to both sexes, compared with ten women (see accompanying figure). This widening gap occurred even though at least one new event was added to the women's program for each of these Olympics, giving Kenyan women increasing opportunities to improve their numbers. Additionally, while the women did not win any Olympic track and field medals during this period, Kenyan men won a total of fourteen.[14]

This comparative underperformance was not for lack of ability. Female teenagers consistently recorded exceptional statistics. In the early 1980s Esther Kocch ran 56.5 seconds for the 400 meters at age thirteen, Jennifer Wanjononi completed the 1500 meters in 4:26 when she was fourteen years old, and Selina Chirchir was thirteen when she ran 2:11 in the 800 meters and 58 seconds in the 400 meters—all impressive times for athletes still in their early teenage years.[15] In 1979 when the Kenya Colleges and Schools Sports Council first allowed primary and secondary schoolgirls to compete directly against women from the teacher training colleges,

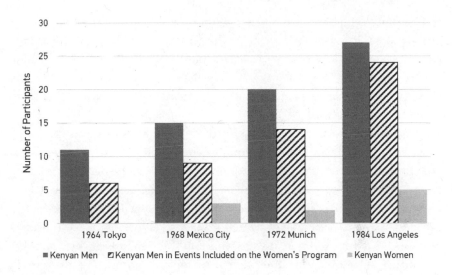

FIGURE 1. Participation of Kenyan Men and Women in Track and Field at the Olympics, 1964–1984. Kenya boycotted the 1976 and 1980 Olympic Games. SOURCE: OLYMPEDIA, HTTP://WWW.OLYMPEDIA.ORG/

the former claimed victories against the college women in every event except the 100-meter hurdles. Primary schools were not expected to enter any athletes in the "grueling" 3000-meters event, yet over that distance, primary schoolgirls "ran their [older] opposition to the ground."[16]

In 1981 Kenyan media outlets such as *Drum* magazine touted thirteen-year-old Justina Chepchirchir, whom the Kenyan sport establishment hoped would "carry the mantle of the Kenyan greats who have made such a mark in international athletics in the past fifteen years" and "not disappear immediately like the other young girls including the 'Petticoat Princess' Sabina Chebichi and Elizabeth Onyambu."[17] *Sports Review*, a Kenyan periodical, acknowledged that "each season brings a new sensation to Kenya track and field," and that in 1981 it had been "the little Nandi schoolgirl" Chepchirchir.[18] She started running for her primary school in Kapsabet as an eleven-year-old and the following year dominated the distance races at the 1980 Kenyan national primary schools meets. In 1981 Chepchirchir received an invitation to take part in a series of events in Japan. Kenyan national coach Walter Abmayr expressed concern that Chepchirchir and her compatriot, Mary Chepkemboi, also aged thirteen, were too young and inexperienced to be exposed to international competition. Competing at the first meet in Kobe only twenty-four hours after arrival, Chepchirchir finished second in the 5000 meters and Chepkemboi third. At the second meet in Hiroshima, Chepchirchir won the 1500 meters event. At the final competition in Tokyo, she won the 3000 meters with a stellar time of 9:11.74 seconds, breaking the Kenyan and African record held by fellow countrywoman Rose Chepyator-Thomson.[19]

Chepchirchir advanced to secondary school at Kapsabet Girls' High School, where she balanced her studies with training for the 1984 Olympic Games. "Right now, I have a great deal to do academically and on the sports field," she told the Kenyan periodical *True Love* in December 1983.[20] At the age of sixteen, Chepchirchir competed at the 1984 Los Angeles games, finishing seventeenth in the 1500-meters event. She would not compete again at a major international meet. Her early promise and abrupt retirement were typical for Kenyan girls at the time who, despite achieving exceptional performances, seldom continued their sporting careers into adulthood.

Secondary Schools and Sport

By the late 1960s a well-organized system of primary schools' competitions identified athletic talent. Cross-country competitions were held at schools, then districts, then provinces across the country, a pattern that repeated during the track and field season. These competitions provided opportunities for coaches to observe a large pool of runners and to recruit talent for their respective high schools. Sport geographers John Bale and Joe Sang also highlight the "significance of the printed word," notably a coaching manual on *Athletics* authored by education officers in Kenya who advocated that track and field be included in the school curriculum starting in the primary school.[21] Kenya Sports Officer Charles Mukora stated that his first aim upon taking up the position of national coach of the Kenya Amateur Athletic Association (KAAA) in April 1968 was to encourage athletes at the school level, and he promised an ambitious campaign to locate "raw potential" in the districts and provinces. "There are several good athletes in the primary schools and last year we discovered Tecla Chemabwai who now holds the Kenya 220 yards women's record," he declared.[22] Regarding her earliest years in the sport, the *Sunday Nation* reported, "When her athletics ability was discovered by her school, she was thrown into every event she could participate in, especially when the competitions involved other schools."[23] Chemabwai subsequently entered divisional competitions, then district championships and national championships, and ultimately competed at the Olympics.[24]

Attending secondary school was essential for continued athletic development. "Only those people in school have a chance of exploiting their talent in sports," declared Naftali Temu, Kenya's first Olympic gold medalist in 1968.[25] British and European 5000 meters champion Bruce Tulloh who trained and coached in Kenya in the early 1970s similarly asserted: "The production of fresh athletic talent depends on the schools."[26] Kenyan national athletics coach in the 1980s, Walter Abmayr, declared, "Many talented young runners find their way to the top in Kenya through the schools. At schools in Kenya, athletics has its nursery," and "credit must be given to the many school teachers who take their time to help young athletes."[27] The daily commute of running many miles between school and home, morning and afternoon, also helped build a strong endurance base for many young people. The *Sunday Nation* reported Chemabwai developed her endurance running to and from her school in Kilibwoni located eleven kilometers away from her village.[28] World cross-country champion Lornah Kiplagat told the *Daily Nation* that she ran to class barefoot for "six and a half kilometres there and as many kilometres back."[29] According to another report, "If frequent lunches at home are considered, then she often covered 25 kilometres a day."[30] Kiplagat explains, "In Kenya if you are late, the teacher will cane you. I was a bit lazy. I didn't see why I should wake up early and walk when I could run to school."[31]

The Kenyan government at independence inherited an education system that educated far more boys than girls. In 1963 roughly one-third of the total Kenyan school-aged population were enrolled in primary education (840,000 out of a total 2.4 million), 34 percent of whom were girls.[32] The first postcolonial Kenyan government established seven years of primary education as the minimum standard for all schoolchildren, replacing the four optional years for African pupils offered during the colonial period. Significant investment into the education system eventually introduced free primary education, school meal programs, and new school buildings to accommodate the enrollment growth.[33] The new policies were effective in widening access to primary school for boys and girls, though many schools struggled to find qualified teachers and lacked books and adequate facilities. By 1965 the number of Kenyan children attending primary school had increased to over one million students. This number continued to rise each year, and a decade after independence, more than 1.8 million children were enrolled in

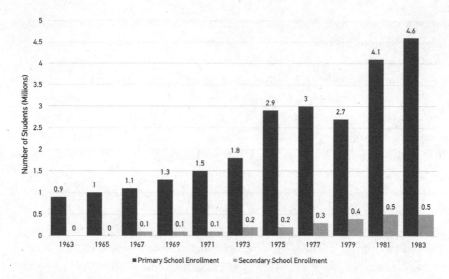

FIGURE 2. Kenyan Students' Enrollment in Primary and Secondary Schools, 1963–1983.

SOURCE: GEORGE S. ESHIWANI. *IMPLEMENTING EDUCATIONAL POLICIES IN KENYA.* WORLD BANK DISCUSSION PAPERS, NO. 85: AFRICA TECHNICAL DEPARTMENT SERIES. WASHINGTON, DC: WORLD BANK, 1990, 21.

primary school. By 1975 enrollment more than tripled that of 1963.[34] Disparity by sex in primary school enrollment had almost disappeared by 1989, when some 4.8 million Kenyan children were enrolled.[35]

Enrollment numbers dropped sharply at secondary schools, however, and many more boys were enrolled than girls at that level, adversely affecting their athletic futures.[36] Cost was a major factor contributing to the drop-off in school attendance at the secondary level. From 1974, the first four years of primary school tuition were free and after 1978, so too were the final three years of primary school, though parents were still required to pay for uniforms, books, and other materials, as well as to contribute to frequent school fundraising activities. Many families were unable to afford secondary school fees and relied on contributions from family and friends or payment by installment to meet educational costs. Figure 2 records the consistent increase of attendance at the primary level and the much slower increase of enrollment at the secondary level.

Faced with limited resources families often chose to continue the education of their boys and not their girls. Education historian Sydney Hall found that the percentage of girls attending secondary school remained less than half that of boys eight years after independence.[37] Anthropologist Regina Oboler, based on her research in Nandi in the mid-1970s, explains: "What people wanted was to get credentials and qualifications that they believed would lead to good salaried employment . . . Higher education was seen as mainly for males, which is not to say that a girl who did extremely well in school could not also be encouraged in that direction. However, higher-level professions were also seen as primarily for males."[38] In addition the World Bank as recently as the mid-1980s evaluated Kenyan girls' schools as being generally less equipped than those for boys and noted that a smaller proportion of girls gained entrance to the better government-aided schools.[39]

A number of factors beyond family support enabled some girls to stay in school and in sport beyond the norm. Opportunities in athletics were often determined by the interest of sports-minded teachers, the most prominent of whom in the early years of independence tended to be male European coaches. Philip Ndoo claimed in the mid-1970s, "It is to British track and field coaches that much of the credit for Kenya's success must go."[40] Cardinal Otunga High School led by the Brothers of Tilburg in the Netherlands and St. Patrick's High School, Iten, founded by the St. Patrick's Brothers from Ireland "exemplify the efforts of overseas organisations and individuals to mould the form of post-independence Kenyan athletics," according to Bale and Sang.[41] At the national level expatriate coaches such as John Velzian, who coordinated the University Games, served as president of the Kenyan Schools' Athletics Association, and started a national secondary schools athletics championship; Ray Batchelor who worked with double Commonwealth Games gold medalist sprinter Seraphino Antao while stationed at the Coast; and United States Olympian and State Department Cultural Affairs Officer Mal Whitfield based in Nairobi made important contributions in the early independence years.[42] Their ranks were filled by Kenyan-born men such as Aish Jeneby, who began his sports career as a teacher in Mombasa in 1952. Five years later, he joined Nottingham University in the United Kingdom for three years' training for a physical education diploma, during which time he also attended Loughborough College (now University), one of Britain's foremost institutions for sport. On his return to Kenya in 1960, he resumed his teaching career in Nairobi before accepting the position of inspector of schools for physical education three years later, a post he held until 1968. Jeneby became principal sports officer in 1969 and served as assistant chef de mission with the Kenyan team to the Mexico City Olympics in 1968, athletics team manager at the Munich Olympics in 1972, and assistant athletics team manager accompanying the Kenyan team to the Montreal Olympics in 1976.[43]

The efforts of sports-minded teachers at times created important opportunities for girls. In 1973, John Blevins of the Rift Valley Schools Sports Association and Graham Parker of Njoro School led a co-educational Rift Valley Secondary Schools track and field team on an ambitious three-week tour of Britain to compete against schools' teams there in a series of meets.[44] One report stated that the groundbreaking tour would "give the young Rift athletes a taste of international competition and the incentive to continue their track careers in the senior ranks."[45] Parker justified the venture on the basis that "in recent years, so many of Kenya's track internationals have come from the schools' nursery that this is now the accepted channel to an Olympic medal."[46] Rift Valley teachers and administrators organized numerous fundraisers to finance the trip.[47] These educators "have done an outstanding job in doing the seemingly impossible task of raising cash to send a full school's athletic team to England," noted one observer.[48] The touring squad selected from that year's Rift Valley Schools championships comprised thirty-two boys and eighteen girls, including future African 3000-meters record holder Rose Chepyator-Thomson.[49]

Among the female educators who made remarkable contributions to girls' athletics was Ank de Vlas of the Netherlands. She first taught at Kapsabet Girls High School in Nandi from 1963 to 1966, after which she completed a degree in education at Bluffton College in Ohio before returning as head teacher at Kapsabet.[50] She then began stints at Kipsigis Girls' High School, Nairobi's Moi Girls' High School, Kapkenda Girls' High School in the Rift Valley, and finally Hekima Girls' High School in Central Kenya. Her career spanned almost forty years until her death in 2001 and included a strong commitment to developing athletics for young women.[51] De Vlas served as treasurer of the Kenya Secondary Schools Sport Association, and during her years in the Rift Valley she collaborated with the brothers of St Patrick's in Iten, who developed many track and field champions. Beginning in 1977, she worked with renowned St. Patrick's coach Brother Colm O'Connell to develop young female runners in the area, including standouts such as Susan Sirma, Esther Kiplagat, and Leah Malot, all of whom represented Kenya at major international competitions. In the mid-1980s, de Vlas recruited American physical education instructor Joanna Vincenti to coach athletics at Kapkenda near Eldoret. Vincenti describes the school as "one of the best in Kenya for running, no doubt, along with Sing'ore Girls." Its curriculum included daily gym classes and training in the afternoons, cross-country meets on weekends, and district, provincial, and national meets during the championship season.[52]

Secondary schools in Kenya offered girls widely varying levels of support for track and field. Sing'ore Girls' High School, the sister school to St. Patrick's in the Rift Valley, began to establish its stellar reputation for athletics in the early 1970s. The school won the first Rift Valley Province Girls Secondary Schools Cross-country Championships in 1972.[53] The following year, while competing in towns across Britain as a member of the Rift Valley Secondary Schools team, 800- and 1500-meters runner Rose Chepyator of Sing'ore recorded outstanding results.[54] Among other accomplished athletes, the school later enrolled Selina Chirchir, who as a student won the 800 meters at the 1985 All Africa championships in Cairo, followed by gold in that event at the 1986 World Junior Track and Field Championships in Athens, and two golds at the 1987 All Africa Games in Nairobi.[55] In 1991, Sing'ore student Lydia Cheromei won the World Junior Cross-country Championships in Antwerp, Belgium, becoming the first Kenyan female runner to win an individual world cross-country title. She had enrolled because her father, a primary school teacher, insisted that she attend Sing'ore High School because of its emphasis on athletics.[56] Arguably the most decorated Sing'ore High School athlete of the twentieth century was Sally Barsosio, who at fourteen took bronze in the 10,000 meters at the 1992 Junior Athletics Championships in Seoul, South Korea, and won the Junior World Cross-Country Championships in 1993. Later that year Barsosio won a bronze medal at the 1993 World Athletics Championships in Stuttgart, Germany, in the 10,000-meters event, becoming the youngest person to claim a senior IAAF medal. In 1995 she won bronze at the senior women's World Cross-Country Championships held in Durham in the United Kingdom, and at the 1997 World Athletics Championships 10,000 meters event in Athens, Greece, she became the first Kenyan female to win a senior-level World Athletics Championship. Barsosio had been a student throughout these competitions and told *Nation* reporters that her progress had been a "delicate balancing act between training, athletics, and books."[57]

By contrast, if a student enrolled at a school that placed little value on sport, even those arriving as highly touted runners could be discouraged. Elizabeth Onyambu as a preteen burst upon the Kenyan racing scene at the 1979 national championships, winning the 1500 meters in front of one of the largest crowds in Kenya ever to witness a track and field meet. Onyambu was a relative unknown, while the favorite to win the national title was Rose Chepyator-Thomson who held the African record in the 3000 meters. The *Daily Nation* reported:

Few noticed the skinny 12-year-old barefoot schoolgirl sprinting behind the powerful and determined Rose Thomson . . . After the first two laps, one began to notice something strange. The diminutive schoolgirl had stuck on the shoulder of Mrs Thomson, and she still looked fresh. In the third lap, the scene changed from that of anticipation to excitement. When the bell went for the final lap, everybody was on their feet, cheering the "never heard of" underdog, for other than her coach, nobody else knew Onyambu's name. On the final stretch, Thomson gave everything she had, engaging the top gear in an effort to put off the little challenger. But Onyambu responded strongly, floating past the now struggling Thomson to win by a whisker . . . The crowd went wild. So excited was everybody that few noticed Mike Boit winning the men's 1500 metres, which was originally billed as one of the feature events of the meeting.[58]

Onyambu became the celebrity of the 1979 season, and her accomplishments featured regularly in the Kenyan press.[59] Describing the East and Central African Athletics Championships held that year in Mombasa contested by more than two hundred athletes representing Ethiopia, Kenya, Malawi, Somalia, Tanzania, Uganda, Zambia, and Zanzibar, the media declared Onyambu who won the 1500-meters event "the darling of the meet, without a shadow of doubt."[60] Later that year she was among a team of Kenyan students selected to travel to the tenth World University Students' Games in Mexico City. Although too young to race, Onyambu's trip was sponsored by Kenyan sport authorities hoping that the early exposure to international competition would encourage her to continue running. "This young girl is no doubt going to compete in the next Olympics," gushed one official.[61] Her best times were outstanding: 100 meters in 12.0 seconds, 200 meters in 24.8 seconds, 400 meters in 56.6 seconds, 800 meters in 2 minutes and 13 seconds, 1500 meters in 4 minutes and 18.9 seconds, and 3000 meters in 9 minutes and 21 seconds. She was the only Kenyan, man or woman, to have won both the shortest race (100 meters) and the longest (3000 meters) at national championship meets.[62]

Two years after her sensational emergence, Onyambu disappeared from national athletics. After completing primary school, she was admitted into the selective government-run Nairobi Moi Girls' School, where academic achievement was exalted and sport was of secondary importance. Philip Ndoo observed in the *Daily Nation* that this was "no Sing'ore High, when it comes to athletics," alluding to the renown of its runners.[63] During her five years there, she raced sporadically, and admitted, "I do not train as hard as I used to."[64] The most academically competitive girls' schools often failed to emphasize sport, causing promising female athletes to quit running altogether. "Keiyo Wonder Girl" Rose Tata-Muya, whose track and field career began in the early 1970s and included selections for four Olympics, three World Championships, and six Commonwealth Games, disclosed: "My sisters, they were runners, but they went up to national schools. They were running up to primary school and then they stopped. It depends on which secondary you go to. Some schools, they are not very keen in running."[65] Even at athletics powerhouse Kapkenda, Coach Joanna Vincenti observed that her athletes took their education seriously because "they didn't know what would happen when they left school. There were no guarantees of anything in sports."[66]

Pressures Facing Young Women as Athletes

In 1973 at a major meet in Kericho, Sabina Chebichi of Kitale won her first race running barefoot and wearing her Mlimani primary school uniform. Dubbed the "Petticoat Princess," the fourteen-year-old was awarded her first pair of spikes, shorts, and running vest after her victory.[67] She recorded excellent times for the 800- and 1500-meters distances. In the 1974 Commonwealth Games she ran the 1500 meters event, the 4x400 relay and won a bronze medal in the 800 meters, becoming the first female Kenyan runner to medal at the Commonwealth Games.[68]

Her efforts captured media attention and instilled bright expectations for her future. One report suggested, "If Sabina can continue training hard, there is no reason why she should not win a medal in the Olympic Games and become the first-ever woman from Africa to do so."[69] Described as "precocious," and dubbed "Kenya's latest track wonder," she routinely defeated more experienced opponents.[70] Only two years later, Finnish sports journalist Pekka Rinne lamented in an editorial in the *Daily Nation*:

> Sabina Chebichi ran a world-class time in Christchurch in 1974. She could have broken the world record in both the 800m and 1500m events the following year. But where was she? She was pregnant. Another unwed mother. It is possible to have children at the age of 40 but one cannot set world records at this age.[71]

Chebichi was no outlier. Fifteen-year-old Cherono Maiyo set an African record in the 1500 meters in 1971 at the Kenyan national championships before going on to become one of two women to represent Kenya at the 1972 Munich Olympic Games.[72] One observer noted:

> It is staggering to think of the potential of this young girl. More seasoned athletes turning in comparable times elsewhere in the world are hammering away at weights, fartlek, parlaaf, cross-country and interval training under the watchful eyes of their coaches. Yet Maiyo, on her four-mile a day run to school, without any advice from a coach can casually catch a bus down to Nairobi and win two gruelling races within an hour.[73]

The following year, Maiyo left school, married Olympic steeplechaser Amos Biwott, and soon gave birth to the first of their five children.[74] Tecla Chemabwai, who with Maiyo represented Kenya at the Munich Olympic Games, noted, "She was a very talented lady who could have done many great things, but [her husband] insisted she stop."[75] Pregnancy, motherhood and social pressure ended the careers of many promising athletes, according to Chemabwai, who in a subsequent interview reflected on what pushed talented peers out of sport:

> You see, for all athletes, with the lack of education, you will never be able to plan ... then women have one weakness. They get pregnant. So you get married and you don't have a job, when will you be able to train? That is one problem that women run into. There are so many of our former athletes who apparently can still run well who are still out there. And even if that man was an athlete and he has told you that he will make you run, it will not work because of the community. We are losing so many girls, athletes because of these problems.[76]

Olympian Ruth Waithera, whose decorated international career spanned more than a decade, echoed these observations, adding that, "Girls who start rising in athletics and are then interrupted by pregnancy never seem to recover."[77] The popular Kenyan women's magazine *True Love* stated, "Our women put a lot of hard work on the track yet they get poor results when it comes to major international events." It cited motherhood as "one problem many young and upcoming athletes have faced over the years," noting that "once they begin to cut a niche a lot of men start advancing, beckoning them to become girlfriends. These boyfriends finally leave them pregnant."[78] Former Kenyan athlete Vicky Okoth in 1987 applauded the few athletes who persevered, noting that, "Past women athletes," referring to Chemabwai and Waithera, "took athletics and education as parallel issues."[79]

A three-day IAAF/Olympic Solidarity conference held in Nairobi in 1990 addressed these and other issues that confronted young female runners as their careers progressed. Acknowledging that "Africa's women athletes have long lived in the shadow of their male counterparts when it comes to major international competitions," attendees noted that limited education for girls, cultural prejudices that inhibited female progression in sport as young women matured, lack of qualified coaches, and insufficient organization of women's track and field on the part of national committees were all contributing factors. Nawal el Moutawakel of Morocco, the first African woman to win an Olympic gold medal at the 1984 Los Angeles games, was one of twenty-one delegates from eleven African countries at the conference. She argued that cultural beliefs opposing participation in athletics by adult women as well as lack of education stymied success for many girls. Kenya sent five female representatives of the KAAA women's subcommittee formed three years earlier. In comments after the event, the Kenyan *Weekly Review* noted that the subcommittee had yet to implement any substantive program for female athletes and suggested inviting athletes long involved in the sport such as hurdler Rose Tata-Muya and thrower Elizabeth Olaba to join the committee. The periodical also suggested holding seminars at which female athletes could discuss the challenges they faced and insisted that the subcommittee "find out why most Kenyan women athletes end their careers prematurely and come up with a solution to this malady."[80]

St. Patrick's coach Brother O'Connell observed that "Often [girls] run well in school, then on returning to the family farm they are faced with all the housework; there is no time or energy left to train."[81] The contributions that women made to rural homesteads have been documented in anthropological studies of the era. Oboler concluded that domestic labor for Nandi women accounted for a larger proportion of time than any other single activity and that housework and childcare were not the province of adult men.[82] Ethnographic accounts of other communities revealed similar divisions of labor.[83] In a 1989 study, the World Bank ascertained that 75 percent of the country's agricultural production was derived from small farms and that women provided roughly three-fourths of that labor. The study estimated that women living in rural areas spent at least twelve hours per day working at home or in the fields.[84] That same year, the *Standard* declared, "In most Kenyan cultures, it is still unthinkable for a man to be seen minding children, preparing food, carrying water or cleaning the house or the compound."[85]

Olympic medalist Mike Boit in 1988 blamed the paucity of female Kenyan athletes on the fact that the demands of "child bearing, cooking, cleaning and washing are exclusively the responsibilities of women," noting that such work in rural regions had to be accomplished without running tap water.[86] Lornah Kiplagat, a three-time Olympian and multi-world-record holder, agreed, stating, "Girls have a difficulty breaking through. They have to do jobs at home. The men have many more opportunities. They don't have to cook or do those other things. It's very tough for women to have a successful career."[87] The 1997 World Athletics Championships 10,000-meters winner Sally Barsosio bluntly captured the reality, noting, "It is hard to find the time for running if you leave school and get stuck with a husband early."[88]

Custom in many parts of Kenya dictated that a bride move from her birth home to the homestead of her in-laws. Not only were her early years of marriage often physically demanding, but travel for training and races could also raise issues of morality and respectability. Olympian Tecla Chemabwai reflected:

> Also, there is influence from the man's side. How can you let your wife go? You have a small baby and then suddenly you are leaving the baby and you are running in the morning. The same husband who understood about training will turn around and say, "Where are you? Where are you coming from? Where are you going at this time? Why are you leaving? Maybe you had gone to see another man." Those kinds of accusations. So it becomes a bit difficult.[89]

Some women returned to athletics later in life, such as Agnes Mwagiru, who became a teacher and coach after her husband passed away. A talented athlete, she set the national record in the high jump event before she stopped competing to focus on her family. After graduating from Kagumo Teachers' Training College, she taught at Kiangoma Primary School in Nyeri, where she coached Rose Nyaguthii who bettered Mwagiru's own national high jump record. Mwagiru coached girls track and field for many years and chaperoned Kenyan women's teams both locally and internationally while still competing. "It is through sheer hard work that I managed to achieve all these, bearing in mind that I had two daughters to bring up and to educate since my husband had died in 1969 . . . I hope they will do even better than I have done both in class and in sports," she told *Drum* magazine.[90]

Rose Owino was another early standout who made her way back to athletics later in life. After leaving school, where she had been an accomplished sprinter at Awas Intermediate School in Nyanza Province, she gave up running, started a family, and later began work at the Nairobi Police Headquarters while her husband served as an assistant police inspector. At the age of thirty in 1967, she "felt she should try her hand again at athletics," according to the *Standard*.[91] Owino returned to competition in two meets in Nairobi, one in the 220 yards distance and the other in the shot put, finishing third in both. She then shifted to race walking, and in May 1968 won the women's section of a twenty kilometers road walk in record time.[92] Three months later she recorded a comfortable victory over a distance of twenty-five kilometers in another record time, more than ten minutes ahead of her closest rival.[93] "To be a mother of six children and at the same time take part in athletics with full dedication and enthusiasm, is indeed a rarity. But Rose Owino . . . has achieved this," declared the *East African Standard*.[94]

In the first decades of independence, women's running in Kenya persisted as a "fragile project" with vastly fewer adult women than men participating. Leaving school prematurely, early pregnancy and motherhood, and familial and community opposition were major impediments to participation by many promising female athletes, contributing to the disparity in international accolades one observes when comparing the achievements of Kenyan male and female athletes of this era. While some women, such as Agnes Mwagiru and Rose Owino, returned to athletics after becoming wives and mothers, persistent barriers to female participation forced an end to the athletic pursuits of most women. Yet some found ways to forge outstanding and lengthy track and field careers even at the international level during the amateur era of running. The following cases show their successes typically relied on a combination of educational, familial, and spousal support, often in the face of community opposition, and in many cases employment by governmental organizations that encouraged their athlete-employees to compete at a high level.

The Front Runners

Rose Chepyator-Thomson devised her own path to success. Raised near the village of Iten in the Rift Valley, the Sing'ore Girls' graduate held Kenyan records for the 800 and 1500 meters. In 1974 she retired from the sport and married American Peace Corps worker Norman Thomson, who taught biology at neighboring St

Patrick's High School. Three years later, after the birth of two sons, she returned to the track and set an African record for 3000 meters and later accepted an athletics scholarship from the University of Wisconsin-Madison, where she became an eleven-time All-American and two-time national champion who "could run well at any distance from 800 meters through cross-country," according to track and field historian Frank Murphy.[95] She made the Kenyan Olympic team in two events in 1980, only to be denied the chance to race when Kenya boycotted the Moscow games, and later earned two master's degrees and a PhD at American universities.[96]

Chepyator-Thomson was among the first married women with children to represent Kenya internationally, and her decision to return to racing as a wife and mother was met with outrage at home. "What is this woman doing robbing our children of prizes; running is for children, not for married with children," was a commonplace sentiment according to one *Daily Nation* report at the time. "To them, Rose should have retired the day she got her wedding ring and she should now devote her time to looking after her children and not running."[97]

Women who sought to combine athletics and family needed active spousal support. Chepyator-Thomson traveled extensively during the first year of her comeback. She competed at a Kapsabet meet in the Rift Valley in February 1977, followed by a competition in Meru in Central Kenya two months later before entering a meet in Mombasa, where she qualified for the Kenya World Cup Trials held in Kisumu in western Kenya. She was then selected to represent Kenya at the Africa World Cup Trials held in Tunisia. Chepyator-Thomson ended a sensational comeback season with a runner-up finish at the East and Central Africa 3000 meters championships in Mogadishu, Somalia.[98] Then twenty-five years old, she stressed that her husband supported her desire to continue competing after starting a family. "He really encourages me, he is the one who made me come back, otherwise it would have been difficult with the kids, besides he is always willing to take care of them when I am away attending meets."[99]

Some women delayed marriage while pursuing their athletic ambitions, such as Alice Adala who dominated the sprints in Kenya from the early to mid-1970s. Born in Nyanza Province she lived for a time in Moscow, where her father Adala Otuko was stationed as Kenya's ambassador. She earned her first selection for a Kenyan national team as a fifteen-year-old at Kerem Girls' High School in Kisii when she competed in the 4x100 meters relay team at the 1967 East African Championships. Among her many honors were two titles won in 1975 at the East and Central Africa Championships, where she set records in both the 100- and 200-meters events and earning Kenyan Sportswoman of the Year honors in 1976.[100] Adala qualified for the Montreal Olympics but due to the Kenyan boycott of those games, she lost the opportunity to compete. "I was ready, I had trained hard and was hoping to win a medal for my country . . . I was really very disappointed when they said that we were not going to compete." Employment in the country's government agencies such as the prisons, posts, ports, and others greatly advanced opportunities for women. These organizations offered coaching and sponsored training for elite adult athletes who benefited from these perquisites while earning a living wage. A 1976 feature story by *Trust* magazine emphasized that Adala's employment in the prisons service was essential for her athletic development. Following her success in high school, the prisons recruited Adala, and she remained in their employ for the duration of her storied athletics career.[101]

Her record as a runner employed by the prisons in the 1970s was emulated by other leading female runners who competed for the major "sports-oriented" parastatal companies in the following years, which, as *Sports Review* noted in 1983, were "always on the lookout for talent budding from schools and at the beginning of each year, school leavers might get into employment due to their sports potential."[102] Mercy Wacuga of Nyeri competed in schools' competitions up to the national level, where she drew the attention of recruiters for the Kenya Posts and Telecommunications Corporation (KPTC). She accepted their offer of employment as a public relations clerk and represented the organization at major events in Kenya. She excelled at the 1983 Kenya Communications Sports Organization (KECOSO) Games, winning the high jump and the 1500 meters at the age of twenty-one. Wacuga told the Kenyan magazine *Sportsworld* that without joining the KPTC she "could not have made it as a sports girl," adding "I joined their athletic club and there I found all the facilities and this encouraged me to engage in sports."[103]

Outstanding sprinter and long jumper Joyce Odhiambo similarly flourished in the employ of the Kenya Posts. She first qualified for the Kenyan national team in 1982 and debuted in international athletics by winning both the 100 and 200 meters that year at the East and Central African Championships. At the East and Central African Championships three years later, she won triple gold in the 100 meters, 200 meters, and long jump events. "I felt on top of the world when I set the new record," said Odhiambo of her East and Central Africa long jump record set at the 1986 Championships.[104] Her track and field career continued into the 1990s as a star athlete for the posts.

The most enduring and one of the most accomplished female athletes of this era was "queen of hurdles" Rose Tata-Muya, whose track and field career spanned twenty years. She first excelled as an athlete in primary school growing up near Kamariny stadium in Iten, where Brother O'Connell recalls her presence at St. Patrick's training sessions.[105] She notes that in her early years of competition, she found a conducive environment for training at her school but that her family offered the least support, as "they thought I might be exploited by not finishing my education or get[ting] married or in a relationship under age."[106] Tata-Muya first competed abroad at the 1974 Commonwealth Games in New Zealand and qualified for the boycotted 1976 and 1980 Olympic Games. She was named the 1978 Kenyan Sportswoman of the Year, earned selection to the team for the 1984 Los Angeles Olympics, though she could not compete due to pregnancy with her second child, and finally in 1988 represented Kenya in the 400 meters at the Seoul Olympic Games before being named the KECOSO Best Woman Athlete of 1990. Tata-Muya sustained her career by accepting a position with the prisons and later the Kenya Ports Authority, which provided her "with an opportunity to maintain her sports talent as she represented her employer at many KECOSO meetings."[107] In 1990 she told the Kenyan *Weekly Review* that "I'll continue running as long as my two feet can carry me."[108] In 1991 a Kenyan magazine noted, "Talented women come to athletics, shine briefly, and then wither out quickly, but not Rose Tata-Muya who started running at a tender age of 11 and still remains a force in 400 metres having been on the track for seventeen years." By then she was the mother of three, and the magazine acknowledged the encouragement she received from her husband, observing, "She is one of the few women athletes who have succeeded despite being in marriage."[109]

Accomplished international athlete Mary Chemweno balanced marriage, motherhood, and athletics with the support of her husband, long-distance international track star Kipsubai Koskei. The first woman in Africa to break two minutes for the 800 meters, Chemweno raced at the All Africa Games and the African Championships and qualified for the boycotted 1980 Moscow Olympics. Growing up in the Rift Valley highlands, she loved to run. "Even when I was going to school, I was running all the time." Chemweno attributed her affinity for athletics to her father, who worked for the Kenya Prisons and had competed at the national level. She noted that "because my father was a great runner, he encouraged me."[110] Chemweno recorded a remarkable time for the 800 meters at the 1978 national championships held on a dirt track in Kisumu. Recalling the reaction of the timekeepers, she described, "They say: 'Oh—2:04, this is wonderful. And if this had been a tartan track, you would have run 1:57.'" Based on that performance, she was invited to tour Australia and New Zealand where, competing internationally for Kenya for the first time, the fifteen-year old ran the 800 meters in 2:03.[111] Competing in the same event two years later in Dusseldorf, Chemweno completed the two-lap race in 1:59.94—the first time the two-minute barrier had been broken by an African woman.[112] She won Sportswoman of the Year in 1980, Kenya's most prestigious sporting award.[113]

Chemweno's husband encouraged her track career. He was one of Kenya's most durable track and cross-country runners whose career spanned from the 1970s to the 1990s and included four East and Central African Championship titles, three World Cross-Country Championships appearances, and a gold medal won at the 1984 African Athletics Championships. Chemweno knew what could happen when spouses were antagonistic to their wives' continued involvement in athletics. "My sister . . . was talented, more than me. But as soon as she got married, the husband said: 'no, no more, forget it.'"[114] Chemweno knew what she wanted in a husband, and agreed to marry Koskei only on the condition that he agree to support her athletic ambitions. For several years the pair competed as the best in Kenya in their respective events.[115]

Far too many promising female athletes ceased competing as teenagers in the decades after independence, depleting the ranks of what portended to be a world-class cohort. Alice Adala, Mary Chemweno, Rose Chepyator-Thomson, Rose Tata-Muya, and Joyce Odhiambo, among others, persisted in a bold departure from social dictates. Their choice to run, familial support for education, and decisions about employment and of when and whom to marry helped to establish a presence for Kenyan women on the international stage. Ruth Waithera, one of the very best of this era, devised her own innovative strategy to stay in the game.

Defying Expectations and the Struggle for Autonomy

In 1977 Ruth Waithera was stationed at the Kenya Air Force Eastleigh base, serving as a corporal in the Women Service Corps (WSC) of the Kenyan Army. She was not only the fastest woman in Africa over 400 meters but as one newspaper reported:

Her times in the 100m, 200m and 400m can only be beaten by competitive men athletes, and the rest of us male chauvinists boasting physical superiority over women have just to swallow our pride as a direct challenge would turn out to be too humiliating.[116]

She was regularly applauded with headlines such as "Waithera and Tata Set Track Records," describing her racing as "magnificent" and referring to her as a "star."[117]

Waithera distinguished herself as an exceptional sprinter as a schoolgirl when she was introduced to formal running competitions. Born in 1957 in Murang'a in Central Province, as a child she and her family moved to Nyahururu in the Rift Valley. She was the fastest girl in Kahero primary school and always joined the boys in competitions. "I started when I was young. I was running all the time—quick, quick, quick, quick!" she recalled. She qualified to compete at the provincial level as a thirteen-year-old.[118]

Waithera's father was a shopkeeper and farmer, and he supported her running, providing bus fare to travel to races. They were not a wealthy family, and her ability to supplement family income through running awards played a role in whether relatives offered support for her efforts. "Me, I have slept with hunger. I have walked without shoes," she said. Her father died when she was young, and her participation in sport became "a big problem" to those around her. "My mom, she didn't want me to run. Other women told my mother, 'Your girl, if she starts running, she will never get a baby! Her body is going to be destroyed,'" she recalled.[119] Their worries about competitive sport and reproductive health evoke warnings elsewhere alleging that vigorous physical activity endangered the female body, not least by depleting women of the vital energy of necessary for childbirth.[120] Undeterred, Waithera continued to race despite the fact that she now had "to hide to go compete" and "when I came back home, my mom used to beat me." She persisted, winning prizes ranging from household goods, such as buckets and blankets, to small cash allowances. She presented these rewards to her mother, and they helped to pay her school fees. The physical punishment stopped, and "we became good friends!"[121]

Women in her community began to intervene with questions about her intentions as she reached marriageable age. "Other women, they were telling [my mom], 'Oh, my son can marry your daughter.' The friend of my mom wanted me to get married to her son." Efforts to solidify the union escalated when the suitor's father offered bridewealth to Waithera's mother, a tempting proposition for a widow without sons. Waithera's refusal of the offer provoked more beatings, and she ran away and lived with her sister for a short while. She declined the marriage proposal because she wanted to protect her running. She had watched as her three older sisters, runners as girls, quit the sport when they married. "They were not going far [in their running]. They were getting married so quickly. That was the problem." She also felt no desire to marry the suitor and declared: "No, no, no, I didn't like the guy at all."[122]

It was customary for a widow to move in with her son and his family. Having no sons, Waithera's mother had to rely on herself. Her husband's family too had refused to provide the support that, according to custom, was owed to her as a widow without sons, a dereliction that as historian Kenda Mutongi notes was not uncommon in western Kenya in the years after independence.[123] In the face of these obstacles, Waithera pursued the best option she felt she had: living with her mother while continuing to compete in sport. In her words, "My mom, she doesn't have anybody to help her. My dad is dead; my sisters, they are all married. So she doesn't have anybody to help her. You know, in Africa, if you have a son, you are welcome into his home. But we were five sisters—no brothers."[124]

At the age of sixteen she gave birth to a son. Not long after, one of her sisters introduced her to the birth control pill, explaining that modern contraception was freely available from the hospital nearby. Her sister advised, "Because you are a good runner and you know these men, somebody can cheat you. So get this medicine—protect yourself." While choosing to stay single had caused conflict, Waithera's decision to take the pill was even more controversial and provoked "a very big drama in the home, to the villagers, to my mom."[125] According to a survey conducted in 1979, 8 percent of women in Kenya were using modern birth control methods.[126] Research undertaken by Oboler around this time in the Rift Valley similarly indicates that although government family planning agencies made a range of devices, such as IUDs, pills, and condoms available at very little cost, such methods were rarely practiced.[127]

The stigma of a family member preventing pregnancy was as much about community honor as reproduction. Waithera's unorthodox choices were antithetical to what was thought necessary of women to achieve the productive households that sustained the community.[128] The observation by historian Tabitha Kanogo about Kenyan womanhood in an earlier period—that "women and their bodies became sites of public, political, and personal struggles"—remained salient, and the life that Waithera chose was exemplary of Kanogo's insight.[129] Although her choices opened her to derision and even ostracism from some in her community, Waithera grew up unencumbered by the authority of father, brother, and husband, which she put to her advantage in a determined pursuit of running. Within a system of constraint on female choices, runners such as Waithera willfully shaped lives for themselves and disregarded traditional expectations of marriage, motherhood, and sport. In so doing, they forged meaningful narratives as athletes outside of the roles they played as wives and mothers.

Like the Bullets She Triggers, Ruth Suddenly Shot to the Top

In 1974 Waithera signed a three-year contract with the armed forces. By the time she joined the army, most of Kenya's best male athletes based within the country were affiliated with the army, police, prisons, or General Service Unit (GSU), which offered coaching, resources, and time to train, all necessary for competing at the highest level. Kalenjin men from the Rift Valley had historically been well represented as athletes in the uniformed services.[130] As a Kikuyu, and the first woman to join the army as a runner, her path diverged from many of her contemporaries. Waithera noted, "I was the first female to run in the army and was in the running team for eight years. I was the only female on the team with fifty male teammates and they were all respectful towards me."[131] Her participation in army athletics spawned infrastructure changes to that previously all-male institution. While based in the army's permanent training camp in Nyahururu, Waithera was given a tent of her own.[132] She expressed joy at the memory of the welcome camaraderie of her friend Sabina Chebichi, employed by and running on behalf of the prisons, who herself was one of Kenya's premier runners and who accompanied Waithera at the Army Championships.[133]

As a soldier, Waithera described herself as "able to concentrate" on her running for the first time. Of her new employment, she declared:

> At the Women's Service Corps, I had all the time. I had quit school when I got pregnant and stayed idle for a year. With that dreaded first pregnancy for schoolgirls behind me, when I started running in the army, it was like I had already completed part of my life. There was nothing to interrupt me.[134]

She emphasized the single-mindedness of her purpose. "I have to run, and after turning twenty-one, I was still running." The fact that she continued her running into adulthood was a rare feat among women of this era. In her first year as a soldier, she earned her first trip outside of Kenya as a member of Kenya's 4x100 meters relay team competing at the 1974 East and Central African Championships held in Kampala, Uganda. Two years later she finished runner-up in the 200 meters at the Kenya national championships behind established star sprinter Alice Adala.[135]

From there, as the *Daily Nation* reported in 1977, "Like the bullets she triggers off at shooting ranges during army manoeuvres, Ruth suddenly shot to the top."[136] The army corporal won all the major meets in Kenya that season and peaked by winning the 100 and 200 meters at the national championships. At the 1977 East and Central Africa Championships in Mogadishu, Somalia, Waithera "stole the limelight, outshining even her male colleagues when she won an unprecedented five medals."[137] She won the 100 meters, 200 meters, and the 400 meters and anchored Kenya to victory in the 4x400 meters relay for her fourth gold medal of the competition. She also anchored the 4x100 meters relay team that finished second. The *Daily Nation* trumpeted, "Cpl. Ruth Waithera being the most decorated athlete (or soldier?) during the East and Central African Athletics Championships held in Mogadishu."[138]

Waithera was now running well enough to compete outside of Africa. Her first opportunity came on a weeklong trip to the USSR, where she "ran with *wazungus* [white people] for the first time."[139] Twenty nations participated in the 1977 Friendship Games held outside of Moscow. Waithera was the only woman from Kenya alongside three male athlete representatives. She placed sixteenth in the 100 meters and eleventh in the 200 meters.[140] Later that year at the World Cup trials in Tunis, Waithera won the 400 meters event, thus qualifying to represent the continent at the inaugural World Cup held in Dusseldorf, West Germany. At that meet, where only one individual was selected to represent their continent in each event, Waithera's time of 53.48 seconds for the one-lap race was the fastest by an African woman that year. She was recognized as Kenya's Sportswoman of the Year in 1977.[141]

She described running in the armed forces as "very good," but stressed that "it wasn't good at the other side, at my mom's home. There was a lot of drama. 'Oh that girl, she is lost! She has gone to the Army, with men. She is on her own, she is lost!'"[142] According to Waithera, "some of them, they talked bad about me when I was gone. Like I'm going to be a prostitute or something like that."[143] Other women who left home to seize new opportunities within a changing society endured similar accusations.[144] Ethnic unions, local native councils, and local authorities had long sought to curb such publicly "deviant" choices, which they alleged shamed the community.[145] The insinuation of prostitution thus connected Waithera's experience to long-standing disputes about gender and community honor.

Waithera remained single and a globetrotting soldier-athlete. In an interview with the *Daily Nation* in 1977, the question of marriage arose. According to the newspaper's portrayal of the conversation, "Ruth refused to discuss it."[146] The journalist concluded by suggesting, "If there are any men who have been attempting to catch-up with the 'Flying Soldier,' they have some running to do as there is no stopping Kenya's sprint heir-apparent."[147] In an interview decades later Ruth was more candid about the compatibility of marriage with involvement in athletics as a woman:

> We [the prominent Kenyan female runners of this generation] succeeded because we didn't get married as a second wife or third wife. And we didn't get married at 22 years old—you are still running! Even today girls should run until you come to 25 or 28. And then if you want to get married, get married by somebody who can run or somebody who does not have another wife or somebody who understands what you are doing.[148]

Waithera recognized that an unsupportive spouse could jeopardize female participation in sport. She also refused to allow rumors about her alleged promiscuity and the media's interest in her personal life to deter her from competing. Waithera declared to the *Daily Nation* in 1977 that when her contract with the army ended the following year, she intended "definitely to renew it" because she "want[ed] to keep in trim shape and keep on winning more medals."[149]

Waithera remained in the security forces until 1981, when she accepted an athletic scholarship from the University of Arizona. Though beset with injuries during much of her time as a student-athlete, her final year was exceptional. She won the NCAA Division I Indoor Track and Field National Championships in the 400 meters. That summer, she represented Kenya in both the 200 meters and the 400 meters at the 1984 Olympics in Los Angeles, becoming the first Kenyan woman to reach the finals of any track or field event at the Olympics. The University of Arizona inducted her into its Sports Hall of Fame in 1990.[150]

Waithera achieved economic independence. As a soldier she earned three hundred shillings a month. Top athletes were also given allowances for food and miscellaneous expenses while away on trips and training camps. As a student-athlete she received tuition, room, board, and a college degree as well as extensive travel and training at high-quality facilities under the direction of expert coaching. President Jomo Kenyatta made it possible for her to buy a house and, in her words, "[Kenyatta] said, 'I want to give the good runners something.' So, Kipchoge Keino was given a big ranch. That was 1977. I went to the office of the Minister of Land. He said, 'Ruth, you know that the President said that you should get a house.'"[151] The new four-bedroom house built in Nyahururu was the latest of many surprises to the people of her community. "They were asking, 'How did Ruth do it? How did she get that house?' Nobody would believe. How did I maneuver it?" Some speculated that the Kikuyu ethnicity she shared with President Kenyatta prompted his generous help in purchasing a house, to which she replied, "But me, I am from Central Province. And from there, I was so happy because I was number one in Kenya, from my tribe, to get the name. And the President gave me the house because of that."[152] While bonds of ethnicity may have helped, the bestowal of gifts in recognition of athletic excellence was not unprecedented including to Kalenjin running luminaries such as Keino.[153] Receiving land was nevertheless exceptional for any runner, as 1968 Olympian Amos Biwott emphasized: "Very few of us, maybe two or three, were given land by the government, but that was all."[154]

Waithera's unconventional choices met with opposition, but her successes rendered her actions honorable and brought enormous prestige to Kenya. She emulated the trajectory taken by many of Kenya's most successful male runners during the amateur era of track and field: embracing sport in school, joining the military to run competitively, and accepting a sport scholarship in the United States, all culminating in qualifying for an Olympic finals race. Waithera overcame the loss of her father at a young age and disapproval at home of her unorthodox choices to achieve an outcome that benefited herself, her community, and her country.

Conclusion

"Fragile project" aptly describes women's running in Kenya from independence in 1963 through much of the 1980s. Track performances of women in this generation failed to equal the high standards set by Kenyan men, and advances in women's running at the international level remained tenuous and stunted. In this period track and field among female Kenyan athletes emerged as a sport pursued by adolescents. International teams often consisted almost entirely of teenagers, and even preteen girls, who won medals and set national records.

Education in Kenya expanded after independence, with more primary and secondary schools built to accommodate rising enrollment. Schools quickly became essential training grounds for the development of Kenya's runners, but only those who enrolled in school and continued their education beyond the primary level could take full advantage of available opportunities. Parents at the secondary level had to pay for tuition, uniforms, books, and other materials, and along with pregnancies and family preference to educate sons rather than daughters, far fewer girls than boys transitioned to secondary school and dropout rates for girls were higher. Leaving school early not only denied prospective athletes a degree but any realistic opportunity for developing their athletic talent as well. Adult female runners faced derision from family and community and lack of support from spouses. Pregnancy, motherhood and the relentless time and effort required for agrarian work also diminished their numbers. Though many teenage and even preteen girls displayed excellence in track and field, disappointingly few among them emerged as adult athletes.

Yet a determined handful of women found inventive ways to create meaningful careers in track and field. Precocious achievement in sport while attending schools that encouraged athletics opened doors to employment in agencies that allowed time for training and racing. The choice of spouse, or whether to marry at all, was critical. Their lives reveal the structure of obligations and expectations confronted by sporting women in the twenty years following independence in 1963, and their actions reshaped the boundaries of gendered behavior. The advances these women made in the face of formidable obstacles set the stage for better days by their successors.

CHAPTER FOUR

The World Beckons

Kenya, Title IX, and the Expansion of Women's Track and Field

Few athletes in Kenya, especially women, can have graduated from provincial to international recognition as fast as 15-year-old Tecla Chemabwai," declared the *East African Standard* in December 1967.[1] Two years after she began running in school competitions, Chemabwai emerged as a teenage sensation who qualified for the 1968 Kenyan Olympic team that competed in Mexico City.[2] "We were very young at that time, and we were so proud to be the first three to represent not only the country but women as well," she declared.[3] Chemabwai in the 400 meters, Elizabeth Chesire in the 800 meters event, and Lydia Stephens in the 100 meters event became the first female runners to represent Kenya at the Olympic Games.

Four years later at the 1972 Olympic Games in Munich, two women competed for Kenya. Cherono Maiyo debuted in the 800- and 1500-meters events and Chemabwai again made the team, this time advancing to the second round in the 400-meters event. It would be her final race in Olympic competition though she qualified for the boycotted 1976 and 1980 games.[4] Kenya sent a total of five women to the 1984 Los Angeles games, including Ruth Waithera attending university in the

United States on an athletics scholarship.[5] Running "the race of my life," Waithera became the first Kenyan woman to qualify for an Olympic final, where she set an African record time of 51.54 seconds in the 400 meters event.[6]

Their Olympic participation contributed to what Kathrine Switzer, the first woman to officially complete the Boston Marathon, has called "the beginning of the competitive age of women's running."[7] Women had long been barred from road races around the world, and the IOC for much of the twentieth century refused to include middle- or long-distance events on the women's Olympic track and field program. A decades-long battle for gender parity at Olympic competitions, buoyed by the thousands of women already running long distances worldwide, finally compelled the IOC, the International Amateur Athletic Federation (IAAF, now World Athletics) and other sport federations to allow women at the 1984 Los Angeles Olympics to compete for the first time at the marathon distance of 26.2 miles.

Although their entry at the games from the late 1960s to the mid-1980s ensured Kenyan women retained a presence on the most important stage during this "fragile period," Olympic success proved elusive. Their participation at the major games of this era remained limited to a handful of athletes, while the numbers for male runners increased, and their performances improved. While the previous chapter of this book looked at local challenges posed to women's running and how a subset of women overcame them, this chapter focuses on the international and national sporting environments which at times restricted and other times opened opportunities for Kenyan women.

Two momentous developments during this period revolutionized women's athletics, though both required many years for full implementation. First was the expansion of the women's program of events at the Olympics and other major championships to include distances from the 1500 meters to the marathon. This expansion of events almost fully realized in 1984 finally allowed women to compete in nearly the same track and field program long allowed for men at the Olympic Games. These changes greatly benefitted female Kenyan runners as the Kenya Amateur Athletic Association (KAAA) promptly followed the lead of the IOC and IAAF in introducing longer distances for women at domestic competition.

The second game-changing development for the very best female Kenyan runners was the passage of legislation in 1972 in the United States that mandated equal funding for men's and women's education at all federally funded American schools and universities. The Kenyan women who gained access to sport scholarships at American universities used the opportunities therein to forge lengthy careers at the international level. However, delays in the enforcement of Title IX meant that far fewer Kenyan women than men could take advantage of these competitive prospects at a time when boycotts of successive Olympic Games heightened their importance in the amateur era of track and field. With a few exceptions, Kenyan men were the predominant beneficiaries of athletic scholarship opportunities while deliberative bodies in the US wrestled with the full reach of that legislation.

Overall Kenyan women continued to be largely limited to domestic competition on inferior tracks during the two decades following their debut at the 1968 Mexico City games. Female runners endured a paucity of opportunities to compete beyond Kenya at competitions conducive for recording qualifying times necessary to compete at major international events. Limits to distances no greater than 800 meters at the Olympic Games until 1972 reduced opportunities to achieve excellence in events at which Kenyan men excelled and Kenyan women of later decades gained worldwide acclaim. For most of the twentieth century, though their options at the international level gradually improved, constraints within one or more of the local, national, and international levels proved inimical to Kenyan women matching the record of success achieved by their male counterparts.

International Women's Track and Field

When Pierre de Coubertin, a primary architect of the modern Olympic Games, brought athletes from around the world together in 1896 for a modern-day revival of the ancient Olympic Games in Athens, Greece, not a single woman competed.[8] He asserted that women's sport defied "the laws of nature."[9] His devotion to that bias was intact in 1935 when he declared: "I personally am against the participation of women in public competition . . . At the Olympics their primary role should be like the ancient tournaments—the crowning of victors with the laurels."[10] Nevertheless, some women competed in upper-class sports at the early Olympic Games, beginning with golf and tennis in 1900 in Paris. The 1904 St. Louis games included archery as the only event for women, and at the 1908 London Olympics women competed in figure skating, sailing, and tennis.[11] Swimming and diving events were added to their program beginning in 1912.[12]

The IOC resisted pressure to add women's track and field to the games, and the all-male IAAF founded in 1912 initially took no account of women.[13] Following World War I and the establishment of separate women's sport organizations in several countries, the inaugural Women's Olympic Games watched by a reported twenty-thousand spectators took place in Paris as the first large-scale women's international track and field meet.[14] The cause of female athletes was linked with campaigns that were committed to women's suffrage, and efforts by leaders such as Alice Milliat, the founder of the first international governing body for women's athletics, the Fédération Sportive Féminine Internationale (FSFI), and many others, finally prompted the IOC to include five women's track and field events in the program for the Amsterdam Olympic games in 1928.[15]

The calamitous events of the 800 meters race in Amsterdam generated intense backlash. The IOC had added the high jump, discus, 100 meters, 4x100 meters, and 800 meters events to the women's program as an "experiment."[16] Some of the runners reportedly collapsed at the conclusion of the two-lap race. Hysterical news coverage of their "poor condition" caused uproar and was used as evidence to insist that women should not be allowed to compete over distances of that length. In 1929 the IOC voted to remove the women's 800 meters event from the program, a decision that held for the next thirty-one years.[17]

Pervasive concerns regarding the safety of "strenuous" sport such as track and field restricted competitive opportunities for women. Proponents of an influential ideology in the early decades of the twentieth century maintained that women possessed finite energy for all physical and intellectual activity and believed that such reserves had to be carefully marshaled, even claiming that the reproduction of the nation was somehow threatened. Some further contended that exercise required close oversight by medical specialists and coaches to prevent women from training and competing too vigorously. These and similar concerns hindered the expansion of the length and duration of women's track and field events. The notion that women's bodies were not suited to excessive physical activity endured well into the twentieth century.[18]

Nor did the greater economic and social freedoms that women gained during World War II prompt an expansion of international track and field events for women. A conservative backlash after the war exalted the family, home, and marriage. Nations struggled economically, and female athletes were often the first left out if team size had to be reduced. Roman Catholic bishops opposed women's involvement in competitive physical sports, claiming that it was both unfeminine and immoral.[19] In 1954 Pope Pius XII warned that many young women did not realize the "harm caused by the exaggerations of certain gymnastic and sporting exercises (which) are not fitting for virtuous young women."[20] Many people viewed participation in track and field in particular as contrary to the ideals of femininity and believed it would make women less attractive. It was not uncommon for athletes to be called "mannish," casting doubt on their appeal to men and their interest in men.[21] Women's involvement in the sport of track and field also threatened some men. Efforts to protect the exclusivity of men's sport were "not just about women—they were about preserving sport as a place for boys and men and guarding masculine qualities as their own," explains sport scholar Jaime Schultz.[22]

By the 1950s expansion of the range of women's track and field events at the highest level was only barely underway.[23] The 100 meters remained the longest distance available to them at the Olympics until 1948 when the 200 meters was added, and the 800-meters event was not restored until 1960. The 400-meters event debuted for women in 1964, and as late as the 1968 Mexico Olympic Games, the only track distances for women were the 100 meters, 200 meters, 400 meters, and 800 meters. Men competed in twenty-four track and field events, and women in twelve at those games. The 1500 meter was added in 1972, and it would take another twelve years for the IOC to add the first long-distance track event, the 3000 meters, and the marathon to the women's 1984 Olympic program. The sustained refusal by decision-makers to provide equivalent competitive opportunities for much of the twentieth century stymied the growth of international track and field for women. Competitive running over middle and long distances was an arena in which men could display their physical prowess, and generations of women were prevented from discovering their athletic talent.

Emerging from the "Wilderness Years"

Distance running for women gradually emerged from what track and field scholar Frank Murphy calls the "wilderness years" from 1928 to 1960.[24] Beginning in the 1960s, women's sport "entered a dramatically new era, a period of tremendous gains and even higher hopes for women athletes," declares historian Susan Cahn.[25] These gains were nevertheless incremental, as the world's international sports governing bodies embarked on what historian Allen Guttmann dubs the "slow trudge" toward full recognition of women's sport.[26]

The Olympic Games continued to set the standard for most track and field programs throughout the world. In 1960, after a gap of thirty-two years and five Olympic games, the IOC at last initiated the first steps of that slow trudge when it reintroduced the 800 meters event to the women's program. In that year Rome hosted the first televised Olympics, and a huge new audience was able to watch the games for the first time. They witnessed irrefutable proof that women could safely run middle-distance events.[27]

Determined female competitors began to challenge their exclusion from long distance running events, and some found innovative ways to participate. In 1963 Lyn Carmen and Merry Lepper hid across the street from the start line before merging into the Western Hemisphere Marathon in Culver City, California. When an official tried to force them off the road, Carman "gave him a good punch, and he landed on the pavement. I kept going, and they left me alone."[28] Some dressed to disguise their sex while others joined races from the crowd of onlookers risking ridicule, penalty, and even violence. American Roberta Gibb emerged from the sidelines of the 1966 Boston Marathon and finished in a reported unofficial time of 3:21:07, ahead of 290 runners in the all-male field.[29] In 1967 Kathrine Switzer entered the Boston marathon using only her initials on the application. During the race an official attempted to tear the numbers from her, shouting at her to leave the competition. With the help of her coach and fellow male track team members who surrounded her and prevented her from being pushed off the course, Switzer became the first officially registered woman to complete the Boston marathon.[30] Individual women around this time also entered marathons in Britain, Canada, and New Zealand.[31] South African women first challenged their exclusion when Frances Hayward of Durban unofficially completed the 1923 Comrades Marathon, a distance of fifty-six miles (ninety kilometers), finishing the race with thirty men. Geraldine Watson, also racing unofficially, completed three consecutive Comrades races from 1931 to 1933. Several South African women unofficially finished the ultra-endurance test from 1966 to 1975, when women were finally authorized to participate officially.[32] West Germany's promotion of women's long-distance running preceded that of many Commonwealth nations and the United States, in part because coaches required female cross-country skiers to prepare for those races by completing long runs in the summer. In 1968 German sports officials arranged for fifty-one women to compete in the Schwarzwald (Black Forest) Marathon, and fifty-three women completed it the following year. When the German Athletic Association (DLV) sanctioned women's participation in 1971, it became the first national athletics federation in the world to allow women to compete officially in the marathon.[33]

By the 1970s, as the "marathon boom" drew many more people into long-distance running, women were justifying their place in the longer distances of the sport.[34] Popular publications such as *People* and *Sports Illustrated* devoted increasing coverage to the achievements of female runners, often bringing focus to the unequal opportunities for women.[35] Rising participation by American sportswomen was highlighted by the *New York Times* in a 1972 article entitled "For-Men-Only Barrier in Athletics Is Teetering," which cited examples of female participation in baseball, crew, football, horse racing, hockey, shooting, and skiing, along with marathon running.[36] These breakthroughs were consistent with a broader cultural and political struggle that historian Susan Ware describes as a critical feminist moment in the United States when the Equal Rights Amendment passed Congress, Shirley Chisholm ran for president, and the Supreme Court upheld a woman's right to control her body in *Roe v Wade*.[37]

A landmark event in 1973 connected the battle for equality in sport with second wave feminism.[38] American tennis star Billie Jean King won one of the decade's most memorable athletic events, a "battle of the sexes" match against self-proclaimed "male chauvinist pig" Bobby Riggs. Riggs had issued the challenge, telling one news source: "Hell, we know there is no way she can beat me . . . When the pressure mounts and she thinks about fifty million people watching on TV, she'll fold. That's the way women are."[39] In the Houston Astrodome, in front of more than thirty-thousand people, the largest crowd ever to witness a tennis match, and the TV audience of approximately fifty million, King won in three straight sets. She used her resources to advocate for gender equality in sport, financing the magazine *WomenSports* in 1974, and joined Olympic swimmer Donna de Varona to establish the Women's Sports Foundation that continues to campaign against sexism in sport.[40]

The Cold War also accelerated change in women's sport when athletic success was held to mirror the superiority of competing ideologies. The annual track and field dual meets between teams from the United States and the Soviet Union beginning in the late 1950s were intensely followed in both nations.[41] American sprinters excelled, but Soviet women won these meets and dominated the middle-distance events, building on a legacy of promotion of female physical activity established long before the 800-meters event was restored to the Olympic program.[42] Recognizing the geopolitical implications of sport, US President Kennedy declared physical fitness a priority during his presidential campaign and established the President's Council on Physical Fitness. Kennedy referred to Americans' lack of physical fitness as "a menace to our security" in a 1960 *Sports Illustrated* article on "The Soft American," reiterating the point two years later in an essay entitled "The

Vigor We Need."[43] For decades, the two Cold War superpowers vied for medal count dominance in efforts to achieve both athletic and ideological supremacy.

During the years leading up to the 1980 Moscow Olympics, Soviet women achieved extraordinary results in middle-distance track events. In 1972, the first year that women contested the 1500-meters event at the Olympics, athletes from East Germany and the USSR won gold and silver, and five of the eight women in the 800 meters final came from communist countries. At the 1976 Montreal games, Eastern women claimed the first five places in the 1500-meters event—still the longest distance race on the women's Olympic program—and filled out the entire 800-meters final. Although depleted by the US-led boycott of the Moscow games, only one Western athlete made the final in either the 800 meters or the 1500 meters at the 1980 Olympics. Such resounding success in track and field reinforced the need to improve athletics for women on the other side of the Iron curtain.[44]

The precociousness of American middle-distance runner Mary Decker, who as a teenager in pigtails kicked past the Eastern bloc's best athletes at the dual meets of the early 1970s, contributed to changing perceptions about track for women in the United States. Her image beamed through televised broadcasts inspired other white, middle-class women and girls to consider taking part in a sport long deemed socially and physically inappropriate for them. As one observer described at the time, "the tremendous growth of women's running in the USA must owe much to the publicity surrounding Mary in 1973 and 1974."[45] By contrast, Black American women had long defended their nation's honor on the track in the rivalry between the superpowers, yet as Susan Cahn argues, racial prejudices meant their "achievements in a 'mannish' sport also reinforced disparaging stereotypes of black women as less womanly or feminine that white women."[46]

Although momentum gathered from the 1960s to the 1980s for an expanded women's track and field program at major international competitions, the all-male leadership of the IOC resisted full participation by women. Before any additional longer distance events at Olympic games could be realized, the IAAF was required to provide evidence that women's health would not be compromised and that these events for women could fit into the existing timetable without being detrimental to the games. The requirement that experimental races be held before events could be sanctioned further slowed progress in the fight for their inclusion.[47] Finally in 1980 the IOC voted to add the 400 meters hurdles and 3000 meters distance to the women's track and field program for the 1984 Los Angeles games and postponed consideration of the women's marathon. Also in 1980 the IAAF resolved that all international marathons would include both men's and women's races and recognized the 5000 and 10,000 meters as official distances for women. In 1983 the inaugural IAAF World Championships in Helsinki became the first major championship to include a women's marathon. After some dispute and with IAAF endorsement, the IOC and the Los Angeles Olympics Organizing Committee decided to include the marathon for women in 1984, marking what Schultz calls "a major occasion in the history of the Olympics."[48] The women's 10,000 meters followed in 1988. By then parity in competitive opportunities for men and women at major track and field championships was nearly complete.[49]

The expansion and interest in women's events at the international level encouraged the growth of women's track and field competitive opportunities generally, and Kenya was no exception. The European Championships first included the 1500 meters distance for women in 1969, and the Commonwealth Games followed suit in 1970. The KAAA then added that event to the Kenya national championships in 1971 in advance of the debut of that distance at the 1972 Olympics. The expansion of the 5000 meters event for women followed a similar pattern. Following its acceptance by the IAAF in 1980, the Kenyan national championships in June of 1981 included the inaugural run of the 5000 meters distance for Kenyan women, which the *Daily Nation* heralded as the first women's championship track race over that distance held officially on the African continent.[50] Full inclusion of these distance events was a gradual process that took the better part of a decade to accomplish. Concurrently the locus of Kenyan men's track and field running was shifting to the colleges and universities of the United States, where another battle over women's sporting participation was being waged.

Title IX and Athletics Scholarships

In 1964 when American tennis star Billie Jean King was a student at California State University, Los Angeles, she had already won two Wimbledon doubles titles. While male players benefited from tennis scholarships, she worked two jobs because women were not eligible for athletic scholarships. "People didn't think much about it," said King in 2007. "Nobody seemed to care that girls didn't have opportunities."[51]

The inertia and gradualism that characterized advancement for women in sport for much of the twentieth century entered its end game with the passage of Title IX in the United States Congress. On June 23, 1972, President Richard Nixon signed the Education Amendments Act of 1972. Title IX of the act states: "No person in the United States shall, on the basis of sex, be excluded from participation in, be denied the benefits of, or be subjected to discrimination under any educational programs or activities receiving federal financial assistance."[52] The initial goal of the comprehensive law was to combat gender inequalities in education, and as originally written, it made no specific mention of sport. With this act, women's right to equal participation with men had been codified in law, and it soon became clear that its ramifications extended beyond the classroom.[53]

Three-time Olympic gold medalist and scholar Nancy Hogshead-Makar and co-author Andrew Zimbalist assert that, "Other than women's suffrage, possibly no other piece of legislation has had a greater effect on women's lives."[54] The number of girls playing American high school sports in 1971 increased from three hundred thousand to more than two million in 1992, disproving claims by opponents of Title IX that the lower numbers of female athletes were due to lack of interest rather than lack of opportunities. At the university level, the number of female athletes increased from sixteen thousand in the early 1970s to more than 160,000 by the late 1980s.[55] In 2010, 193,232 women competed at the university level, and a decade later, that number had reached 221,212.[56]

Such encouraging statistics belie the contested and uneven progression of Title IX's implementation in the 1970s and 1980s that ultimately involved all three branches of the United States government. Many schools did not begin to comply with the law until 1975, after policy interpretations had been published by the US government.[57] "The administrative regulators of Title IX, under congressional oversight, strolled cautiously toward equality in sport," observes legal scholar Catharine Stimpson, who points out that "even as a series of regulations governing sports equity took hold, arguments about it persisted."[58] A well-organized campaign to reverse Title IX combined with delaying tactics by some officials charged with its enforcement stalled its full implementation. The NCAA opposed Title IX from its inception and even filed a lawsuit in 1976 to have the act overturned.[59]

By the late 1970s compliance remained irregular and dependent on further court rulings and additional legislation. One of the country's largest athletic programs, Ohio State University, did not award any women's track and field scholarships until four years after President Nixon signed Title IX into law.[60] In 1978 the University of Wisconsin's first full scholarship awarded to a female track and field athlete went to Pat Johnston, who won three national championships in the long jump.[61] Some universities were unwilling to admit that Title IX pertained to sport, and in a 1984 ruling, the United States Supreme Court went so far as to exempt athletics from the law's reach. In 1988 Congress at last mandated that all programs, including athletics, at federally funded institutions were indeed subject to the stipulation in Title IX requiring complete gender equality.[62]

For athletes of any nationality or gender, a sport scholarship from an American university constituted a life-changing opportunity, and for prospective Kenyan runners, that financial support was essential. Scholarship athletes receive tuition-free education, coaching, state-of-the-art equipment, and ample competitive opportunities. Until the early 1970s, however, coaches faced restrictions when recruiting international athletes that did not apply to American athletes. Athletes from overseas were subjected to an "over-age foreigner rule," which caused them to lose one year of NCAA eligibility for every year in which they participated in organized competition in their home countries past the age of twenty.[63] International athletes could be recruited out of high school (or its equivalent) and enrolled for four years, though, as one coach noted in a 1974 report published by the *Eugene Register-Guard*, "if you waited and tried to pluck off some Olympic gold medal winner from Kenya, then you would have him for considerably less time."[64] Sport scholar John Manners declares, "the rule had all but stopped the recruiting of Africans before it ever really got under way." He notes that in the 1950s and 1960s, English-speaking international-caliber athletes who had completed high school and passed college entrance examinations were "rare enough . . . athletes who could meet these requirements before turning 20 were practically non-existent."[65]

On December 10, 1973, a federal court suspended the over-age rule that applied only to international athletes on grounds that it did not comply with the equal protection provision in the Fourteenth Amendment to the US Constitution. Removing all constraints on recruiting older athletes from abroad quickly altered the composition of leading men's collegiate track and field and cross-country programs, and Kenya became a major source of recruited athletes. Sport geographer John Bale points to the swelling numbers of outstanding Kenyan runners at US colleges and universities after the NCAA retracted its rule on age limit eligibility. No more than three male Kenyan athletes competed at NCAA championships held between 1971 and 1973. In 1974 that number rose to twelve, doubled to twenty-four in 1975, reached thirty-one in 1976, thirty-seven in 1977, and fifty-four in 1978.[66] In 1976 twelve Kenyan men were competing for the University of Texas at El Paso (UTEP) alone. The ruling benefited smaller and less renowned collegiate programs that had often been at a recruiting disadvantage. With twenty-five international athletes on his forty-man roster from East and Southern Africa as well as Scandinavia, Canada, and the United Kingdom, UTEP head coach Ted Banks declared in 1977, "There's no way I'm gonna out-recruit big schools with big campuses and big reputations unless I bring in foreigners. I'm in the desert."[67]

College sports recruiting continued to revolve around male athletes in the years after IX was signed into law. NCAA schools could pay prospective male students to visit campus whereas the Association of Intercollegiate Athletics for Women (AIAW), established in 1971 to oversee women's sport, barred coaches from doing the same for prospective female athletes. University of New Mexico (UNM) women's athletic director Linda Estes noted in 1981 that her university budgeted $175,900 for men's recruiting and none for female recruitment.[68] Only four years before, the UNM had become one of the first universities in the country to offer women athletic scholarships, one of which went to Kenyan star Tecla Chemabwai soon thereafter. That year the UNM women's athletics budget of $35,000 was dwarfed by the men's of $700,000, and only eight scholarships were offered, split between the eight women's teams, but these gains were significant compared to the $5,000 budget and zero scholarships available to female athletes in the past.[69]

While athletic directors and other leaders battled over the future of women's collegiate sport in the United States, efforts accelerated to recruit male athletes from Anglophone African nations to universities in the United States. The beginnings of such pipelines can be traced to 1970, when Ghanaian sprinter George Daniels and Kenyan triple jumper Patrick Onyango were each awarded athletic scholarships to major NCAA sports programs.[70] Americans Bill Toomey and Mark Winzenried had met them the previous year during a US Information Services tour of Africa. Toomey recruited Daniels for his University of Colorado alma mater and Winzenried persuaded Onyango to join him at the University of Wisconsin.[71] Onyango and Daniels performed credibly but with the over-age rule still in place, coaches at other schools remained cautious about recruiting other African athletes. Kenyans Julius Sang and Robert Ouko arrived at North Carolina Central University (NCCU) in 1971 and competed in the 400 and 800 meters, respectively. The medals they won at the 1972 Munich Olympic Games, and the success of the Kenyan men's team at the 1968 and 1972 Olympics sent American coaches scrambling to establish connections with male Kenyan athletes in the wake of the 1973 ruling that lifted all age restrictions. From 1975 through 1985, Kenya sent the greatest number of male track and field athletes to the NCAA championships of any country other than the United States.[72] Some of these men won NCAA titles and were among the best runners in the world. In 1982, arguably the peak year of Kenyan presence in American intercollegiate athletics, twenty-four of the fifty top male Kenyan 5000 meters runners were attending colleges in the United States.[73]

Several factors contributed to the rapid increase of male Kenyan runners. The allure of a scholarship to the United States was especially important for preserving interest in the sport during the period in which Kenya boycotted the Olympics of 1976 and 1980 while running was still an amateur pursuit. The Cold War also created openings, as the US government sought to build goodwill in nonaligned African nations by funding sport exchanges and clinics with athletes and coaches. Sang and Ouko, two of the earliest notable Kenyan runners to attend a US university, had been contacted by North Carolina Central University's coach while he was on a visit to Kenya funded by the US State Department, which had stationed American Olympic gold medalist Mal Whitfield in Nairobi to develop Kenyan athletes. Whitfield served as a liaison between American universities and Kenyan track and field athletes.[74]

Their swelling numbers drew the ire of many American coaches who opposed the recruitment of foreign athletes. They contended that US colleges and universities were developing international talent for the benefit of other countries at the Olympic Games to the detriment of American athletes.[75] Age was another contentious issue. Criticism emerged alleging that overseas athletes enrolled as freshman in their late twenties or even thirties thereby placing domestic athletes who started college at age eighteen or nineteen at a disadvantage. In a 1986 interview with the *Los Angeles Times*, Coach Banks, who brought many East Africans to UTEP admitted that "because the guys were older, they would beat down young Americans. They'd discourage them. You've got to be mentally mature to take that."[76]

These objections eventually resulted in reinstatement of age eligibility rules that applied to both men and women in the early 1980s. The NCAA amended its over-age rule to mandate that all athletes, Americans included, who entered a Division I university would lose one year of collegiate eligibility for each year in which they took part in organized competition after turning twenty. Years of military service were initially exempted, but in 1984 the NCAA amended the rule again to remove that clause for Division I schools, thus eliminating an important loophole for Kenyan athletes, many of whom—including Ruth Waithera—had previously competed as soldiers in Kenya. These changes applied to American and international recruits alike but because relatively few US-born athletes started university after age twenty, the rule succeeded in limiting the recruitment of older international athletes.

When given the opportunity Kenya's best male and female runners often chose to leave Kenya to pursue four years of free university education and well-supported competitive opportunities. According to Philip Ndoo, who won championships for Eastern New Mexico University in the 1970s, "I don't know any[one] who regrets having come."[77] Kipchoge Keino in 1983 noted that conditions at home motivated many Kenyan athletes to obtain a university degree that upon return opened opportunities as journalists, university professors, civil servants, and business leaders. "They all work for U.S. track scholarships. They have to be worried for their future employment and security and that is a difficult thing in Kenya right now."[78] Fred Hardy, who coached several outstanding Kenyan runners at Richmond University in Virginia, similarly observed that "the motivation for many African runners is clear. When Western-educated graduates return home, they can expect rapid advancement in government, private business or education."[79] During this period, however, far fewer women received scholarship offers, and as Bale notes, "recruitment of foreign sportswomen to American universities was almost nonexistent."[80]

Comparing the team affiliation of the best Kenyan runners demonstrates that Kenyan men of this era were taking full advantage of the opportunities in the United States while the vast majority of leading female athletes represented Kenyan primary and secondary schools. The tables below show annual rankings for 1984 compiled by Kenyan national coach Walter Abmayr of the top ten performances by Kenyans in the 800 meters, 1500 meters, and 3000 meters distances, including their affiliations with educational institutions, whether Kenyan primary schools, secondary schools, or American universities.

Female athletes primarily represented schools and occasionally institutions such as the railway, prisons, and post. The fastest men of this era, in contrast, were most often university students in the United States, and only one male secondary school athlete ranked in the top ten of each of the three track events. For the 3000 meters distance, half of the fastest Kenyan men were attending American universities that year. Among the top ten female runners for the 3000 meters, seven were students in primary or secondary schools. In 1984 not a single top ten time for Kenyan women, at these distances, was attained by a student at an American university that year.

Though rare, exceptions in this era did exist for the very best female Kenyan athletes. Olympian Tecla Chemabwai, African 3000-meters record-holder Rose Chepyator-Thomson, and standout sprinter Ruth Waithera were among the first female Kenyan recipients of college running scholarships in the United States.

TABLE 1. Ten Best Performances with Institutional Affiliations: Women and Men's 3000 Meters (1984)

KENYAN WOMEN'S 3000 METERS 1984 BEST PERFORMANCES			KENYAN MEN'S 3000 METERS 1984 BEST PERFORMANCES		
TIME	NAME	AFFILIATION	TIME	NAME	AFFILIATION
8:57	Helen Kimaiyo	Secondary School	7:49	Joseph Chesire	Army
9:19	Mary Chepkemboi	Primary School	7:51	Ibrahim Hussein	USA
9:22	Regina Chemeli	Primary School	7:52	Julius Kariuki	Army
9:23	Esther Kiplagat	Secondary School	7:54	Kipsubai Koskei	Unattached
9:31	Theresa Chesang	Primary School	7:54.5	Paul Rugut	USA
9:35	Alice Mokeira	Posts	7:56.6	Patrick Sang	USA
9:54	Mary Wagaki	Prisons	7:59.1	Joseph Chelelgo	USA
9:57	Florence Maisiba	Railway	7:59.3	Charles Cheruiyot	Secondary School
9:58	Florence Maisiba	Secondary School	7:59.8	Paul Kipkoech	Army
9:58.4	Susan Sirma	Secondary School	8:00	Joseph Nzau	USA

Source: Walter Abmayr, *Track & Field Best Performances: Kenya 1984* (Nairobi: AFTS, 1985), 36, 66.

TABLE 2. Ten Best Performances with Institutional Affiliations: Women and Men's 1500 Meters (1984)

KENYAN WOMEN'S 1500 METERS 1984 BEST PERFORMANCES			KENYAN MEN'S 1500 METERS 1984 BEST PERFORMANCES		
TIME	NAME	AFFILIATION	TIME	NAME	AFFILIATION
4:18	Mary Chepkemboi	Secondary School	3:34	Joseph Chesire	Army
4:18	Justina Chepchirchir	Secondary School	3:37	Kipkoech Cheruiyot	Secondary School
4:20	Alice Mokeira	Posts	3:37.2	Mike Boit	USA
4:21	Esther Kiplagat	Secondary School	3:39	Josphat Muraya	Army
4:22	Prisca Chemeli	Secondary School	3:39	Samson Obwocha	USA
4:24	Wayua Kiteti	Prisons	3:40	Sisa Kirati	Army
4:27	Susan Sirma	Secondary School	3:40.8	Sammy Koskei	USA
4:27	Helen Kimaiyo	Secondary School	3:40.8	Paul Rugut	USA
4:29	Mary Chemweno	Unattached	3:41	Peter Koech	USA
4:32	Grace Chepchumba	Army	3:42	Julius Korir	USA

Source: Abmayr, *Track & Field Best Performances*, 36, 65.

TABLE 3. Ten Best Performances with Institutional Affiliation: Women and Men's 800 Meters (1984)

KENYAN WOMEN'S 800 METERS 1984 BEST PERFORMANCES			KENYAN MEN'S 800 METERS 1984 BEST PERFORMANCES		
TIME	NAME	AFFILIATION	TIME	NAME	AFFILIATION
2:04	Justina Chepchirchir	Secondary School	1:42	Sammy Koskei	USA
2:05	Selina Chirchir	Secondary School	1:44	Billy Konchellah	USA
2:06	Florence Wanjiru	Railway	1:44	Edwin Koech	USA
2:07	Susan Sirma	Secondary School	1:45	Juma Ndiwa	Army
2:07	Wayua Kiteti	Prison	1:46	James Maina Boi	Army
2:08	Helen Kimaiyo	Secondary School	1:47.1	Charles Onsare	Post
2:08.	Rose Tata-Muya	Cargo	1:47.1	Joseph Chesire	Army
2:09	Florence Njeri	Posts	1:47.8	Kipkoech Cheruiyot	Secondary School
2:09.1	Mary Chemweno	Unattached	1:48	Kiprono Chepkwony	Army
2:09.2	Alice Mokeira	Posts	1:48	Julius Korir	USA

Source: Abmayr, *Track & Field Best Performances*, 33, 63.

Chemabwai became the "second woman in Africa to receive and accept a Track and Field scholarship outside Africa," noted a Chicago press report in 1975.[81] She enrolled at Chicago State University in 1974, followed by Chepyator-Thomson at the University of Wisconsin at Madison from 1979 to 1983, and Waithera at the University of Arizona from 1981 to 1984. All three had been accomplished athletes prior to joining US collegiate teams and were exceptional in having competed for US universities prior to the widespread enforcement of Title IX.

Chemabwai was in her early teens when she ran in Mexico City at the 1968 Olympic Games. When her primary school discovered her running ability, she was invited to take part in multiple events in competitions against other schools: "I was an over-active youngster. I would run the 100 meters sprint, then go do the long jump, and then run 400 meters and so on."[82] She quickly reached the national level where she won the 400 meters at both the 1967 national championship and the East African Championships with record-setting marks.[83] Recalling that time, Chemabwai describes how she "used to run for fun and just to ensure I was defeating the other people in the race with me. Before I even knew what was going on, they told me that I had qualified for the 1968 Olympics." Her experience left an excitement palpable decades later, when she recalled, "I didn't care whether I was going to run or not, I was getting on a plane to visit a new place!" Describing the games, she remembered: "I was meeting new people and for the first time I was in close quarters with white people and even eating with them in the same dining hall; I wasn't used to these things."[84]

After enrolling at Kapsabet Girls' High School, Chemabwai was introduced to interval training, which boosted her performance but not enough to contend with the best sprinters in the world. "By the time I [reached] the 1972 Olympics, I had improved to progress to the second round but still got eliminated. You have countries like the US, Jamaica and Cuba, so Kenya could not feature for sprints because I didn't have a coach. However, due to the experience I was getting, I managed to get gold at the All Africa Games in 1973," she recalled.[85] At that second edition of the continental sport festival held in Lagos, she won the 200 meters in the fastest time ever recorded by a Kenyan woman.[86] Upon her return from the Olympics, she reflected, "My community was so excited. They were always very supportive . . . when we got home from international competition, we used to go around to all the provinces and there was a party. By the time we reached all the provinces, it would take two months!"[87]

Chemabwai built an extraordinary fifteen-year athletics career before marrying Olympian Julius Sang, one of the most decorated runners of the era. Sang passed away in 2004 and Chemabwai glowingly reminisced in a 2011 interview: "Remember the 1972 Olympics. He got the baton when we were last in the 4x400. He ran and we won gold. He was my husband." The pair had much in common and often competed at the same meets, from those in Kenya to the Olympic Games. "We knew each other back home. His parents knew my parents. We were neighbours."[88]

Both Chemabwai and Sang were part of the exodus of accomplished runners from Kenya to American universities. He left for North Carolina Central University in 1971 as one of the first Kenyan men to compete as a collegian in the United States. Chemabwai met Chicago State University (CSU) coach Dorothy Richey while competing in Australia in 1972, and in 1973 she accepted an offer to attend that university, though not on an athletics scholarship because CSU lacked a budget for women's athletics but rather through a foreign aid program.[89] She joined the university midway through the year after representing Kenya at the 1974 Commonwealth Games held in Christchurch, New Zealand, in January. "I was totally unprepared for the weather," she admitted. "I went there during winter. It was terrible. In fact, it was my first time to step on the snow to see the snow and feel the cold . . . I couldn't take it and I went to Los Angeles. It was also terrible, very humid. With the pollution, I could not breathe. So, then I landed in New Mexico."[90]

Chemabwai ended her collegiate search in 1976 when she accepted an athletic scholarship from the University of New Mexico (UNM), where women's athletics director Linda Estes and her allies had fought for recognition of women's sport and worked to increase the number of scholarships for female athletes.[91] Chemabwai competed with distinction for the UNM Lobos and for her country, recording the fastest 800 meters time by an African woman for that distance in 1977 and earning an invitation to Tunisia for the African trials for the World Cup, where she gained a place on the continental team in the 4x400 meters relay. She competed at the World Cup held in Dusseldorf, West Germany, that year. "After the World Cup, I was tempted and fell homesick, so instead of going back to school in the States, I boarded the homebound plane together with other Kenyans," she informed the *Daily Nation*.[92] Leaving school for a semester without permission cost her the scholarship from UNM, but Chemabwai obtained private sponsorship to complete her studies at UNM and graduated with a BS degree in physical education.[93] She then chose to return to Kenya for good, first taking a coaching job at the Rift Valley Institute of Technology, then moving to Mosoriot Teachers Training College, before accepting a position at Moi University in Eldoret to teach sports and physical education. After retiring from running in 1984, she married Sang in 1986, and together they had five children.[94]

Chemabwai was one of very few female athletes from her country to make full use of the competitive opportunities beginning to emerge for women in the United States. She was at the forefront of such participation not only among women in Kenya but also the continent, showing on an individual level how athletes found ways to compete in places and contexts previously not recognized as suitable for them. It was at the level of policy, however, that wider changes could be wrought, and Title IX sought to redress gender inequality in education ultimately including athletics programs in its reach. The passage of the act in 1972 one year before the removal of the age eligibility constraint on international athletes should have allowed Kenyan women to benefit from the same opportunities that Kenyan men were quickly taking advantage of at American universities. However, the long delay caused by the initially limited scope of Title IX, as well as its inconsistent enforcement, significantly postponed entry by female Kenyan athletes into collegiate track and field. Kenya's boycotts of the 1976 and 1980 Olympic Games further reduced competitive opportunities available to Kenyan women during the late seventies and early eighties while recruitment of male athletes boomed.

Chasing World-Class Times in Challenging Conditions

"Kenya female athletes cannot be expected to perform wonders when they are not accorded the same opportunities as their male counterparts," declared veteran international runner Rose Tata-Muya in an interview with the *Standard* in 1992, insisting on the "the need for sports officials to give Kenyan women opportunities to run overseas and measure themselves against the standards of those overseas."[95] Her lament stemmed from the fact that all Kenyan athletes were required to meet minimum performance standards achieved at officially sanctioned events in order to qualify to compete at the Olympics and other major international events. Beyond this Kenyan sport officials in the previous three Olympic cycles had set national qualifying standards even more rigorous than Olympic standards, staring in January 1980, when KAAA chairman Sam Ongeri announced that to compete in Moscow, athletes not only had to attain the Olympic qualifying standard once but do so "continuously with improved standards."[96] These heightened standards were in response to the surfeit of male Kenyan runners able to achieve these times.

Since so few Kenyan women competed outside the country in these years, it was especially difficult for them to attain qualifying standard times. Referring to runners based in Kenya, the *Daily Nation* noted ahead of the 1976 Montreal Olympic Games "it is almost practically impossible that any athlete will hit the set marks from 1500m. and above. The reason is altitude." Nairobi, at 5500 feet above sea level, offered athletes the lowest altitude of the major domestic track and field venues, outside of the one in coastal Mombasa. The others were Kisii (6000 feet), Nyeri (6200 feet), Embu (7000) feet, and Kapsabet (7200 feet). The report suggested that athletes who hoped to qualify would likely have to wait until the 1976 Olympic trials in Mombasa. Those without opportunities to compete abroad had only that competition to achieve the Olympic standard at a venue near sea level.[97]

Compounding this burden was the paucity of state-of-the-art tracks in Kenya. All races were conducted on grass or dirt until 1983, when the first all-weather track was constructed in Nairobi. In the famous running hub of Iten in the Rift Valley, generations of runners competed on a dirt track laid in 1959 that remains in heavy use today.[98] Unreliable track surfaces posed a significant challenge to achieving qualifying times required for international meets. At an important meet in October 1973, athletes seeking qualifying marks for the upcoming Christchurch Commonwealth Games blamed their disappointing performances on the rain-soaked grass track.[99] A February 1976 KAAA meet had to be relocated due to critical shortages of water and the poor state of the stadium track, most of which had been washed away during the previous year's rainy season.[100] The following month athletes hoping to qualify for the Montreal Olympics learned that renovations to the Kericho Stadium track had been delayed due to disagreement between two ministries over financing for the project, which resulted in athletes having to compete on a grass track, rather than the anticipated upgraded murram version.[101] A "rain-sodden" Kapsabet track also produced no qualifying times at the KAAA meet held there that season.[102] Four years later, many of Kenya's best athletes converged in front of a capacity crowd for the momentous 1980 Kenyan national championships on a rainy day that loosened the surface of the track of Kakamega's Bukhungu Stadium. By the end of the first day, "only two Kenyan records had fallen," both before the downpour, noted a *Daily Nation* reporter, adding, "This gives a misleading impression of the performances put up by the athletes. They did enough to deserve more."[103]

Meet logistics did not always proceed as planned. Athletes complained of "little food and lack of accommodation" at a meet in Bungoma in western Kenya in 1978, and three marathoners resorted to sleeping in the KAAA bus before waking up four hours later to compete in the event.[104] Though often marginally funded and disorganized, these meets were crucial, and one official noted, "Kenya Amateur Athletic Association organised competitions sometimes are the only challenge for the many talented young Kenyan runners who cannot make their way overseas."[105] British coach and top athlete Bruce Tulloh who lived in Kenya in the 1970s was less circumspect, declaring that, "To speak bluntly, Kenya has derived an immense amount of prestige in the world from the performances of a handful of runners, but has done nothing for the sport in return."[106] Tulloh cited one nearly seven-month stretch from the All Africa games selection meet in early December 1972 to the Brooke Bond-sponsored meet in late May 1973 in which not a single track and field meet took place, despite salaried sport officers and KAAA executives being stationed in every province. The dearth of regular local competitions limited Kenyan athletes, leaving them overly reliant on the handful of meets that rotated across the country and almost always required lengthy travel.

The *Sunday Nation* as early as 1969 raised the issue of improving the caliber of domestic competition, arguing that the "main problem facing talented African athletes was a lack of top-flight competition."[107] It reported that although "courage and determination have always spurred our African athletes to reach the top . . . they really have to struggle against the more experienced and established world-class runners."[108] European and American athletes were seen as having the chance to compete routinely against their "opposite numbers on other continents," while the only opportunity for Kenyan athletes to face international competition came at the Commonwealth Games and the Olympics. Highlighting the adverse consequences for women, a *Daily Nation* reporter observed in 1971, "Our track Cinderellas have had all too few opportunities of overseas competition."[109] Directing similar complaints at the KAAA a full sixteen years later, one female Olympian lamented to the *Standard*, "How do you expect us to perform miracles when we are never even considered for any international meetings. It is only our men who get exposed. It is very bad."[110]

While Kenya's best female athletes fought weather, altitude, and track conditions to achieve the qualifying times necessary to compete on the world's biggest stage, the *Daily Nation* regularly reported marks achieved by the fleetest Kenyan men as student-athletes in the United States. James Munyala, competing at the Penn Relays in Philadelphia in April 1976 as a UTEP sophomore, became the fifth Kenyan that year to attain an Olympic qualifying mark in the 5000 meters, adding it to the qualifying standard he had already achieved in the 3000 meters steeplechase. Two days later competing on the same all-weather track, UTEP teammate Wilson Waigwa attained a qualifying mark in the 1500 meters event, becoming the sixth Kenyan that year to attain the Olympic standard for that event. Tariq Mahmood of the University of Wisconsin became the third Kenyan based in the United States within a week to attain an Olympic qualifying mark when he ran under the standard for the 200 meters distance.[111] These achievements of US-based Kenyan runners contrasted with those competing only in Kenya in the same period. "There were no qualifiers in the countrywide Kenya inter-district championships, mainly because of weather and altitude, but the effort put out by most of the performers was outstanding," observed the *Daily Nation* in May 1976, one month after reporting the spate of Olympic qualifications by male runners.[112]

Kenya's running men also benefited from the practice of inviting individuals or small groups of athletes to international matches. "The Kenya Amateur Athletic Association is choked with overseas invitations for Kenya athletes!" proclaimed the *Daily Nation*, noting that the month of May 1976 alone had drawn requests for participation by Kenyan men in competitions in five countries. KAAA secretary Isaiah Kiplagat added, "There seems to be a big rush for our athletes and although we have received numerous invitations in the past, this month will go down as a record." Meet organizers in China, Czechoslovakia, Jamaica, Japan, and Poland sought participation of Kenyan male athletes, many of whom at these competitions attained Olympic standard times.[113] The press and archival record are replete with similar requests and plans for their participation in meets around the world. Three-time Olympic gold medalist and US Department of State Sports Affairs officer for Africa Mal Whitfield observed, "Kenyans have a better natural ability. But they just may not have the necessary facilities to enable them to get the best out of their talent. There are some things that one may not be able to achieve if devoid of facilities."[114]

Conclusion

Participation by Kenyan women in track and field expanded unevenly and incrementally in the decades between independence and the professionalization of the sport that unspooled in the 1980s. As women around the world justified their place as runners, overturned medical myths, and fought for opportunities, two institutional changes at the international level accelerated their participation. One was the expansion of distance events that were finally allowed for women at the Olympic Games and the other was the passage and implementation of Title IX legislation in the United States.

From the early 1970s, following the court-mandated elimination of age-based eligibility rules for collegiate athletes, competing for an American university on scholarship became a path taken by most top Kenyan male runners. Throughout the 1970s and early 1980s, steadily increasing numbers of Kenyan men benefited from ample opportunities to compete against world-class competition at state-of-the-art facilities while receiving a tuition-free education. The fleetest Kenyan women remained in the country representing primary and secondary school teams and domestic employers. Far fewer received track and field scholarships while the three branches of American government wrangled over the full reach of Title IX. After years of delays in attaining the full definition of the law, the 1980s finally saw NCAA universities begin to provide the same scholarship opportunities in numbers for women as men.

While Kenyan women were forced to wait, they were confined to domestic track events to attain the qualifying standards necessary for international competition. These meets failed to offer an optimal environment for fast times as they were contested on substandard surfaces usually at altitude. The omission of longer distance events also denied Kenyan women opportunities to compete over the same distances at which their male counterparts excelled. Kenyan female runners did benefit from successful efforts from the 1960s to the mid-1980s to include a nearly full program of women's races at major international events, but for the most part, progress in these years was stunted. Most international victories instead went to athletes from the Soviet bloc that emerged as a track and field powerhouse along with a resurgent American team in response to the politicized sporting achievements of the Cold War.

Nevertheless, a determined handful of Kenyan women managed to compete at American universities and the major international games. These women excelled in NCAA competition, attained the standards required to represent Kenya at Commonwealth and Olympic games, and established important precedents helpful for the next generation of running women in Kenya for whom the professionalization of sport opened new possibilities. Favorable environments prevailing concurrently at local, national, and international levels allowed women's running in Kenya to transition from exclusion to inclusion, and changes at the global level of sport were critical to that shaping that progression.

CHAPTER FIVE

I Have a Whole Battalion that Depends on Me

Professionals, Patrons, and Pioneers of Women's Running in Kenya

When Tegla Loroupe crossed the finish line to win the 1994 New York City Marathon, the twenty-one-year-old was $50,000 wealthier and the owner of a $35,000 Mercedes Benz.[1] Starting in the early 1980s, the international governing body of track and field had finally begun to reverse its long-standing official prohibition of monetary compensation for athletic success.[2] A decade of transition ensued and by the early 1990s running became a fully professional pursuit in which the most talented performers, many of whom were Kenyan, earned significant financial rewards. With her win in New York City, Loroupe became the first Kenyan woman to claim such a large prize at a major marathon. She and her peers and predecessors faced many obstacles as committed athletes that the professionalization of the sport helped them to overcome.

In defiance of gender norms, Loroupe and many of the small cadre that joined her in the 1990s created an avenue for change by honoring long established expectations about social behavior and civic virtue, confirming the insights of scholars of Kenyan history such as John Lonsdale that older ideas about community and belonging could prove both durable and fluid.[3] Loroupe's improved economic circumstances allowed her to become a redistributive patron, a role traditionally performed by men. In many Kenyan societies the attainment of civic virtue rested on the redistribution of wealth to family and community in order to improve the lives of others. Sharing her newfound wealth, which she willingly did, replicated established notions of moral authority and in so doing she quelled criticism often directed at women who dared to pursue athletic careers.

A confluence of changes in this era greatly benefited Kenya's running women. The program of women's track and field events at the Olympics expanded to nearly that of the men just as the professionalization of the sport gathered momentum, resulting in new competitive opportunities for women in track and field, cross-country, and road racing. The professionalization of the sport spawned the entry of sport agents whose negotiating skills became increasingly important as the goal of running transformed from competing for pride to competing for profit. Tegla Loroupe was one of the first women to benefit from these changes, and the choices she made in her running career provided a valuable template for the many who followed her. The potential for international success and substantial wealth drove a new motivation for running, inspiring growing numbers of Kenyans to take up the sport that now offered the possibility of greater socioeconomic mobility.

Pay for Play Finally Finds Track and Field

For twelve days in August 1987, a capacity crowd filled the Moi International Sports Centre in Kasarani, outside of Nairobi, to watch the fourth All Africa Games.[4] The newly constructed multimillion dollar sports center financed by the Chinese government and the Nyayo National Stadium in Nairobi, completed a few years earlier, both featured all-weather tracks.[5] Kenyan president Daniel arap Moi was present to observe the 1987 games involving fourteen sport disciplines and attracting five thousand athletes from thirty-nine African countries. "This is the first time in the games history that a head of state gives the festival top priority," declared Supreme Council for Sport in Africa secretary general Amadou Lamina Ba.[6] Dignitaries from across the continent filled the VIP section as the events unfolded before a packed house at the sixty-thousand-seat Kasarani venue.[7] Vendors took advantage of the "stupendous crowds" to inflate the price of food and drinks.[8] Television broadcasts reached viewers across the nation. In the city of Mombasa, streets were deserted as fans everywhere were "glued to their radios and televisions sets." People filled the social halls, the Swahili gardens in Old Town and Majengo, and bars with televisions sets, reported the *Daily Nation*. Tourists joined Mombasa residents in cheering for Kenyan athletes such as Sing'ore Girls' High School student Selina Chirchir who won the 1500 meters on the final day of competition.[9]

The host nation dominated the track and field events. Kenyan athletes won fourteen titles, ranging from the 200 meters to the 10,000 meters for both men and women. "Kenyans found an amazing winner," declared the *Daily Nation*, in fifteen-year-old Leah Malot who won the inaugural women's 10,000 meters event running barefoot.[10] Francisca Chepkurui set a games record in the 400 meters previously held by Tecla Chemabwai. A trio of Kenyan athletes, Selina Chirchir, Florence Wanjiru, and Mary Chemweno, swept the 800 meters event. In a front-page story titled "Kenya Continues to Pile Up Gold Medals," the *Daily Nation* declared that "perhaps the greatest effort" of the third day came from Elizabeth Olaba, whose shot put throw gave Kenya its first gold in the field events.[11] Susan Sirma won gold in the 3000 meters ahead of teammate Helen Kimaiyo. The quartet of Geraldine Shitandayi, Florence Wanjiru, Francisca Chepkurui, and Esther Kavaya astounded the crowd with a new games record in the 4x400 meters relay.[12]

In the decades prior to this sport festival, Kenyan women had been generally limited to domestic meets at substandard venues that handicapped their ability to achieve international qualifying standards necessary to compete on the world stage. Completion of the country's first synthetic track ahead of hosting the 1987 All Africa Games in Nairobi opened more realistic opportunities for them to attain the necessary qualifying times. When Kenya hosted and won the five-nation 1988 East and Central Africa Athletics Championships in its new, state-of-the-art facilities, Francisca Chepkurui recorded an Olympic qualifying time for the 1988 Seoul games, running the 800 meters in 2:01.2 seconds, and one month later at the Kenyan Olympic Trials set a new African 800 meters record with a time of 1:58.1 on the same track.[13]

Many of the female runners who raced at the international level during the "fragile period" of Kenyan women's running began to retire in the late 1980s and early 1990s, such as hurdler Rose Tata-Muya, who retired in 1992 at age thirty-three. Dubbed "the grand old lady of the Kenya athletics team," she had qualified for her fourth Olympics at the 1988 Seoul games. A new generation was rising with opportunities that exceeded their forerunners, led by athletes such as Susan Sirma, graduate of Kapkenda Girls' High School, and the Ngotho sisters, Jane and Margaret, who helped Kenya to win the women's World Cross-Country team title for the first time in 1991 in Antwerp, Belgium, a feat they repeated the next two years.[14] In 1994 Hellen Chepng'eno became the first African woman to claim the individual World Cross-Country Championship senior women's title in Budapest, Hungary.[15] The rapid success enjoyed by Kenyan women in the 1990s contrasted with the precarity and outright exclusion that their predecessors had endured.

What track and field historian Jörg Krieger calls "the slow turn toward professionalization in athletics" underpinned this shift. Competing for financial remuneration had long been proscribed. Even though many athletes took money under the table from race organizers, the international governing body of track and field, the International Amateur Athletic Federation (IAAF, now World Athletics) remained committed to official principles of strict amateurism. Since the beginning of the modern Olympic movement in 1896, officials had harbored fears that track and field would be tainted by the intrusion of monetary rewards for athletic achievement. Over time the concept of amateurism as "something which was infinitely worthwhile" began to be criticized as obsolete by defiant and increasingly outspoken athletes, coaches, meet organizers, and sport entrepreneurs, such as those who established the short-lived International Track Association, a professional track and field organization, in the mid-1970s.[16] As television coverage of sport expanded, corporations realized the economic benefits of advertising during track and field events. The infusion of money and escalation of profits spurred athletes to organize collectively for the right to receive compensation for their athletic achievements, which they argued was required to train, travel, and compete in events around the world.[17]

The IAAF began to abandon amateurism with a momentous decision in 1982 that permitted remuneration for athletic accomplishments, though for years thereafter, restrictions remained on how athletes received payments, including through trust funds controlled by national sport-governing bodies that doled out earnings for athletes' living and training expenses only. Television networks paid the IOC and other major sport organizations increasingly large sums for broadcast rights. Ahead of the first World Athletics Championships in 1983 held in Helsinki, the IAAF, led by President Primo Nebiolo, negotiated several lucrative television and advertising contracts.[18] The revenue these generated financed a plethora of new competitions, incentive schemes, and high-profile championships. Between 1988 and 1992, track and field competitions were among the twenty most-watched sporting events, with the 1991 World Athletics Championships in Tokyo attracting 152 million TV viewers.[19] The budget of the IAAF ballooned to $120 million for the years between 1992 and 1996.[20] "Many competitions generate a lot of television sponsorship which oils the wheels of world athletics," noted the *Standard* in 1993.[21] The exorbitant financial value of sport brought the utility of preserving amateur status under increased scrutiny.

The IAAF Grand Prix (now Diamond League) track and field circuit, the World Cross-Country Challenge, and the World Athletics Championships emerged as critically important venues for runners. Introduced in 1985, the IAAF Grand Prix consisted of a linked series of the world's elite and most lucrative track and field competitions. In its inaugural year, 632 athletes competed, and by 1993, over two thousand men and women were vying for $2.3 million in prize money.[22] The program varied from year to year, and top finishers received increasing payouts. Athletes accumulated points throughout the season for each event, and the individual with the most points at the end of the season was awarded upwards of $50,000. By 1997 the Grand Prix had grown to include twenty-nine track and field meets that commenced in February in Melbourne, Australia, continued mainly in Europe throughout the Northern hemisphere summer, and ended in September in Fukuoka, Japan. Fifteen years after the IAAF first loosened official restrictions on remuneration, almost $4 million in prize money was awarded to athletes over the course of a Grand Prix season. Track and field athletes benefited from this plentiful and mushrooming array of rewarding opportunities. The Grand Prix "has been an important innovation in athletics and has helped develop young talent," reported the *Standard* in 1993.[23]

Following the success of the Grand Prix events, the IAAF launched the World Cross-Country Challenge in November 1990 using a formula similar to that of the Grand Prix circuit. The world's top cross-country runners competed for roughly $100,000 in prize money in ten races between November and April of the following year.[24] Runners accumulated points, and at the end of the season, the athlete with the most points earned the World Cross-Country Challenge title and $10,000.[25] In the inaugural 1990–1991 season, the winner was Susan Sirma of Kenya two points ahead of compatriot Jane Ngotho, a soldier in the Kenya Armed Forces Women's Service Corps who received $8000 for second place.[26]

The Grand Prix and the Cross-Country Challenge competitions offered lucrative prospects for runners, but the hallmark meet for all track and field athletes came in the form of the World Athletics Championships. The Kenyan press declared, "The World Championships is the second most important event in any athlete's life, after the Olympic Games."[27] The first World Athletics Championships in 1983 featured athletes from 153 nations, including Kenya, and the number of athletes and nations increased in successive competitions.[28] In the 1990s, that event became one of the most widely watched sporting events, surpassed only by World Cup soccer and the Olympic Games.[29]

The IAAF's approach to athlete remuneration at the World Championships shows how it sought to "carefully tiptoe between opening the door for professionals while maintaining firm control of the sport," as Krieger puts it.[30] Nebiolo clung to the principle that athletes should receive no direct prize money for participation in either the World Championships or the Olympics, and the first three World Athletics Championships from 1983 to 1991 awarded no rewards for performance.[31] Some athletes declined to compete. World 10,000 meters record-holder Yobes Ondieki of Kenya preferred to "concentrate his energies on the lucrative Grand Prix Circuit events on either side of the World Championships," according to the Kenyan press.[32]

After the IAAF signed a four-year television contract worth $91 million in April 1992, athletes demanded prize money for excellence at the championships, arguing that they were the reasons for the governing body's new wealth.[33] Amid threats of athlete boycotts before the 1993 World Championships in Stuttgart, Germany, the IAAF compromised and awarded a Mercedes Benz 190E sedan to all gold medalists, each worth $28,000 at the time.[34] Reflecting on the breakthrough concessions five years later, the *Standard* noted that "Kenyans still recall the trio of Paul Ruto (800 meters champion), Ishmael Kirui (5000 meters champion), and Moses Kiptanui (3000 meters steeple-chase champion) being handed over their Mercs at the Moi Kasarani Stadium by President Moi."[35] Athletes continued to push for cash rewards for success at the World Athletics Championships, demands to which the IAAF finally acquiesced in 1997. The IAAF Competition Awards were introduced, and for the first time, prize money was distributed directly to medal-winning athletes at all the major IAAF championships (see accompanying table).[36]

The $91-million television deal signed in 1992 promised to deliver large audiences, which was an attractive advertising opportunity for corporations. Private sports investment in Kenyan athletics exploded once professionalism became the norm. The dominance of Kenyan distance runners attracted the attention of the largest shoe companies and others. Mizuno, Adidas, Reebok, and Nike competed for sponsorship, and on January 6, 1993, Nike signed its first contract with the KAAA.[37] Although corporate support of individual athletes had long been a Nike tradition, direct sponsorship of national track and field governing bodies was relatively new to the firm.[38] The Nike contract with the KAAA amounted to nearly $1 million for

TABLE 4. Prize Money Distribution at IAAF World Championships (1997)

PLACE	CROSS COUNTRY	INDOOR TRACK AND FIELD	OUTDOOR TRACK AND FIELD
1st	$40,000	$50,000	$60,000
2nd	$20,000	$20,000	$30,000
3rd	$15,000	$10,000	$20,000

Source: Omolo Okoth, "Rewarding Performers," *The Standard,* March 31, 1997, 29.

the period from 1993 though 2000.[39] Nike also agreed to award a $7500 bonus to the Kenyan governing body for each individual gold medalist, male or female, at the World Athletics Championships and the Olympic Games.[40]

This sponsorship, along with funds from the IAAF and international meet promoters, combined to make the KAAA the wealthiest sport federation in Kenya in the 1990s. One Kenyan press report expressed delight that the Nike contract "opened the financial floodgates for the KAAA."[41] According to association officials, their budget covered the costs of the local, national, continental, and international competitions, residential training camps prior to major championships, and coaching seminars.[42] By structuring its financial rewards in a gender-neutral fashion, Nike provided the ability and incentive for the KAAA to increase the quality and quantity of competitions, camps, and coaching clinics for male and female competitors. This intervention helped to ensure that the exclusion of women that occurred at the 1989 World Cross-Country Championships, when the Kenyan senior women's team was left out, would not recur.[43]

The rapid monetization of the sport and parity of remuneration by gender brought major changes to distance running in Kenya. Women proved, in short order, that their late arrival to the winning circle was a function of denied opportunity, not of inferior talent. Susan Sirma became the first Kenyan woman to excel in the Grand Prix circuit of competitions in 1991, leading the women in her specialty, the 3000 meters. That same year she became the first Kenyan woman to medal at the World Athletics Championships. Sally Barsosio also medaled for Kenya at the World Athletics Championships two years later, and Tegla Loroupe recorded consecutive victories in the New York City Marathon in 1994 and 1995. Ahead of the 1996 World Cross-Country Championships held in Cape Town, KAAA secretary David Okeyo declared, "We are going for a clean sweep, especially with the senior women's team, which is no doubt the best in the world at the moment." That team

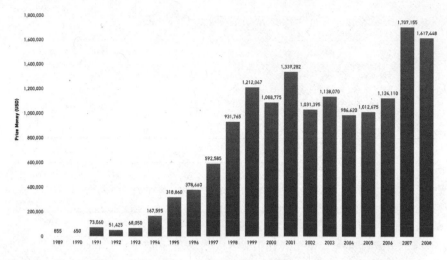

FIGURE 3. Kenyan Women's Prize Money by Year, 1989–2008.

SOURCE: "PRIZE MONEY DISTRIBUTIONS BY YEAR," ASSOCIATION OF ROAD RACING STATISTICIANS, HTTPS://WWW.ARRS.RUN/PM_BYYR.HTM.

consisted of Chepkemoi Barsosio, Sally Barsosio, Rose Cheruiyot, Lornah Kiplagat, Noam Mugo, and Jane Ngotho, several of whom were considered capable of winning the individual world title.[44] Both the senior women's and the junior girls' teams finished first. Cheruiyot and Mugo claimed the silver and bronze, respectively, and the trio of Ngotho and the Barsosio sisters finished in the top-fifteen, representing a sea change from previous generations of female Kenyan runners. Also that year, Paulina Konga won her historic silver medal in the 5000 meters at the Atlanta Olympics, becoming the first woman to win an Olympic medal for Kenya. Before competing in Atlanta, the prisons officer had limited international exposure and had not joined the lucrative European circuit where "other top women athletes are minting cash," according to the Kenyan press.[45] Mary Chege, head of the KAAA women's subcommittee, declared, "Her success is a manifestation of the fact that Kenyan women athletes have come of age and can compete and win against the best in the world provided they continue getting the necessary support and exposure as is given to our successful male athletes."[46]

According to the Association of Road Racing Statisticians, between 1982 and 2008 Kenyan men collectively earned more than $50 million in prize money from track and field and road running events. As of 2008, American men were distantly second in the world with roughly $22 million. Over the same period, Kenyan women

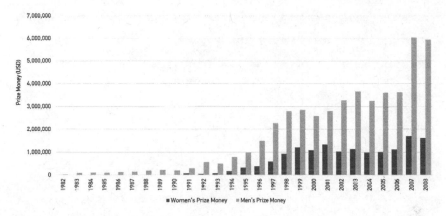

FIGURE 4. Comparing Kenyan Men's and Women's Prize Money by Year, 1982–2008

SOURCE: "PRIZE MONEY DISTRIBUTIONS BY YEAR," ASSOCIATION OF ROAD RACING STATISTICIANS, HTTPS://WWW.ARRS.RUN/PM_BYYR.HTM.

were second to American women with nearly $15 million, almost all of it since 1991.[47] The accompanying tables illustrate the progression of female runners' prize money since 1989 (the first year of earnings recorded for Kenyan women) as well as earnings by women relative to those of men.

The first year that a woman from Kenya achieved a top ten world ranking in a distance event was 1991, which was also the first year in which Kenya became one of the top eight countries in the world in terms of total prize money earned by women.[48] By 1994 Kenyan women were third in the world in prize money winnings, and by 2013 they were first, with total annual recorded earnings of more than $3,500,000, while their numbers in the world top ten rankings for distance events swelled.[49]

The new wealth generated by male and female athletes greatly enhanced local economies across the Rift Valley, the region in which many of the fleetest runners were raised and where many others trained. The Kenyan press noted that these winnings were often converted into tangible investments in Eldoret, the major commercial hub of that region, to the effect that:

Rental houses have sprung up all around the area, shops are stocking goods that the best money can buy while new schools and hospitals are gradually being put

TABLE 5. Top-Ten World Rankings of Kenyan Women by Track and Field News, 1989–1997

EVENT	1989	1990	1991	1992	1993	1994	1995	1996	1997
800									
1500			9th						4th
5000			4th				5th, 8th	4th, 10th	2nd, 4th
10,000					3rd, 4th		4th	8th, 10th	1st, 7th
MARATHON						7th	5th, 9th	10th	2nd, 6th

Source: "Track & Field News Rankings," *Track and Field News,* http://www.trackandfieldnews.com/rankings/.

up. It's all a result of the millions of shillings pumped into the zone by the talented athletes that have emerged from the area.[50]

From a 2007 survey of the economic impact on Eldoret, the *Daily Nation* conducted that:

> The money in prizes is fast turning the region from an agricultural zone into a massive investment destination. Eldoret town and the surrounding areas are witnessing a property boom as the sportsmen and women, many of them from the area, set the pace in investing their earnings at home.[51]

Government and sports officials in these areas confirmed the positive impact of this new wealth. Keiyo North Sports Officer George Obumba noted that in 2011, "the heavy presence of the multi-millionaire athletes has changed the socio-economic landscape."[52] Owner of a thriving sports store in Eldoret and former professional athlete Martin Keino added, "I would say they make a pretty big contribution to this town [Eldoret]. They are the ones who drive the demand for housing, office space in town, new construction. They are really driving the boom in this town.[53]

Women were increasingly matching men in track and field success and earnings. "The 1991 Tokyo World Athletics Championships saw the rise of African women athletes. Although the women did not win as many gold medals [as the men] they firmly established their presence," noted the *Standard*.[54] According to the *Daily Nation*, "In a nation that especially reveres long-distance runners, the rise of Kenya's women into the global running elite has enormous potential to open doors for women and improve economic conditions for everyone."[55] Their ascent continued, and in 1993, the *Standard* observed that the trend of male Kenyan distance runners overshadowing their female counterparts "has been reversing in the past three years."[56] In 1995, one *Standard* reporter enthused that "Ladies have performed exceptionally well in sports in Kenya and abroad . . . In athletics, we have household names like Hellen Chepng'eno who was the first black woman to win the world cross-country title, Sally Barsosio, Susan Sirma and Tecla Lorupe all have won medals to their credit. No wonder Kenyan woman athletes are a threat to the world at large."[57] Kenyan women as professional athletes were emerging as respected equals with their male counterparts in international competitions. The livelihoods available through sport opened new pathways at home for ambitious, wealthy sportswomen, as the exceptional life of Tegla Loroupe reveals.

Tegla Loroupe and the Accountability of Power

Tegla Chepkite Loroupe was one of the first female Kenyan runners to rise to international prominence while earning substantial wealth from long-distance running. She became a two-time world marathon record holder and held world records over distances of twenty-five and thirty kilometers while twice being named the world's best performer in the marathon.[58] Other successes included victories in ten of the twenty-two international marathon races that she entered between 1994 and 2003 and outstanding performances recorded in cities "from New York to Berlin, Tokyo to Lisbon, from Boston to Cologne," according to a report by the IAAF.[59] During her fifteen-year career as a professional athlete, Loroupe competed in three Olympics and five World Athletics Championships, twice winning a bronze medal in the latter. In four World Half-Marathon Championships, she won three times. Loroupe also served as an ambassador of running in its early professional years to many Kenyan women. "She has been very important to me," stated two-time Olympian, two-time World Champion gold medalist, and former marathon world-record holder Catherine Ndereba. "When I started running in 1994, I learned about her in magazines. I knew she was a star in our country, and I was copying her."[60]

Born on May 9, 1973, Loroupe grew up with twenty-two siblings in the hills of West Pokot in the Rift Valley. She worked in the fields as a child and looked after younger brothers and sisters. Loroupe was six when she began to run, barefoot, the four miles along a dirt road to and from Kapsait Primary School each day, an experience familiar to many Kenyan runners.[61] "Those teachers would beat you if you were late," she explained in a 2006 interview.[62] When she was nine, she competed for the first time at a school sports day, winning the 1500 meters, 5000 meters, and 10,000 meters events against boys and girls.[63]

Her father, Loroupe Losiwa, discouraged her interest in sport but allowed her to run in primary school if she earned higher math grades than her brother.[64] At age twelve, she entered boarding school at Nasokol Girls' Secondary School in nearby Kapenguria, and her father again advised that she stop running because "it was not very ladylike."[65] Without appropriate running attire, training in blouse and skirt, she continued to run. Fellow pupils wondered what "sort of woman I wanted to be in the future," Loroupe disclosed in an interview years later.[66] She credited the negativity she encountered from family and peers with hardening her resolve, referring to herself as having "a wooden head" at that time.[67] "I have two arms and legs and I came out of the same stomach as my brothers. Why can't we do the same things?" she declared in 1999.[68]

Loroupe credits her mother, Mary Lotuma, who had been orphaned, with teaching her the value of independence and supporting her interest in sport.[69] Her mother and older sister Albina insisted that she attend school, where she developed as an athlete.[70] She first competed at the 1987 national schools athletics championships as a member of the Nasokol Girls' School team.[71] Her rise to fame began the following year when she traveled to Japan as a member of the national junior cross-country team. In 1989, she won the Kenyan National Cross-Country Championships, despite stepping on a sharp piece of wood during the race, and also helped the Kenyan team win the junior women's race at the World Cross-Country Championships in Stavanger, Norway.[72]

As her running career progressed, her father softened his opposition, but many in her community did not. She had to publicly dismiss allegations that she was not a woman, declaring "I am pleased to show I am all woman. Some people have been suggesting otherwise, things like I am half man and half woman," further adding that she was "speaking out after cruel gossips questioned her gender after her impressive times in races against men."[73] Such allegations evoked the barbs about their physical appearance endured by female running pioneers in the United States, Britain, and elsewhere from critics who contended that "strenuous" sport rendered women overly masculine.[74] Remaining single also brought disapproval. Looking back on that period in a 2006 interview, Loroupe stated, "At this point, I was so fed up with men, I thought of becoming a nun."[75] She deflected questions about her unmarried status with humor, saying "perhaps I run too fast for any man to catch up with me."[76] On another occasion, she observed: "You know when you age, you might not be able to run. For now I want to concentrate on that. One can join university at any age to study for a degree course of choice or settle down in marriage any time but it is not the case with athletics. I will wait until my legs refuse to run."[77] Striving for sporting and economic opportunities beyond the norm placed her at the center of conflict, yet Loroupe had a precocious understanding of the implications that certain choices would have for her and stayed single while competing in races across Kenya and beyond.

Her career peaked as monetary rewards and performance incentives were exploding when female runners could take advantage of the new economic opportunities being offered. Victories at major marathons allowed Loroupe to become the first runner in her Pokot community, male or female, to fulfill a role as patron. She purchased several properties, with homes in Nakuru and Kitali, while also providing for many others, noting: "I have a whole battalion that depends on me. I come from a family of 22, who virtually depend on me for many things. A good number of my community members, too, look up to me for economic support."[78] She paid for siblings' education in Kenya and financed two sisters to study in the United States, helping Emily Chebet pursue a master's degree in Community Health and Gladys Loroupe to complete a degree in medicine.[79] She also funded scholarships for two women and one man from her community to study medicine abroad.[80] While training in Germany, Loroupe shared her earnings with several athletes who joined her there, including friend and training partner Joyce Chepchumba who would become an Olympic medalist and two-time winner of both the Chicago and the London marathons. On one occasion, Loroupe met the cost of the operation, flights, and overseas accommodation for a neighbor in Kapenguria who needed urgent medical attention. She also cared for the six children that her sister left behind when she passed away just days before the 1995 New York City Marathon, which Loroupe won in her honor.[81] Her running career replicated a pattern common to successful male athletes in Kenya and elsewhere in Africa. Accomplished runners gaining accolades at the international level, Loroupe among them, were now able to support aspiring young athletes and to fulfill wider kinship obligations and even to create jobs for the wider community.

Patronage relationships had long been vital elements in the attainment of civic virtue within East African communities which depended on reciprocity and mutual respect from members of the community. The arrival of colonial capitalism posed a significant challenge to this moral economy with its embedded norms of reputational accountability, leading to what Lonsdale calls "subjection, household conflict and social unease."[82] In return for the promise of support for future marriages, sons had traditionally remained obedient to elders in their communities on whom they relied for land and resource allocation. The demands of the colonial economy often forced young men to abandon older traditions, which upset the conditional nature of relationships. The advent of waged work on settler farms and in urban centers allowed young men to find alternative ways to achieve self-mastery and independence. The ensuing migrancy of men and some women presented a challenge to the existing social order. Alliances between colonial officials and African collaborators devalued long-established moral economies and expected obligations between people. According to Lonsdale, these changes raised critical questions that persisted beyond the colonial era, such as "to whom was duty now owed, at what cost, for whose benefit"?[83]

Loroupe's loyalty never veered from her Pokot community. By the end of 2011, she had invested $150,000 in the Tegla Loroupe Peace Foundation, which went toward building a boarding school and sport center in Kapenguria for disadvantaged youth from the region.[84] Although little precedent existed for patronage by a Pokot woman, by choosing to "pour hundreds of thousands of dollars of her prize money" into her community, she achieved the civic virtue historically expected of prosperous men in the Rift Valley. Loroupe recognized that as a person of means, she was accountable to others. She adhered to values that made a "good Pokot" while her choices helped to redefine what constituted a "good woman."

Loroupe also organized local athletic competitions with a peace-making agenda. Accomplished Kenyan men such as Olympic medalist Paul Tergat had sponsored races in his home in the Rift Valley in the 1990s. Loroupe was the first woman from the region to do so when in 2003 she financed the first Race for Peace in Kapenguria, West Pokot's largest town, inspired by a visit to Indonesia the previous year as an ambassador for peace. "I told myself that if I could fly for thousands of kilometres to help restore confidence in a country hit by terrorists, why can't I do it at home?" she explained to the *Daily Nation*.[85]

The Race for Peace brought together runners from Pokot, Marakwet, Turkana, South Sudan, and the Karimojong of Uganda, communities with a long history of deadly conflict.[86] Clashes among these groups "have continued claiming innocent lives, ravaged the poor people's fragile livelihoods, disrupted learning, and ruined health facilities," Loroupe told the *Daily Nation*.[87] In a brochure advertising the race, she proclaimed that the competition aimed to give communities, their leaders, and government agents the opportunity to work toward peaceful solutions to sustained traditions of enmity.[88] Describing her motivation, she declared: "It is not an easy task but I have vowed to use my track and field achievements, skills and friends to promote peaceful co-existence and development of poor and marginalised pastoralists in my community of West Pokot and Africa at large."[89] By building goodwill between warring groups through the races she financed with generous prize money, Loroupe showed a determined commitment to inherited ideas about bettering her community in the traditionally male role of patron.

The solidarity of female athletes, an achievement made possible by their athletic excellence and the new economics of the sport, received warm acknowledgment at home as Loroupe's efforts indicate. The *Daily Nation* declared that "there is no doubt that Tegla enjoys the respect and admiration of her people" and that her "sporting achievements had earned her respect and gave her clout even among men with traditional mindsets."[90] Loroupe thought her contributions at home and abroad also underpinned the positive reception the Race for Peace received. "They considered me their successful daughter who has brought glory and pride to the local communities, and my initiative was not met with any hostility."[91]

In a magazine published by the IAAF, Ottavio Castellini covered the "welcome home" parade organized in Loroupe's honor after her second consecutive New York City Marathon victory, noting that "one of the main aspects I recall during the event is the unbelievably strong admiration for Tegla that one could sense flowing from all the men and women present." Castellini quoted Rodda Rotino, a head teacher of a local secondary school for girls, who said, "Thanks to Tegla, today is an important day for the women of Kapenguria."[92] Loroupe's international victories and her efforts to promote change within her local community gained her widespread respect. "After I won, the women came to me and said, 'You were wise to resist our words. We are proud of you' . . . It gave a lot of motivation to many people," she said, adding that her village "gave me an ostrich feather. They usually give the feather to the warriors who come home victorious."[93] For a woman to receive an ostrich feather symbolizing a victorious warrior was extraordinary. Her community respected her effort to pay respectful homage to its mores while meaningfully challenging the gender constraints that she faced.

Political scientist Nic Cheeseman observes that communities in Kenya assess patrons on their willingness and ability to use their wealth for the benefit of the group.[94] The obligations that men and women, rich and poor, and young and old owed each other had long been a governing dynamic of interpersonal relationships and society. Evaluation of this interplay rested on what Lonsdale calls the "accountability of power, that which makes inequality socially responsible and thus justifiable in practice."[95] Loroupe sought to make her choices respectable by serving her community as a patron and a peacemaker. Wealth was a reward for hard work that came with obligations, and the means of material acquisition mattered less than the extent to which, and with whom, resources were shared.

Transitions in Track and Field for Kenyan Women

The professionalization of track and field created lucrative careers for athletes who came after Loroupe, such as Pamela Jelimo. In September of 2008, Jelimo returned to her Rift Valley home of Kaptamok as Kenya's first female Olympic gold medal winner.[96] She paired that breakthrough achievement in Beijing with earning over $1,000,000 in prize money during her widely publicized four-month streak of victories in Golden League competitions across three continents. The eighteen-year-old middle-distance athlete became one of Kenya's running celebrities in her first season of racing at the international level. Men greeted her return holding "Pamela Marry Me" signs, Kenyan president Mwai Kibaki granted her a private audience, and the road that connected her village with the Kipchoge Keino stadium in Eldoret was renamed Pamela Jelimo Road.[97]

Catherine Ndereba, inspired by the enormous success of Loroupe, began her running career as the professionalization of the sport was reaching maturity. The Kenya Prisons recruited her in 1994 and provided an environment conducive to her athletic development.[98] She married fellow prisons employee and training partner, Anthony Maina, who supported her athletic ambitions. After giving birth to a daughter, Ndereba continued her employment and training with the prisons.[99] When she broke the world record in the Chicago marathon in October 2001, she received a $75,000 prize purse, $100,000 for breaking the world record, a Volkswagen Jetta valued at over $26,000, and a significant appearance fee.[100] Her victory in the marathon at the 2003 World Athletics Championships was worth $60,000 and opened other lucrative avenues in terms of appearance fees and professional sponsorship by a major shoe company.[101] Ndereba followed Loroupe's example and sponsored a half-marathon in her home region of Nyeri in Central Kenya, transforming the small event into a national and later an international competition with prize money commensurate to its increasing stature. She paid many children's school fees, including those of her younger siblings, bought land and built a house for her parents, and purchased properties in Nairobi and Philadelphia.[102]

Other female runners from the early years of professional sport similarly emphasize that remuneration allowed them to undertake new ventures while supporting their extended families and communities. World-class athlete Rose Cheruiyot, who came to stardom in the 1990s, purchased property in Eldoret and funded the education of her two sisters and one brother in secondary school.[103] World Championships medalist Susan Sirma sponsored siblings and cousins after she "won good prize money on the international circuit and bought, among other things, a new pickup truck for driving in Kenya."[104] She also supported her cousin, Lornah Kiplagat, who would go on to win the 2007 World Cross Country Champion and become a three-time Olympian. Kiplagat started running in 1995, a time when, she recalls, "It was very hard for a woman to reach the top."[105] Two years later she used her earnings from athletics to purchase a piece of land at 8000 feet above sea level in Iten, one of the hubs of running in the region. She built a High Altitude Training Centre, completed in 1999, guided by her vision to create a dedicated space for female Kenyan athletes entering secondary school to live, train, and study, and then organized an annual all-woman's race to celebrate its anniversary. Kiplagat additionally financed the education of other younger girls, helped to send women to universities in the United States and Holland, and in 2000 established the Lornah Kiplagat Foundation with a focus on girls' education.[106]

Female athletes embarking on a running career today acknowledge that they concentrate on the materially transformative power that athletics would confer on themselves, their children, and their extended families. Monica Cheruiyot, mother of two small boys and aspiring 10,000 meters runner living in Iten, describes her motivation:

> I run to change my life. I run for my children, not only these two but also for the brother. He is nine years old, still in Class Eight [Primary School]. I want to have a *shamba* [small farm] someday, for these children. I do not want a man, never again. I want my own *shamba* and I want to have enough to send my children, or the brother, to college someday.[107]

Fellow athlete Eunice Jelimo trains so that someday she can earn enough to purchase a plot of land, declaring: "A piece of land. And then I build a very good house [*sic*]. And then after, after I would build rental houses in town. Money is everything. With money, you can do anything."[108] As these comments indicate, running offered a shortcut to transformative wealth, far more lucrative than small-scale agriculture or selling goods in the village marketplace. According to a 2011 report, after four or five years on the European or North American road race circuit with average earnings of one million shillings a year (around $11,000), a Kenyan athlete could "build a house, buy a farm and join the mainstay of the area—agriculture. Or they can start a business with the running winnings and, if managed properly, it can sustain them and their families for the rest of their lives."[109]

Aspiring women runners face a fierce market packed with other determined athletes. They hope to gain a position on a state-sponsored team that comes with a regular salary and support for training ultimately to catch the attention of agents who can aid their entry to international competitions. Kenyan running, especially for men but also for women, has become so hyper-competitive that athletes who could win competitive road races in Europe or the United States may not even qualify for the Kenya trials. Running as a career is risky, with unpredictable flows of income. For most, an athletic career is short-lived and only the very best achieve material success. Subelite Kenyan athletes scavenge road race circuits in the United States, Europe and Asia. Injury and economic precarity are commonplace for many.[110]

Other challenges arise when athletes from humble backgrounds achieve great success. As Patrick Sang, the 1992 Olympic steeplechase silver medalist, explains:

> Depending on your level of education and the level of exposure of the people surrounding you, then if it's low, the chances of getting professional advice [about how to invest the prize money] are low. If [the runners] are exposed and well-connected, level of education high, the chances of going for the professional level for advice is high. So, the bulk, what are the levels of most of these people? Their background? Low.[111]

In a dramatic example of the rise and fall that can ensue, Richard Chelimo, a soldier who in 1992 broke the 10,000-meters world record in Stockholm and won silver medals at the World Championships and the Olympic Games, died a pauper at age thirty-four, despite sponsorship by Nike and a bank account that, according to the *Daily Nation*, once held some Ksh 60 million ($860,000). In 2011 Loroupe explained to the Kenyan magazine *Management* why investing wisely cushions the transition from a sport career to life beyond: "We invest because you cannot run all your life, there comes a time when you slow down. Athletics is dynamic, new stars are born every day and age catches up with you at some point and you slow down. Investing is a cushion when the cheques are no longer coming in."[112]

Ruth Waithera, 1984 Olympic Games 400 meters finalist, notes that many female athletes emerge as champions, only to disappear as swiftly as they rose in the international ranks, lamenting the fact that "a person who is in this business, it is quick money—like that [snaps her fingers]. Lot of money. But they don't go many years. They get the money so quick, and the money then get finished so quick."[113] Leah Malot, star of the 1987 All Africa Games, veteran World Cross-Country team champion, and winner of three major marathons, attributes the negative consequences that professional sport has wrought, in part, to youth and a stubborn refusal to take financial advice:

> The problem with the girls at this age, they do not want to listen. If you tell her something, she says "I know it." She doesn't want to listen to somebody like me. She wants to do everything for herself. There are so many girls who run together who are younger than me. And when they run in Europe and when you tell her, "When you get money, you do this, A, B, C, D" and then later on, you will hear that she has failed. Because she has issues with the money, because she will not listen to your advice.[114]

Concerns regarding the vastness and suddenness of newly acquired wealth trouble female athletes who competed during the amateur era, and many expressed frustrated by their inability to pass on the wisdom they had gained.

Their reasons for competing also varied from women runners of today. Tecla Chemabwai, a standout athlete of the amateur era who competed at the 1968 and 1972 Olympics and qualified for both boycotted games of 1976 and 1980, addressed her motivation for running, describing how her keen interest in all sports emerged as a young girl:

> I was a talented athlete. As a sports person, when I look back on my history, the way I know myself, I did almost everything in school. I was a netballer, I was a soccer player. I played with the boys, volleyball, and I was playing in the center with men

. . . This was at the beginning. So as I continued, I continued liking, loving running so much. I started running 100 meters, 200 meters, doing long jump, field events, everything except hurdles. So when I was running, I was running because I liked to run.[115]

Rose Tata-Muya, whose international career spanned from 1974 to 1992 including competing in the 400 meters at the inaugural 1983 World Championships, shared Chemabwai's avid interest in sport. Tata explained that she was motivated to continue by the opportunity to travel, among other reasons, and that "My reason, it was just a challenge. Competing with others. Interacting with others. Travelling all over the country, all over the world! You know? . . . So it was amazing."[116]

Many female runners who competed during the amateur era derived pride from representing their nation. As Chemabwai notes, it was important that "you have a uniform with a Kenya patch, the medals."[117] Waithera refers to her choice to run as motivated by fame and "to be protected." In her words, "[I ran] to change my life. To get the name, which means to be protected. Because if you have a name, it means you are protected. And people, they know you. And even in your life, you are going to be happy."[118] The sport of running made Waithera a national icon, provided the means to gain a powerful patron within her community, and once in possession of her own house and land, allowed her to enter obligations of her own.

In the amateur years, small material rewards buoyed many athletes. Recalling awards received in the 1960s, Chemabwai explains: "We used to be given so many presents. Cooking pots and knives. There were teabags. I'm talking about appreciation. You know like Coca Cola would bring so much drinks, many crates. I remember sugar, sugar factories. You would be given so many kilos of sugar. I got two crates of beer."[119] Referring to her first races in the 1970s, Waithera recalls: "So they give me the rubber shoes. Even I didn't have the shoes. I was barefooted. So they gave me the bed-sheet, the towel, buckets. When I went abroad, they gave me allowances."[120] Despite these testimonials, amateur sport did not permit sufficient economic reward or sufficient personal gratification to attenuate the pervasive set of obstacles confronting young women, leaving the vast majority of them to exit the sport before adulthood.

Noting the contrast of current realities with those of the amateur era in which she competed, Chemabwai stressed that "if you remove the money, you will not have sports."[121] Waithera added, "Nowadays, running is like a business. Because you can see it is how they are getting money. It is like a business because they are making a lot of money."[122] Susan Sirma echoed that "athletes from 2000 until now are different from the ones before. Nowadays everyone is training for that jackpot."[123]

Margaret Muret adds the perspective of an athlete from an earlier generation who ran and high jumped in her youth and has maintained a lifelong interest in the sport but never herself competed beyond Kenya. Her niece, Sally Barsosio, was Kenya's first female World Athletics Championship gold medalist in 1997, and Muret has long been a strong advocate of Barsosio's running career. Her perspective on the changes wrought by prize money is that:

> Of course, it has changed a lot, trust me. You know, money has changed everything. Because I do see now our beautiful friends here . . . they run because they have seen the athletes owning property, vehicles, everything. Because of money. But during my time, it was because of interest. We were few but these days, so many of them! Because they see their fellow friends, who have run and who have come out rich.[124]

The lucrative opportunities catalyzed a wave of women runners also because most aspirants lacked alternative career prospects from which to earn significant money. The *Standard* noted in 1995 that "it is so evident that other than the dollars that athletes make on the track, their livelihood here at home is at best erratic given the general shortage of financially rewarding opportunities."[125] In 2006 Kenyan sport scholar Vincent Onywera and his colleagues administered a questionnaire to 404 accomplished male and female athletes and reported that financial rewards were most frequently cited as their primary motivation to run. They note that in the context of the challenging economic environment of rural areas, "It would stand to reason that economic reasons would act as an important contributing factor to the success of East African athletes in distance running."[126] Not unlike aspirants around the world who find in baseball, boxing, basketball, soccer and other sports an opportunity for social mobility, women in Kenya seized the opportunities that the professional running made available to them.[127]

The publicity surrounding large prize payouts created other challenges for successful athletes when returning home. In 1997, Loroupe called on the press to cease publishing the amounts of money earned by athletes in various meets for "security reasons." Addressing a KAAA dinner gala at an Eldoret hotel, she said the announcements of enormous cash awards won at major world meets left athletes vulnerable. "You could even be marked by bad people," Loroupe asserted.[128] Petitioners also sought out newly minted stars. Patrick Sang describes the many appeals made of successful runners. "When you arrive in the morning, you'll have maybe ten, twenty people. The next day, it goes to thirty. And these people, they come in two forms. One, to ask for support. The other one—to volunteer advice."[129]

He contends that female standouts enjoy an ironic form of protection compared to male stars in that pride limits what people ask of women. "Women are a bit sheltered. Our culture is a macho culture. They look at themselves and say: 'I'm a man. I'm going to a woman to ask for support? No, no, no, no.' So, in that way the women are more sheltered than men . . . because of the shame of the potential people who are coming to ask. They do [still ask] but they have to be very cheap." Such "protection" did not apply to Pamela Jelimo, however, whose wealth after winning $1 million (USD) on the Golden League circuit brought her so much attention that when approached by journalists in the weeks after returning home, she told them in one of her few public statements: "Don't ask about the money," and Marcel Kipkorir, then a twenty-one-year-old man who went to primary school with Jelimo, stated, "Guys want her now because of her fat wallet."[130]

Competing in sport nevertheless remains a contested issue for many married women for whom athletic achievements failed to provide monetary rewards. Some still do not race because their husbands will not allow it. The case of Ann Jepkosgei offers a glimpse of the ongoing challenges. When asked in 2011 why she had ceased to run, she replied, "I ask [my husband] . . . I pray for him to tell me yes. I like running! I love to join them—women runners! But if he says no, I stay. I will not force him because I am in the house. I am married. But if I am free, I will run!"[131] The substantial economic rewards of running available to a privileged few have so far failed to fully close Kenyan athletics' "gender gap."

The wealth Kenya's running women shared with their communities provided social mobility for many. The strategies that they employed took many forms. Lornah Kiplagat invested some of her earnings into the formation of the High Altitude Training Centre, which provides sophisticated facilities for aspiring athletes. Runners from all over the world come to train in the high altitudes of the Rift Valley and their spending stimulates the local economy. The Tegla Loroupe Peace Academy currently enrolls over four hundred students. Others have seeded start-up ventures or invested in real estate and construction providing employment in the greater community. The possibility that athletic success will provide financial security has catalyzed recent waves of female athletes to pursue running as a career.

Conclusion

Starting in the 1990s, Kenya's running women were increasingly successful in entering the highest levels of athletics in meaningful numbers. Remarkably talented runners achieved international standing in sport, became citizens of the world, and attained a standard of living beyond the norm. Success was the consequence of the efforts of individual athletes and their families, the gradual increase in the number of events for women, and the long-delayed granting of monetary rewards to athletes.

Female Kenyan runners benefited enormously as did their communities by way of the imaginative investments of their newfound wealth that many of them devised. Kenyan men had long been successful runners on every stage in the world. For decades longer than women and in far greater numbers they had gained entry to highly beneficial government employment and scholarship opportunities at American universities. The incentivization that "pay for play" introduced quickly leveled the playing field for women. Because a woman could transform her family's standard of living as well as her own opportunities through running, the prize money earned from racing increasingly motivated Kenyan women to run.

Accomplished women who comprised the first generation of professional runners manipulated the social and cultural resources available to them in order to achieve their goals. Their persistence in this traditionally masculine domain often dictated decisions to delay, refuse, or subvert marriage. Early professionals such as Tegla Loroupe challenged long-held standards of behaviors and, in so doing, exemplified the successful few who broke the mold and expanded their own personal empowerment to a previously unimaginable degree of acceptance. The best of these runners functioned as community patrons whose stature was equivalent to men by way of sharing the wealth they earned, ultimately benefitting themselves, their families, and their communities.

Enough Kenyan women have emerged as international running stars to suggest that real and positive change for women is happening. This is not to say that gender equality in the sport has been fully realized or that entrenched ideas about the incompatibility of athletics, marriage, and motherhood have been erased. The issue remains a contested and dynamic area of contention. Some women still do not race because their families will not allow it. While antagonism to female participation has not yet been fully silenced, the numbers of Kenyan women pursuing careers in track and field has advanced from bare sustainability to become an enterprise pursued by many women. Families and communities have increasingly come to regard women as athletes in their own right, widely respected for their many accomplishments. Translating that success to all Kenyan women is a challenge awaiting fulfillment and these sportswomen are inspirational for that goal.

Conclusion

I n 1989, historian Eric Hobsbawm posed the question, "How could women compete as women in a public sphere formed by and in terms suited to a differently designed sex?"[1] He suggested that women would face this question in different ways in every generation, dependent on its own historical contingencies. Pioneering Kenyan women answered it gracefully and determinedly in the public sphere of running by changing the meaning of womanhood itself. They challenged the many obstacles in that wholly masculine sphere and made that world their own, gaining respect for themselves, adding value to their community, and gaining recognition for their country.

Today Kenyan women emerge as international and Olympic champions with the same frequency as Kenyan men in track, cross-country, and marathons. Victories in races across Europe, Asia, and North America have earned them international respect. The Kenyan press routinely reports news of Diamond League and World Championship victories such as those by four-time World Champion 1500-meters medalist Faith Kipyegon, the most recent marathon title claimed by world record holder Brigid Kosgei, the latest 5000 meters event won by World Cross-Country champion Hellen Obiri, and other previously unimaginable accomplishments by Kenyan women. Girls with the ambition to become global stars join running camps, some of which pay for school fees and provide shoes and other resources. Young women represent university teams in the United States, and recent college graduates such as Sally Kipyego and Sharon Lokedi chase world records and international titles as professional athletes sponsored by major shoe companies. At the 2020 Summer Olympics, Kenyan women claimed medals in the marathon, 5000 meters, 3000 meters steeplechase, and 1500 meters. Of the six marathons that comprised the 2022 Abbott World Marathon Majors, four were won by Kenyan women: Peres Jepchirchir in Boston, Ruth Chepngetich in Chicago, Brigid Kosgei in Tokyo, and Sharon Lokedi in New York City.

Although there is much to celebrate, such accomplishments should not obscure the difficulties that still confront girls and women runners in Kenya. Among the most pressing are insufficient protection from abuse and sexual harassment, and exploitation by coaches, spouses, and agents that rob girls and young women of their autonomy as they ascend to the highest echelons of the sport. A clarion call for addressing these concerns came after the fatal stabbing in October 2021 of twenty-five-year-old Olympian and women-only 10,000 meters road record holder Agnes Tirop. Officials quickly charged her estranged husband with murder. Her death galvanized attention around gender-based violence, led by elite Kenyan women runners who sought to raise awareness of the safety of their compatriots who win races around the world. Speaking at Tirop's funeral, 2016 Olympian Viola Cheptoo declared, "We are here because we are putting our sister to rest, but we are also here to raise our voices. We need to be heard as women."[2] In response to this tragedy, elite marathoner Mary Ngugi launched an all-women running camp in October 2022, aiming to provide women with a safe space to train and, in her words, "empower them outside of athletics."[3]

Chroniclers of Kenyan running have so far missed the opportunity to examine women's athletics history with the nuance it deserves—perhaps reflecting how gender and the issues surrounding it have been overshadowed in Kenyan sporting cultures. As *Kenya's Running Women* demonstrates, the athletes of today build on the progress and determination of the women who came before them. From the first Women's Individual Athletics Championship in 1959, Kenyan women have been drawn to the sport of track and field, first introduced by Britain in the colonial era. Unlike Kenyan boys and men, however, women had limited opportunities to compete. The British promoted an exclusively male culture of track and field. They viewed the sport as a tool for the furtherance of imperial control and believed in the "civilizing" influence that Western forms of sport could bring to the enterprise. Government institutions, schools, churches, the army, and sport associations all encouraged track and field among boys and men. African communities, too, possessed their own long-standing traditions of games and human movement, and many young men embraced the sports introduced by the British. Both cultures brought gender bias to these activities, allowing African and European men to preserve older cultures while jointly building the foundations of international track and field success. In contrast, by independence in 1963 Kenyan women had yet to compete in events outside the country.

Some women, such as 1965 All Africa Games bronze medalist Diana Monks and 1968 Olympians Tecla Chemabwai, Lydia Stephens, and Elizabeth Chesire, were able to surmount these obstacles in the early postcolonial years as they debuted for Kenya at international games in the latter half of the 1960s. However, they still did not receive the same opportunities or leniency as their male counterparts. Monks's experience in particular demonstrated the gendered limits to athletes' power, even as their ability to win medals on the global stage took on greater political value. As Kenya strove to Africanize its workforce, sport administrators followed the same template in their aggressive stance toward Monks in track and field when she missed a major international meet. Although they claimed her two-year suspension protected the honor of the sport-governing body, and of the nation itself, her enforced exit was in fact a show of power that established the command of administrators over athletes.

While running gained greater popularity and national importance, Kenyan women's progress during the 1970s and 1980s could be best described as a "fragile project." Girls like Sabina Chebichi and Justina Chipchirchir blew away their competition but faced myriad challenges that hindered their progression. Girls were less likely than boys to transition to secondary school, seriously curtailing their opportunities in sport. Women often faced unsupportive spouses and derision from members of their community causing many to abandon competitive running. Participation by Kenyan women at the international level remained limited and tenuous, while the number of male runners increased and their performances vastly improved.

Despite many obstacles, some female Kenyan runners of this era were able to achieve international success by resisting established ideas about respectable womanhood. Many chose to delay or refuse marriage and gained employment in institutions conducive for running. These organizations offered coaching and sponsored training for elite athletes while also allowing them to earn a living wage. These athletes established a record of excellence and demonstrated an ability to flourish in profoundly male track and field environments—in the army, prisons, police, and other government institutions; at domestic competitions in Kenya; and on overseas trips with the national team. Starting in the 1970s, two momentous developments outside of the country greatly accelerated international opportunities for women runners. First, the International Olympic Committee (IOC) expanded the women's Olympic track and field program to include distances from the 1500 meters to the marathon. This expansion had a trickle-down effect on national competitions in Kenya. Second, top-down legislation, such as the passage of Title IX in the United States, also allowed a select few Kenyan women to gain access to sport scholarships at American universities. They used these opportunities to forge long-lasting careers at the international level.

After persisting at the margins of the sport for decades, Kenyan women's running exploded with the arrival of commercial incentives in the 1990s. As running became a fully professional pursuit, Kenyan woman competing in this era took advantage of the new reality to gain power, wealth, mobility, and status. The prospect for financial gain along with the expansion of long-distance events greatly spurred women's participation in a domain that had long witnessed excellence by Kenyan men. Women runners' income generation and investment in education improved opportunities for wider social mobility. Tegla Loroupe, a leader in this regard, established the Tegla Loroupe Peace Foundation, which has funded and supported the construction of schools in her home region of West Pokot. Others have invested back into running, notably Lornah Kiplagat, who built a High Altitude Training Centre in Iten, and Catherine Ndereba, who sponsored the Nyeri Half Marathon. These professional sportswomen made the best of difficult conditions, devising ways of competing to meet their needs. The enhanced financial opportunities available to top women runners allowed them not only to attain a standard of living beyond what was previously imaginable but also to become patrons who used their newfound wealth to advantage family and community. The example set by these trailblazers legitimized their role as athletes and spurred greater participation by women in the sport.

Taken together, the history of Kenyan women runners reveals how women used the sport of track and field to expand the boundaries of acceptable female behavior. Ruth Waithera, for example, defied conventions when she became the first woman in Kenya to join the armed forces as a runner in the 1970s. She then emerged as the fastest woman in Africa over 400 meters as a soldier-athlete. Waithera achieved economic independence through running before winning a sport scholarship to complete her undergraduate education in the United States, all culminating at the 1984 Los Angeles Olympic games, where she became the first Kenyan woman to qualify for an Olympic final. Other women faced hostility when choosing to run as a wife and mother, such as Jepkorir Rose Chepyator-Thomson, who despite resistance at home returned to competition, setting an African record for 3000 meters and later becoming an eleven-time All-American and national champion as a scholarship athlete at the University of Wisconsin–Madison. For many elite runners such as Mary Chemweno, spousal support and an international milieu increasingly receptive to women's running were foundational to the meaningful careers they forged in track and field. On the other end of the spectrum, Loroupe's decision to make her earnings respectable by serving her community as a patron and a peacemaker echoes older dynamics of the accountability of power. These women carved out niches as exceptions to the general pattern of gender dynamics that limited opportunities for many girls. Their successes in male-dominated track and field teams, in American institutions of higher education, and in professional employment with the government, para-statals, and security forces marked these women as the founders of a generation determined to challenge what was expected of them.

In shedding light on womanhood and postcolonial Kenyan gender relations, *Kenya's Running Women* makes a case for incorporating sport into mainstream histories of gender, showing how the embodied nature of sport makes it a useful tool for tracking changes and continuities in gendered practices and relations. As scholar of African sport Martha Saavedra notes, "For the larger field of Gender Studies, a focus on sport pushes the issue of the body, physicality, and embodied power to the front, where the meaning of physical sexual difference, in biological 'fact,' in cultural belief, or in social practice, can be scrutinized."[4] This book also contends that sport deserve greater attention from historians of Africa. Scholar of Kenyan history Tom Cunningham has argued that the topic has been limited to the realm of sport studies and sport history and has yet to be accepted into broader historical projects.[5] However, as scholars Todd Cleveland, Tarminder Kaur, and Gerard Akindes note, "Sports activity on the continent at both local and national levels highlights a range of enduring and novel dynamics between various actors and entities."[6] For the case of Kenya, as *Kenya's Running Women* shows, studying sport history gives us a unique perspective on gender dynamics, local communities, colonial life, and postcolonial transformations, confirming the insight by anthropologist Bea Vidacs that "studying sports activity can provide insights into social, cultural, political and historical processes which go beyond the sporting arena."[7]

Even more so, *Kenya's Running Women* is an argument for incorporating women's experiences into the study of sport. The history of how Kenyan runners reached this level of dominance has neglected the struggles and achievements of previous generations of women runners. For too long, in both popular and scholarly work on Kenyan sports, male athletes have served as the reference point for everyone else, thereby leaving our understanding of all Kenyan runners' struggles and triumphs incomplete. By centering women, this book provides a more complete history of running in Kenya overall.

The day after Paulina Konga won the 5000 meters silver medal at the 1996 Atlanta Olympic games, the front page of the *Daily Nation* proclaimed "Konga's 'Golden' Moment for Kenya," celebrating the first Olympic medal won by a woman from all of East Africa.[8] The race marked the first women's 5000 meters event in Olympic history, replacing the 3000 meters and bringing the men's and women's programs into greater alignment. Konga and her husband Paul Bitok became the first married couple to win medals at the Olympics for Kenya, both earning silver in their respective 5000 meter events. In a 2012 interview with the *Daily Nation*, Konga shared that "the two silver medals we brought home is something I hold dear to this day."[9] Since her historic achievement and as of the publication of this book, Kenyan women have won twenty-eight Olympic track and field medals, the most of any African country. The stories of their trailblazing predecessors such as Tecla Chemabwai, Ruth Waithera, and Tegla Loroupe expand our understanding of historical, social, and cultural dynamics in African history, including the role of sport in nation building and the connection between local and global sport institutions, while showing how power is produced through sport and how some women were able to tap into that power. *Kenya's Running Women* argues that the study of women should be neither secondary nor subordinate to the study of men. Documenting women's experiences is integral to the study of sport. This book retrieves some of that history from the margins and offers a glimpse of the excellence that has been achieved by women at the epicenter of international running.

Notes

Introduction

1. Eric Odanga, "Little Known Runner Becomes a Heroine," *Daily Nation*, July 30, 1996, 39.
2. Peter Njenga, "Konga Wins Silver," *Daily Nation*, July 30, 1996, 39.
3. "Konga's Success Hailed," *Daily Nation*, July 30, 1996, 39.
4. "Marathon Women: Senior Outdoor 2021," World Athletics, https://www.worldathletics.org.
5. Adharanand Finn, *Running with the Kenyans: Discovering the Secrets of the Fastest People on Earth* (London: Faber and Faber, 2012), 14–15.
6. Dave Prokop, ed., *The African Running Revolution* (Mountain View, CA: Runner's World Magazine, 1975); John Bale and Joe Sang, *Kenyan Running: Movement Culture, Geography and Global Change* (London: Frank Cass, 1996); Toby Tanser, *Train Hard, Win Easy: The Kenyan Way*, 2nd ed. (Mountain View, CA: Tafnews Press, 2001); Paul Rambali, *Barefoot Runner: The Life of Marathon Champion Abebe Bikila* (London: Serpent's Tail, 2006); Tim Judah, *Bikila: Ethiopia's Barefoot Olympian* (London: Reportage Press, 2008); Ed Caesar, *Two Hours: The Quest to Run the Impossible Marathon* (New York: Simon & Schuster, 2015); Finn, *Running with the Kenyans*; and Michael Crawley, *Out of Thin Air: Running Wisdom and Magic from Above the Clouds in Ethiopia* (London: Bloomsbury, 2021). An

exception for its focus on both male and female Kenyan runners is Toby Tanser, *More Fire: How to Run the Kenyan Way* (Yardley, PA: Westholme Publishing, 2008. For Keino's comments, see Hezekiah Wepukhulu, "The Secret Behind the Kenyans Track Success," *Daily Nation*, August 6, 1988, 11.

7. Studies of Kenyan men's long-distance runners have appeared in publications in fields ranging from biology, exercise physiology, and genetics to anthropology, history, psychology, and demography. See, for instance, Bengt Saltin et al., "Aerobic Exercise Capacity at Sea Level and at Altitude in Kenyan Boys, Junior and Senior Runners Compared with Scandinavian Runners," *Scandinavian Journal of Medical Science and Sports* 5, no. 4 (1995): 209–21; Henrik Larsen, "Kenyan Dominance in Distance Running," *Comparative Biochemistry and Physiology Part A: Molecular and Integrative Physiology* 136, no. 1 (2003): 161–70; Robert Scott and Yannis P. Pitsiladis, "Genotypes and Distance Running: Clues from Africa," *Sports Medicine* 37, no. 4–5 (2007): 424–27; and John Bale, "Kenyan Running before the 1968 Mexico Olympics," in *East African Running: Towards a Cross-Disciplinary Perspective*, ed. Yannis Pitsiladis, John Bale, Craig Sharp, and Tim Noakes (Abingdon, UK: Routledge, 2007), 11–23. On diet and nutrition, see Dirk L. Christensen, Gerrit Van Hall, and Leif Hambraeus, "Food and Macronutrient Intake of Male Adolescent Kalenjin Runners in Kenya," *British Journal of Nutrition* 88, no. 6 (2002): 711–17. On geography, see John Bale, "Lassitude and Latitude: Observations on Sport and Environmental Determinism," *International Review for the Sociology of Sport* 37, no. 2 (2002): 147–58. On Kalenjin runners' notable successes, see John Manners, "Kenya's Running Tribe," *The Sports Historian* 17, no. 2 (1997): 14–27; and Vincent Onywera, Robert A. Scott, Michael K. Boit, and Yannis P. Pitsiladis, "Demographic Characteristics of Elite Kenyan Endurance Runners," *Journal of Sports Sciences* 24, no. 4 (2006): 415–22.

8. Bale and Sang, *Kenyan Running*, 96.

9. Craig Sharp and John Bale, "Introduction," in *East African Running: Toward a Cross-Disciplinary Perspective*, ed. Yannis Pitsiladis, John Bale, Craig Sharp, and Tim Noakes (Abingdon, UK: Routledge, 2007), 7.

10. Bea Vidacs, "Through the Prism of Sports: Why should Africanists Study Sports?," *Afrika Spectrum* 41, no. 3 (2006): 336.

11. On boxing, see Loïc Wacquant, *Body & Soul: Notebooks of an Apprentice Boxer* (Oxford: Oxford University Press, 2006); and Louis Moore, *I Fight for a Living: Boxing and the Battle for Black Manhood, 1880–1915* (Urbana: University of Illinois Press, 2007). On basketball, Darcy Frey, *The Last Shot: City Streets, Basketball Dreams* (New York: Mariner Books, 1994); Jay R. Mandle and Joan D. Mandle, *Grass Roots Commitment: Basketball and Society in Trinidad and Tobago* (Parkersburg, IA: Caribbean Books, 1988); and Damion Thomas,

Globetrotting: African American Athletes and Cold War Politics (Urbana: University of Illinois Press, 2012). On baseball, see Alan Klein, *Sugarball: The American Game, the Dominican Dream* (New Haven, CT: Yale University Press, 2001); and Jules Tygiel, *Baseball's Great Experiment: Jackie Robinson and His Legacy* (New York: Oxford University Press, 1983). On football, Gary Armstrong and Richard Giulianotti, eds., *Football in Africa: Conflict, Conciliation, and Community* (Basingstoke, UK: Palgrave Macmillan, 2004).

12. David MacDougall, "The Women Who Became Athletes to Escape Forced Marriage," *Look*, February 1, 2010, 51.

13. Steve Bloomfield, *Africa United: How Football Explains Africa* (New York: Harper Perennial, 2010), 15.

14. Weldon Johnson, "2007 World Cross Country Championships Recap in Mombasa, Kenya: Controlled Chaos," LetsRun, March 24, 2007, http://www.letsrun.com/news/2007/03/2007-world-cross-country-championships-recap-in-mombasa-kenya-controlled-chaos/.

15. Karin Barber, "Popular Arts in Africa," *African Studies Review* 30, no. 3 (1987). 1, 75.

16. Emmanuel Akyeampong and Charles Ambler, "Leisure in African History: An Introduction," *The International Journal of African Historical Studies* 35, no. 1 (2002): 1–16.

17. Paul Ocobock, *An Uncertain Age: The Politics of Manhood in Kenya* (Athens: Ohio University Press, 2017), 6.

18. Ibid., 7.

19. A growing body of scholarly work on African sport attests to the vibrancy of this field, though its focus largely falls on men. Recent edited collections include Augustine E. Ayuk, ed., *Football (Soccer) in Africa: Origins, Contributions, and Contradictions* (Cham, Switzerland: Palgrave Macmillan, 2022); Michelle M. Sikes, Toby C. Rider, and Matthew P. Llewellyn, eds., *Sport and Apartheid South Africa: Histories of Politics, Power and Protest* (London: Routledge, 2022); Todd Cleveland, Tarminder Kaur, and Gerard Akindes, eds., *Sports in Africa: Past and Present* (Athens: Ohio University Press, 2020); Chuka Onwumechili, ed., *Africa's Elite Football: Structure, Politics, and Everyday Challenges* (New York: Routledge, 2020); Michael J. Gennaro and Saheed Aderinto, eds., *Sports in African History: Politics, and Identity Formation* (London: Routledge, 2019); and Francois Cleophas, ed., *Exploring Decolonising Themes in SA Sport History: Issues and Challenges* (Stellenbosch, South Africa: Sun Press, 2018). Notable recent monographs include Katrin Bromber, *Sports and Modernity in Late Imperial Ethiopia* (Suffolk, UK: James Currey, 2022); Derek C. Catsam, *Flashpoint: How a Little-Known Sporting Event Fueled America's Anti-Apartheid Movement* (Lamham, MD: Rowman & Littlefield, 2021); Itamar Dubinsky, *Entrepreneurial Goals: Development and Africapitalism in Ghanaian Soccer Academies*

(Madison: University of Wisconsin Press, 2022); Uroš Kovač, *The Precarity of Masculinity: Football, Pentecostalism, and Transnational Aspirations in Cameroon* (New York: Berghahn Books, 2022); and Joshua D. Rubin, *Animated by Uncertainty: Rugby and the Performance of History in South Africa* (Ann Arbor: University of Michigan Press, 2021); as well as recent co-authored books by Paul Darby, James Esson, and Christian Ungruhe, *African Football Migration: Aspirations, Experiences and Trajectories* (Manchester: Manchester University Press, 2022); and Peter Hain and André Odendaal, *Pitch Battles: Sport, Racism and Resistance* (Lanham, MD: Rowman & Littlefield, 2021).

20. Richard Holt, *Sport and the British: A Modern History* (Oxford: Oxford University Press, 1989); James A. Mangan, *The Games Ethic and Imperialism: Aspects of the Diffusion of an Ideal* (New York: Viking, 1986); Allen Guttmann, *Games and Empires: Modern Sports and Cultural Imperialism* (New York: Columbia University Press, 1994).

21. James A. Mangan, *Athleticism in the Victorian and Edwardian Public School: The Emergence and Consolidation of an Educational Ideology* (Cambridge: Cambridge University Press, 1981); James A. Mangan, "Ethics and Ethnocentricity: Imperial Education in British Tropical Africa," in *Sport in Africa: Essays in Social History*, ed. William J. Baker and James A. Mangan (New York: Africana Publishing Company, 1987), 138–71; André Odendaal, "South Africa's Black Victorians: Sport and Society in South Africa in the Nineteenth Century," in *Pleasure, Profit, Proselytism: British Culture and Sport at Home and Abroad 1700–1914*, ed. James A. Mangan (London: Frank Cass, 1988), 193–214; André Odendaal, *The Story of an African Game: Black Cricketers and the Unmasking of One of Cricket's Greatest Myths, South Africa, 1850–2003* (Cape Town, South Africa: David Philip, 2003); Michael Gennaro, "'The Cause Is a Worthy One, So Come along with Your Sixpence and Enjoy Yourselves with One Hour of Lusty Sport': Sport in Lagos, Nigeria during WWII," *Journal of African Military History* 4, no. 1–2 (2020): 41–65. See also Anthony Clayton, "Sport and African Soldiers: The Military Diffusion of Western Sport throughout sub-Saharan Africa," in *Sport in Africa: Essays in Social History*, ed. William J. Baker and James A. Mangan (New York: Africana Publishing Company, 1987), 114–37.

22. For the Kenyan context, see Tom Cunningham, "'These Our Games'—Sport and the Church of Scotland Mission to Kenya, c. 1907–1937," *History in Africa* 43 (2016): 259–88; and Matthew Carotenuto, "Grappling with the Past: Wrestling and Performative Identity in Kenya," *The International Journal of the History of Sport* 30, no. 16 (2013): 1889–902. On various forms of muscular Christianity, Islam and Judaism in variety of contexts, see Peter Levine, *Ellis Island to Ebbets Field: Sport and the American Jewish Experience* (New York: Oxford University Press, 1992); John Nauright, "Masculinity, Muscular Islam and

Popular Culture: 'Coloured' Rugby Cultural Symbolism in Working-Class Cape Town c. 1930–70," *The International Journal of the History of Sport* 14, no. 1 (1997): 184–90; Clifford Putney, *Muscular Christianity: Manhood and Sports in Protestant America, 1880–1920* (Cambridge, MA: Harvard University Press, 2003); and William J. Baker, *Playing with God: Religion and Modern Sport* (Cambridge, MA: Harvard University Press, 2007); and John J. MacAloon, ed., *Muscular Christianity and the Colonial and Post-colonial Worlds* (London: Routledge, 2009).

23. Markku Hokkanen, "'Christ and the Imperial Games Fields' in South-Central Africa— Sport and the Scottish Missionaries in Malawi, 1880–1914: Utilitarian Compromise," *The International Journal of the History of Sport* 22, no. 4 (2005): 745–69. On sport and its "civilizing" influence, see Norbert Elias and Eric Dunning, eds., *Quest for Excitement: Sport and Leisure in the Civilizing Process* (Oxford: Blackwell, 1986); and as the antidote to "over-civilization," see Mark Dyreson, "Nature by Design: American Ideas about Sport, Energy, Evolution and Republics," *Journal of Sport History* 26, no. 3 (1999): 447–70.

24. Shoko Yamada, "'Traditions' and Cultural Production: Character Training at the Achimota School in Colonial Ghana," *History of Education* 38, no. 1 (2009): 29–59; Jan Dunzendorfer, "The Early Days of Boxing in Accra: A Sport Is Taking Root (1920–1940)," *The International Journal of the History of Sport* 28, no. 15 (2011): 2142–58; Hamad Ndee, "Western Influences on Sport in Tanzania: British Middle-Class Educationalists, Missionaries and the Diffusion of Adapted Athleticism," *International Journal of the History of Sport* 27, no. 5 (2010): 905–36; Francois Cleophas, "A Historical Social Overview of Athletics in 19th Century Cape Colony, South Africa: Sport History," *African Journal for Physical Health Education, Recreation and Dance* 20, no. 2 (2014): 585–92; Roderick Willis, "A Historical Narrative of High School Athletics Amongst 'Coloured' Communities in Cape Town, South Africa, with Special Reference to the Western Province Senior Schools Sports Union, 1956–1972," *The International Journal of the History of Sport* 39, no. 2 (2022): 174–92.

25. Laura Fair, *Pastimes and Politics: Culture, Community, and Identity in Post-Abolition Urban Zanzibar, 1890–1945* (Athens: Ohio University Press, 2001), 226–64. On sport as an instrument of colonial purpose, see also Anthony Kirk-Greene, "Imperial Administration and the Athletic Imperative: The Case of the District Officer in Africa," in *Sport in Africa: Essays in Social History*, ed. William J. Baker and James A. Mangan (New York: Africana Publishing Company, 1987), 81–113.

26. Peter Alegi, *Laduma! Soccer, Politics and Society in South Africa, from its Origins to 2010*, 2nd ed. (Scottsville, South Africa: University of KwaZulu-Natal Press, 2010); and Nuno Domingos, *Football and Colonialism: Body and Popular Culture in Urban Mozambique*

(Athens: Ohio University Press, 2017). Other accounts that emphasize the embrace of European forms of sport by local peoples for their own ends include Terence Ranger, "Pugilism and Pathology: African Boxing and the Black Urban Experience in Southern Rhodesia," in *Sport in Africa: Essays in Social History*, ed. William J. Baker and James A. Mangan (New York: Africana Publishing Company, 1987), 196–213; Anne Leseth, "The Use of *Juju* in Football: Sports and Witchcraft in Tanzania," in *Entering the Field: New Perspectives on World Football*, ed. Gary Armstrong and Richard Giulianotti (Oxford: Berg, 1997), 159–74; Emmanuel Akyeampong, "Bukom and the Social History of Boxing in Accra: Warfare and Citizenship in Precolonial Ga Society," *International Journal of African Historical Studies* 35, no. 1 (2002), 39–60; Laura Fair, "Ngoma Reverberations: Swahili Music Culture and the Making of Football Aesthetics in Early Twentieth-Century Zanzibar," in *Football in Africa: Conflict, Conciliation and Community*, ed. Gary Armstrong and Richard Giulianotti (Houndmills, UK: Palgrave Macmillan, 2004), 103–11; Peter Alegi, *African Soccerscapes: How a Continent Changed the World's Game* (Athens: Ohio University Press, 2010); and Todd Cleveland, *Following the Ball: The Migration of African Soccer Players across the Portuguese Colonial Empire, 1949–1975* (Athens: Ohio University Press, 2017).

27. Paul Darby, "'Let Us Rally Around the Flag': Football, Nation-building, and Pan-Africanism in Kwame Nkrumah's Ghana," *The Journal of African History* 54, no. 2 (2013): 221–46; Hikabwa D. Chipande, "The Structural Adjustment of Football in Zambia: Politics, Decline and Dispersal, 1991–1994," *The International Journal of the History of Sport* 33, no. 15 (2016): 1847–65; Paul Darby, "Politics, Resistance and Patronage: The African Boycott of the 1966 World Cup and its Ramification," *Soccer & Society* 20, no. 7–8 (2019): 936–47. See also Wycliffe W. Simiyu Njororai, "Players of African Descent Representing European National Football Teams: A Double-edged Sword," *Soccer & Society* 22, no. 4 (2021): 411–28; and James Rosbrook-Thompson and Gary Armstrong, "Fields and Visions: The 'African Personality' and Ghanaian Soccer," *Du Bois Review* 7, no. 2 (2010): 293–314.

28. Mark Dyreson, "Sport," in *New Dictionary of the History of Ideas*, vol. 5, ed. Maryanne Cline (New York: Charles Scribner's Sons, 2004), 2248.

29. David Goldsworthy, *Tom Mboya: The Man Kenya Wanted to Forget* (Nairobi: Heinemann, 1982), 218.

30. Alegi, *African Soccerscapes*, 55. For a discussion of Kenya's first independence day celebrations in 1963 that featured a variety of sporting events, see Michelle M. Sikes, "Sprinting Past the End of Empire: Seraphino Antao and the Promise of Sport in Kenya,

1960–63," in *Sports in Africa: Past and Present*, ed. Todd Cleveland, Tarminder Kaur, and Gerard Akindes (Athens: Ohio University Press, 2020), 219–32.

31. Katrin Bromber, "The Stadium and the City: Sports Infrastructure in Late Imperial Ethiopia and Beyond," *Cadernos de Estudos Africanos* 32, no. 1 (2016): 53–72. On physical education, leisure, and sport in Ethiopia from the 1920s to the 1970s that shaped ideas about modernity and nation-building and efforts to engineer what she calls the country's "New Men," see Bromber, *Sports and Modernity*.

32. Alegi, *African Soccerscapes*, 56.

33. Phyllis M. Martin, *Leisure and Society in Colonial Brazzaville* (Cambridge: Cambridge University Press, 1995), 125.

34. Kevin S. Fridy and Victor Brobbey, "Win the Match and Vote for Me: The Politicisation of Ghana's Accra Hearts of Oak and Kumasi Asante Kotoko Football Clubs," *Journal of Modern African Studies* 47, no. 1 (2009): 19–39; Rosbrook-Thompson and Armstrong, "Fields and Visions," 306–7.

35. Susann Baller and Martha Saavedra, "La Politique du Football en Afrique: Mobilisations et Trajectoires," *Politique Africaine* 118 (2010): 10.

36. Wycliffe W. Simiyu Njororai, "Colonial Legacy, Minorities and Association Football in Kenya," *Soccer & Society* 10, no. 6 (2009): 866–82.

37. Solomon Waliaula and Joseph Basil Okong'o, "Performing Luo Identity in Kenya: Songs of Gor Mahia," in *Identity and Nation in African Football Fans, Community, and Clubs*, ed. Chuka Onwumechili and Gerard Akindes (London: Palgrave Macmillan, 2014), 83–98. For an insightful analysis of radio football commentary as oral performance and site of public influence in Kenya, see Solomon Waliaula, "Envisioning and Visualizing English Football in East Africa: The Case of a Kenyan Radio Football Commentator," *Soccer & Society* 13, no. 2 (2012): 239–49.

38. Gary Armstrong, "The Global Footballer and the Local War-zone: George Weah and Transnational Networks in Liberia, West Africa," *Global Networks* 7, no. 2 (2007): 230–47.

39. Chris Bolsmann and Andrew Parker, "Soccer, South Africa and Celebrity Status: Mark Fish, Popular Culture and the Post-apartheid State," *Soccer & Society* 8, no. 1 (2007): 109–24.

40. Women, gender, and the state in independent Africa have been the focus of several edited volumes, albeit without reference to sport, including Jane L. Parpart and Kathleen A. Staudt, eds., *Women and the State in Africa* (Boulder, CO: Reinner, 1989); Dzodzi Tsikata, *Lip-Service and Peanuts: The State and National Machinery for Women in Africa* (Accra, Ghana: Third World Network-Africa, 2000); Anne Marie Goetz and Shireen

Hassim, eds., *No Shortcuts to Power: African Women in Politics and Policy Making* (New York: Zed Books, 2003); Gretchen Bauer and Hannah Britton, eds., *Women in African Parliaments* (Boulder, CO: Lynne Rienner, 2006); Aili Mari Tripp, Isabel Casimiro, Joy Kwesiga, and Alice Mungwa, *African Women's Movements: Transforming Political Landscapes* (New York: Cambridge University Press, 2009); and Alicia Decker, *In Idi Amin's Shadow: Women, Gender, and Militarism in Uganda* (Athens: Ohio University Press, 2014).

41. On women's football in South Africa, see Jennifer Hargreaves, *Heroines of Sport: The Politics of Difference and Identity* (London: Routledge, 2000), 14–45; Cynthia F. Pelak, "Negotiating Gender/Race/Class Constraints in the New South Africa: A Case Study of Women's Soccer," *International Review for the Sociology of Sport* 40, no. 1 (2005): 53–70; Cynthia F. Pelak, "Local-Global Processes: Linking Globalization, Democratization, and the Development of Women's Football in South Africa," *Afrika Spectrum* 41, no. 3 (2006): 371–92; Mari Haugaa Engh, "Tackling Femininity: The Heterosexual Paradigm and Women's Soccer in South Africa," *The International Journal of the History of Sport* 28, no. 1 (2011): 137–52; and Mari Haugaa Engh and Cheryl Potgieter, "Hetero-sexing the Athlete: Public and Popular Discourses on Sexuality and Women's Sport in South Africa," *Acta Academica* 50, no. 2 (2018): 34–51. For histories of other women's sports in southern Africa, see Denise E. M. Jones, "In Pursuit of Empowerment: Sensei Nellie Kleinsmidt, Race and Gender Challenges," in *Freeing the Female Body: Inspirational Icons*, ed. James A. Mangan and Fan Hong (London: Frank Cass, 2001), 219–36; Christopher Merrett, "Race, Gender and Political Dissent in the Comrades Marathon, 1921–1981," *South African Historical Journal* 59, no. 1 (2007): 242–60; Marianne Meier and Martha Saavedra, "Esther Phiri and the Moutawakel Effect in Zambia: An Analysis of the Use of Female Role Models in Sport-for-Development," *Sport in Society* 12, no. 9 (2009): 1158–76; Cynthia F. Pelak, "Women and Gender in South Africa Soccer: A Brief History," *Soccer and Society* 11, no. 2 (2010): 63–78; André Odendaal, "'Neither Cricketers nor Ladies': Towards a History of Women and Cricket in South Africa, 1860s–2000s," *The International Journal of the History of Sport* 28, no. 1 (2011): 115–36; and Christopher Merrett, "Perpetual Outsiders: Women in Athletics and Road Running in South Africa," in *Routledge Handbook of Sport, Gender and Sexuality*, ed. Jennifer Hargreaves and Eric Anderson (London: Routledge, 2014), 139–48. For a landmark study of women's football in South Africa as well as Nigeria and Senegal, see Martha Saavedra, "Football Feminine—Development of the African Game: Senegal, Nigeria and South Africa," *Soccer and Society* 4, no. 2–3 (2003): 225–53.

42. Claire Nicolas, "From Handball Courts to Ministries: The Cousins of Côte d'Ivoire,"

Histories of Women's Work in Global Sport: A Man's World?, ed. Georgia Cervin and Claire Nicolas (Cham, Switzerland: Palgrave Macmillan, 2019), 217–44; Denise E.M. Jones, "Women and Sport in South Africa: Shaped by History and Shaping Sporting History," in *Sport and Women: Social Issues in International Perspective*, ed. Ilse Hartmann-Tews and Gertrud Pfister (London: Routledge, 2003), 130–44.

43. Hannah Borenstein, "Labouring Athletes, Labouring Mothers: Ethiopian Women Athletes' Bodies at Work," in *Sport, Migration, and Gender in the Neoliberal Age*, ed. Niko Besnier, Domenica Gisella Calabrò, and Daniel Guinness (London: Routledge, 2021), 65–82.

44. Jepkorir Rose Chepyator-Thomson, "African Women Run for Change: Challenges and Achievements in Sports," in *African Women and Globalization: Dawn of the 21st Century*, ed. Jepkorir Rose Chepyator-Thomson (Trenton, NJ: Africa World Press, 2005), 239–58.

45. Prisca Massao and Kari Fasting, "Women and Sport in Tanzania," in *Sport and Women: Social Issues in International Perspective*, ed. Ilse Hartmann-Tews and Gertrud Pfister (London: Routledge, 2003), 124–25.

46. Much of the English-language historical literature on women's track and field concerns American and European athletes. See Susan K. Cahn, *Coming on Strong: Gender and Sexuality in Women's Sport* (New York: Free Press, 1994); Jennifer H. Lansbury, *Spectacular Leap: Black Women Athletes in Twentieth-Century America* (Fayetteville: University of Arkansas Press, 2014); Jaime Schultz, *Qualifying Times: Points of Change in U.S. Women's Sport* (Urbana: University of Illinois Press, 2014); Jaime Schultz, "Going the Distance: The Road to the 1984 Olympic Women's Marathon," *The International Journal of the History of Sport* 32, no. 1 (2015): 72–88; Rita Liberti and Maureen M. Smith, *(Re)presenting Wilma Rudolph* (Syracuse: Syracuse University Press, 2015); Lindsay Parks Pieper, *Sex Testing: Gender Policing in Women's Sports* (Urbana: University of Illinois Press, 2016); Anne M. Blaschke, "Running the Cold War: Gender, Race, and Track in Cultural Diplomacy, 1955–1975," *Diplomatic History* 40, no. 5 (2016): 826–44; Colleen English, "'Beyond Women's Powers of Endurance': The 1928 800-Meter and Women's Olympic Track and Field in the Context of the United States," *Sport History Review* 50, no. 2 (2019): 187–204; Jaime Schultz, "Breaking into the Marathon: Women's Distance Running as Political Activism," *Frontiers: A Journal of Women Studies* 40, no. 2 (2019): 1–26; Rita Liberti and Mary G. McDonald, "Back on Track: Wyomia Tyus, Breaking Historical Silences, and the Sporting Activist Legacies of 1968," *The International Journal of the History of Sport* 36, no. 9–10 (2019): 796–811; Cat M. Ariail, *Passing the Baton: Black Women Track Stars and American Identity* (Urbana: University of Illinois Press, 2020); and Jörg Krieger,

Michele Krech and Lindsay Parks Pieper, "'Our Sport': The Fight for Control of Women's International Athletics," *The International Journal of the History of Sport* 37, no. 5–6 (2020): 451–72.

47. On the history of amateurism and rise of commercialism in track and field, see Joseph Turrini, *The End of Amateurism in American Track and Field* (Urbana: University of Illinois Press, 2010); Austin Duckworth, Thomas M. Hunt, and Jan Todd, "Cold Hard Cash: Commercialization, Politics, and Amateurism in United States Track and Field," *Sport in History* 38, no. 2 (2018): 145–63; Aaron Haberman, "'We're All Professionals Now': Frank Shorter, Deregulation, and the Battle to End 'Shamateurism' in the 1970s," *The International Journal of the History of Sport* 36, no. 15–16 (2019): 1414–32; April Henning and Jörg Krieger, "Dropping the Amateur: The International Association of Athletics Federations and the Turn Towards Professionalism," *Sport History Review* 51, no. 1 (2020): 64–83; Michelle M. Sikes and Jacob J. Fredericks, "'It's a Policy Matter, Not a Racial Matter': Athlete Activism and Symbiotic Struggles against Apartheid in US Track and Field of the Early 1970s," *The International Journal of the History of Sport* 39, no. 8–9 (2022): 938–58; and Michelle M. Sikes, A 'Rebel' on the Run: Kenyan Gambles on Intercollegiate Athletics, Apartheid Sport, and US Road Racing of the 1980s—The Case of Samson Obwocha," *The International Journal of the History of Sport* 39, no. 8–9 (2022): 959–86. On amateur sport in the Olympic movement, see Matthew P. Llewellyn and John Gleaves, *The Rise and Fall of Olympic Amateurism* (Urbana: University of Illinois Press, 2016). For the IAAF's own spin see International Amateur Athletic Federation, *IAAF: 80 Years for Athletics* (Monaco: IAAF, 1992). For a scholarly history of the organization, see Jörg Krieger, P*ower and Politics in World Athletics: A Critical History* (London: Routledge, 2021).

48. For a classic account, see John Lonsdale, "Moral Ethnicity and Political Tribalism," in *Inventions and Boundaries: Historical and Anthropological Approaches to the Study of Ethnicity and Nationalism*, ed. Preben Kaarsholm and Jan Hultin (Denmark: Institute for Development Studies, Roskilde University, 1994), 131–50; and for a recent study focused on Tanzanian women, see Jan Bender Shetler, *Claiming Civic Virtue: Gendered Network Memory in the Mara Region, Tanzania* (Madison: University of Wisconsin Press, 2019).

49. On this practice in the Kenyan context, see Christine Obbo, "Dominant Male Ideology and Female Options: Three East African Case Studies," *Africa* 46, no. 4 (1976): 371–89; Regina S. Oboler, "Is the Female Husband a Man? Woman/Woman Marriage among the Nandi of Kenya," *Ethnology* 19, no. 1 (1980): 69–88; Regina S. Oboler, *Women, Power, and Economic Change: The Nandi of Kenya* (Stanford: Stanford University Press, 1985),

69–88; and Wairimũ Ngarũiya Njambi and William E. O'Brien, "Revisiting 'Woman-Woman Marriage': Notes on Gĩkũyũ Women," *NWSA Journal* 12, no. 1 (2000): 1–23. For studies focused elsewhere on the continent, see Eileen J. Krige, "Woman-Marriage, with Special Reference to the Lovedu–its Significance for the Definition of Marriage," *Africa* 44, no. 1 (1974): 11–37; R. Jean Cadigan, "Woman-to-Woman Marriage: Practices and Benefits in Sub-Saharan Africa," *Journal of Comparative Family Studies* 29, no. 1 (1998): 89–98; Ifi Amadiume, *Male Daughters, Female Husbands: Gender and Sex in an African Society*, second edition (London: Zed Books, 1998); Joseph M. Carrier and Stephen O. Murray, "Woman-Woman Marriage in Africa," in *Boy-wives and Female Husbands: Studies in African Homosexualities*, ed. Stephen O. Murray and Will Roscoe (New York: Palgrave Macmillan, 2008), 255–66; Nwando Achebe, *Farmers, Traders, Warriors, and Kings: Female Power and Authority in Northern Igboland, 1900–1960* (Portsmouth, NH: Heinemann, 2005); Nwando Achebe, *The Female King of Colonial Nigeria: Ahebi Ugbabe* (Bloomington: Indiana University Press, 2011); and Nwando Achebe, *Female Monarchs and Merchant Queens in Africa* (Athens: Ohio University Press, 2020). For an insightful discussion of these ideas in conjunction with Western gender scholarship, see Lorelle Semley, "When We Discovered Gender: A Retrospective on Ifi Amadiume's Male Daughters, Female Husbands: Gender and Sex in an African Society," *Journal of West African History* 3, no. 2 (2017): 117–23.

50. An extensive literature exists on "Big Man" politics in Kenya. See Gabrielle Lynch, "Moi: The Making of an African 'Big-Man,'" *Journal of East African Studies* 2, no. 1 (2008): 18–43; Daniel Branch and Nic Cheeseman, "Democratization, Sequencing and State Failure in Africa: Lessons from Kenya," *African Affairs* 108, no. 430 (2008): 1–26; Johan de Smedt, "'No Raila, No Peace!' Big Man Politics and Election Violence at the Kibera Grassroots," *African Affairs* 108, no. 433 (2009): 581–98; Daniel Branch, *Kenya: Between Hope and Despair, 1963–2011* (New Haven, CT: Yale University Press, 2011), 67–88; Jean-François Médard, "Charles Njonjo: The Portrait of a 'Big Man' in Kenya," in *Neopatrimonialism in Africa and Beyond*, ed. Daniel C. Bach and Mamoudou Gazibo (Abingdon: Routledge, 2012), 58–78.

51. Lynn M. Thomas, *Politics of the Womb: Women, Reproduction, and the State in Kenya* (Berkeley: University of California Press, 2003).

52. Luise White, *The Comforts of Home: Prostitution in Colonial Nairobi* (Chicago: University of Chicago Press, 1990); Tabitha Kanogo, *African Womanhood in Colonial Kenya: 1900–1950* (Oxford: James Currey, 2005); Kenda Mutongi, *Worries of the Heart: Widows, Family, and Community in Kenya* (Chicago: University of Chicago Press, 2007). Among other

histories that show how Kenyan women contested the constraints that authorities sought to impose on them throughout the twentieth century, see Claire C. Robertson, *Trouble Showed the Way: Women, Men, and Trade in the Nairobi Area, 1890–1990* (Bloomington: Indiana University Press, 1997); Cora Ann Presley, *Kikuyu Women, the Mau Mau Rebellion, and Social Change in Kenya* (Abingdon: Routledge, 2018); and Brett L. Shadle, *"Girl Cases": Marriage and Colonialism in Gusiiland, Kenya, 1890–1970* (Portsmouth, NH: Heinemann, 2006).

53. Kara Moskowitz, *Seeing Like a Citizen: Decolonization, Development, and the Making of Kenya, 1945–1980* (Athens: Ohio University Press, 2019), 107, 115. On Onyango's life and career, see Phoebe Musandu, "Drawing from the Wells of Culture: Grace Onyango and the Kenyan Political Scene (1964–1983)," *Wagadu* 6: *Journal of International Women's Studies* 10, no. 1 (2009): 108–24. On Kenya after independence, see also Bethwell A. Ogot and William R. Ochieng', eds., *Decolonization and Independence in Kenya, 1940–93* (London: James Currey, 1995); Branch, *Kenya*; and Charles Hornsby, *Kenya: A History Since Independence* (London: I.B. Tauris, 2012).

54. Kathleen Sheldon, *African Women: Early History to the 21st Century* (Bloomington: Indiana University Press, 2017), xi.

55. Jack H. Driberg, "The Status of Women Among the Nilotics and Nilo-Hamitics," *Africa* 5, no. 4 (1932): 407, 409. For a review of Driberg's ethnographic research, see Nancy J. Schmidt, "Jack H. Driberg: A Humanistic Anthropologist before His Time," *Anthropologica* 31, no. 2 (1989): 179–94.

56. On the portrayal of women and men in *Viva* and in South African editions of *Drum* and *True Love*, see Dorothy Driver, "*Drum* Magazine (1951–9) and the Spatial Configurations of Gender," in *Text, Theory, Space: Land, Literature and History in South Africa and Australia*, ed. Kate Darian-Smith, Liz Gunner, and Sarah Nuttall (London: Routledge, 1996), 227–38; Lindsay Clowes, "To Be a Man: Changing Constructions of Manhood in *Drum* Magazine, 1951–1965," in *African Masculinities: Men in Africa from the Late Nineteenth Century to the Present*, ed. Lahoucine Ouzgane and Robert Morrell (New York/Scottsville, South Africa: Palgrave Macmillan/University of Kwa-Zulu-Natal Press, 2005), 89–108; Tom Odhiambo, "The Black Female Body as a 'Consumer and a Consumable' in Current *Drum* and *True Love* Magazines in South Africa," *African Studies* 67, no. 1 (2008): 71–80; and Beth Ann Williams, "'Call Us Ms.': *Viva* and Arguments for Kenyan Women's Respectable Citizenship 1975–80," *Women's History Review* 26, no. 3 (2017): 414–32. See also Michael Chapman, ed., *The Drum Decade: Stories from the 1950s* (Pietermaritzburg: University of KwaZulu-Natal Press, 1989).

Chapter 1. The Gendered Development of Athletics in Colonial Kenya: Warriors, Raiders, and Gentleman Amateurs

1. Community Development Report, Baringo, January-June 1958, Kenya National Archives, Nairobi (hereafter KNA) DO/ER/2/3/7.

2. Ibid.

3. KAAA Secretary to all Provincial Associations, "Second Annual Kenya Women's Individual Championships 1960," October 31, 1960, KNA/CSO/5/11/58.

4. Dorothy L. Hodgson, "Pastoralism, Patriarchy and History: Changing Gender Relations among Maasai in Tanganyika, 1890–1940," *The Journal of African History* 40, no. 1 (1999): 42. See also Bonnie Kettel, "The Commoditization of Women in Tugen (Kenya) Social Organization," in *Women and Class in Africa*, ed. Claire Robertson and Iris Berger (New York, 1986), 45–61.

5. Richard Holt, *Sport and the British: A Modern History* (Oxford: Oxford University Press, 1989), 14.

6. Allen Guttmann, *From Ritual to Record: The Nature of Modern Sports*, 2nd ed. (New York: Columbia University Press, 2004); Wray Vamplew, "Playing with the Rules: Influences on the Development of Regulation in Sport," *The International Journal of the History of Sport* 24, no. 7 (2007): 843–71.

7. Tony Collins, *Rugby's Great Split: Class, Culture and the Origins of Rugby League Football*, 2nd ed. (London: Routledge, 2006); Tony Mason, *Association Football and English Society, 1863–1915* (Brighton, UK: Branch Line, 1982).

8. William Mandle, "Games People Played: Cricket and Football in England and Victoria in the Late Nineteenth Century," *Historical Studies* 15, no. 60 (1973): 511.

9. Robert Lake, *A Social History of Tennis in Britain* (London: Routledge, 2014); Eric Halladay, *Rowing in England: A Social History: The Amateur Debate* (Manchester: Manchester University Press, 1990); John Lowerson, *Sport and the English Middle Classes 1870–1914* (Manchester: Manchester University Press, 1995).

10. Eric J. Hobsbawm, *Age of Empire, 1875–1914* (New York: Pantheon Books, 1987), 174.

11. On the early history of athletics in Britain, see Jeremy Crump, "Athletics," in *Sport in Britain: A Social History*, ed. Tony Mason (Cambridge: Cambridge University Press, 1989), 44–77; Martin Polley, "'The Amateur Rules': Amateurism and Professionalism in Post-War British Athletics," in *Amateurs and Professionals in Post-War British Sport*, ed. Adrian Smith and Dilwyn Porter (London: Frank Cass, 2000), 81–114; Neil Carter, "From Knox to Dyson: Coaching, Amateurism and British Athletics, 1912–1947," *Sport in*

History 30, no. 1 (2010): 55–81; and Matthew P. Llewellyn, "'The Best Distance Runner the World Has Ever Produced': Hannes Kolehmainen and the Modernisation of British Athletics," *The International Journal of the History of Sport* 29, no. 7 (2012): 1016–34. On amateurism and British track and field history, see also Holt's *Sport and the British*, Lowerson's *Sport and the English Middle Classes*, and Llewellyn's *Rule Britannia*, as well as biographies, notably John Bale's *Roger Bannister*, Bill Jones's *Ghost Runner*, and Jeffreys's examination of Olympian and sport administrator Lord Burghley's career. Holt, *Sport and the British*, 109–11, 275–76; Lowerson, *Sport and the English Middle Classes*, 162–80, 263, 275; Matthew P. Llewellyn, *Rule Britannia: Nationalism, Identity and the Modern Olympic Games* (London: Routledge, 2012); John Bale, *Roger Bannister* (London: Routledge, 2004); Bill Jones, *The Ghost Runner: The Tragedy of the Man They Couldn't Stop, The True Story of John Tarrant* (Edinburgh: Mainstream Publishing Company, 2011); and Kevin Jeffreys, "Lord Burghley, *Chariots of Fire* and the Gentleman Amateur in British Athletics," *Sport in History* 33, no. 4 (2013), 445–64.

12. Derek Birley, *Sport and the Making of Britain* (Manchester: Manchester University Press, 1993), 280. See also Peter Lovesey, *The Official Centenary History of the Amateur Athletic Association* (Enfield, UK: Guinness Superlatives, 1979).

13. Jones, *Ghost Runner*.

14. Lowerson, *Sport and the English Middle Classes*, 162.

15. Allen Guttmann, *Women's Sports: A History* (New York: Columbia University Press, 1991), 166–71. On the interwar battle for control over women's international track and field, see Jörg Krieger, Michele Krech, and Lindsay Parks Pieper, "'Our Sport': The Fight for Control of Women's International Athletics," *The International Journal of the History of Sport* 37, no. 5–6 (2020): 451–72; and Florence Carpenter and Jean-Pierre Lefevre, "The Modern Olympic Movement, Women's Sport and the Social Order during the Inter-war Period," *The International Journal of the History of Sport* 23, no. 7 (2006): 1112–27.

16. Lowerson, *Sport and the English Middle Classes*, 159–61; Thierry Terret, "From Alice Milliat to Marie-Thérèse Eyquem: Revisiting Women's Sport in France (1920s–1960s)," *The International Journal of the History of Sport* 27, no. 7 (2010): 1154–72; and Mary H. Leigh and Thérèse M. Bonin, "The Pioneering Role of Madame Alice Milliat and the FSFI in Establishing International Trade and Field Competition for Women," *Journal of Sport History* 4, no. 1 (1977): 72–83. On British women's sport during the interwar period, see Fiona Skillen, *Women, Sport and Modernity in Interwar Britain* (Oxford: Peter Lang, 2013).

17. Domestic institutions such as the civil service, armed forces, and universities introduced the sport to British women. One of the first recorded track championships was a 4x110 yard relay for female members of the British armed services held in September 1918 at

Stamford Bridge in London. The civil service maintained a women's athletics section from the 1920s that held an annual national championship while private enterprise promoted athletics for women by organizing races during their sports days. See Lynne Robinson, "'Tripping Daintily into the Arena': A Social History of English Women's Athletics 1921–1960" (PhD diss., University of Warwick, 1996), 65–72.

18. Ibid.

19. John Stevenson, *British Society, 1914–1945* (Harmondsworth: Penguin Books, 1984), 252.

20. Robinson, "Tripping Daintily," 82.

21. Thomas Hughes, *Tom Brown's School Days* (Oxford: Oxford University Press, 1999). See also Timothy J. L. Chandler, "Emergent Athleticism: Games in Two English Public Schools, 1800–60," *The International Journal of the History of Sport* 5, no. 3 (1988): 312–30; and Bruce Kidd, "Muscular Christianity and Value-Centred Sport: The Legacy of Tom Brown in Canada," *Sport in Society* 16, no. 4 (2013): 405–15.

22. Eric J. Hobsbawm, *Industry and Empire: The Birth of the Industrial Revolution, from 1750 to the Present Day*, 2nd ed. (London: Penguin Group, 1999), 147.

23. Quote in James A. Mangan, *The Games Ethic and Imperialism: Aspects of the Diffusion of an Ideal* (New York: Viking, 1986), 18. See also James A. Mangan, *Athleticism in the Victorian and Edwardian Public Schools: The Emergence and Consolidation of an Educational Ideology* (Cambridge: Cambridge University Press, 1981); James A. Mangan, ed., *The Cultural Bond: Sport, Empire, Society* (Abingdon: Routledge, 1992); and James A. Mangan, "Britain's Chief Spiritual Export: Imperial Sport as Moral Metaphor, Political Symbol and Cultural Bond," *The International Journal of the History of Sport* 27, no. 1–2 (2010): 328–36. See also Mike Huggins, *The Victorians and Sport* (London: Bloomsbury Academic, 2004), and Holt, *Sport and the British*.

24. On Muscular Christianity and its adaptation over the last 150 years, see John J. MacAloon, ed., *Muscular Christianity and the Colonial and Post-Colonial Worlds* (London: Routledge, 2009). See also Brian Stoddart, "Sport, Cultural Imperialism and Colonial Response in the British Empire," *Sport in Society* 9, no. 5 (2006): 809–35.

25. In Peter Alegi, *African Soccerscapes: How a Continent Changed the World's Game* (Athens: Ohio University Press, 2010), 14.

26. John Bale, "Kenyan Running Before the 1968 Mexican Olympics," in *East African Running: Toward a Cross-Disciplinary Perspective*, ed. Yannis Pitsiladis, John Bale, Craig Sharp, and Tim Noakes (Abingdon: Routledge, 2007), 13.

27. Tom Cunningham, "'These Our Games'—Sport and the Church of Scotland Mission to Kenya, c. 1907–1937," *History in Africa* 43 (2016): 259–88.

28. John Lonsdale, "The Conquest State of Kenya, 1895–1905" and "The Politics of Conquest:

The British in Western Kenya, 1894–1908," in *Unhappy Valley: Conflict in Kenya and Africa, Book One: State and Class*, Bruce Berman and John Lonsdale (Athens: Ohio University Press, 1992), 13–44, 45–74.

29. M. F. Hill, *Permanent Way: The Story of the Kenya and Uganda Railway*, 2nd ed. (Nairobi: East African Railways and Harbours, 1961); R. T. Ogonda, "Transport and Communications in the Colonial Economy," in *An Economic History of Kenya*, ed. William R. Ochieng' and Robert M. Maxon (Nairobi: East African Educational Publishers, 1992), 129–47.

30. Joanna Lewis, *Empire State-Building: War and Welfare in Kenya, 1925–52* (Oxford: James Currey, 2000), 29.

31. On the contradictory demands that confronted the Kenyan state, see Bruce Berman and John Lonsdale, *Unhappy Valley: Conflict in Kenya and Africa*, Book 1: State and Class (London: James Currey, 1992); and Bruce Berman, *Control and Crisis in Colonial Kenya: The Dialectic of Domination* (London: James Currey, 1990).

32. Caroline Elkins, *Britain's Gulag: The Brutal End of Empire in Kenya* (London: Jonathan Cape, 2005), 3; Maurice P. K. Sorrenson, *Origins of European Settlement in Kenya* (Oxford: Oxford University Press, 1968); Brett L. Shadle, *The Souls of White Folk: White Settlers in Kenya, 1900s–1920s* (Manchester: Manchester University Press, 2015).

33. Bruce Berman and John Lonsdale, "Coping with the Contradictions: The Development of the Colonial State in Kenya, 1895–1914," in *Unhappy Valley: Conflict in Kenya and Africa*, Book 1: State and Class, Bruce Berman and John Lonsdale (London: James Currey, 1992), 77–100; Robert Maxon, *Struggle for Kenya: The Loss and Reassertion of Imperial Initiative, 1912–1923* (Rutherford, NJ: Farleigh Dickinson University Press, 1993).

34. Anthony Clayton and Donald C. Savage, *Government and Labour in Kenya, 1895–1963* (London: Frank Cass, 1974); Gavin N. Kitching, *Class and Economic Change in Kenya: The Making of an African Petite-Bourgeoisie, 1905–1970* (New Haven, CT: Yale University Press, 1980).

35. Quoted in Caleb E. Owen, "Lands of Leisure: Recreation, Space, and the Struggle for Urban Kenya, 1900–2000" (PhD diss., Michigan State University, 2016), 65.

36. Ibid., 60–61.

37. Jacob S. Nteere, "A Comparative Assessment of the Central Organizations for Amateur Sport in England and Kenya" (PhD diss., University of Manchester, 1990), 119.

38. For consistency this chapter follows Bale and Sang who in *Kenyan Running* refer to the organization throughout its existence as the Arab and African Sport Association; however, Malcolm Anderson shows that it was first known as the Arab and African Athletics Association before being reconstituted as the Arab and African Sports

Association of Kenya in 1936. See John Bale and Joe Sang, *Kenyan Running: Movement Culture, Geography and Global Change* (London: Frank Cass, 1996); and Malcolm Anderson, "The Development of Athletics in 1950s Kenya: Order or Leisure?" (master's thesis, Oxford University 2008), 28.

39. Anderson, "Development of Athletics."

40. Bale and Sang, *Kenyan Running*, 77.

41. Bale, "Kenyan Running Before the 1968 Mexico Olympics," 13; Bale and Sang, *Kenyan Running*, chap. 4.

42. Sydney O. Hall, "The Role of Physical Education and Sport in the Nation-building Process in Kenya" (PhD diss., Ohio State University, 1973), 138.

43. Ross Tucker, Vincent Onywera, and Jordan Santos-Concejero, "Analysis of the Kenyan Distance Running Phenomenon," *International Journal of Sports Physiology Performance* 10, no. 3 (2014): 285–91.

44. John Manners, "Raiders from the Rift Valley: Cattle Raiding and Distance Running in East Africa," in *East African Running: Towards a Cross-Disciplinary Perspective*, ed. Yannis Pitsiladis, John Bale, Craig Sharp, and Tim Noakes (Abingdon: Routledge, 2007), 40–50.

45. John Manners, "Kenya's Running Tribe," *The Sports Historian* 17, no. 2 (1997): 18.

46. On the importance of studying the "pre-colonial" for understanding more recent African history, see Richard Reid, "Past and Presentism: The 'Precolonial' and the Foreshortening of African History," *The Journal of African History* 52, no. 2 (2011): 135–55.

47. Jane Guyer, "Household and Community in African Studies," *African Studies Review* 24, no. 2/3 (1981): 91.

48. Matthew Carotenuto makes a similar point in his history of wresting in Kenya. See Matthew Carotenuto, "Grappling with the Past: Wrestling and Performative Identity in Kenya," *The International Journal of the History of Sport* 30, no. 16 (2013): 1890.

49. Bale and Sang, *Kenyan Running*, 47.

50. Ian Q. Orchardson, *The Kipsigis* [original manuscript of 1929–1937 abridged, edited and partially re-written posthumously by A. T. Matson] (Kampala: East African Literature Bureau, 1961), 34. Other accounts of the Kipsigis of this era include Ian Q. Orchardson, "Some Traits of the Kipsigis in Relation to their Contact with Europeans," *Africa* 4, no. 4 (1931): 466–74; and John G. Peristiany, *The Social Institutions of the Kipsigis* (New York: Humanities Press, 1964). For early histories, see S. C. Lang'at, "Some Aspects of Kipsigis History before 1914," in *Ngano: Studies in Traditional and Modern East African History*, ed. Brian G. McIntosh (Nairobi: East African Publishing House, 1969), 73–94; and Henry A. Mwanzi, *A History of the Kipsigis* (Nairobi: East African Literature Bureau, 1977).

51. G. W. B. Huntingford, *The Nandi of Kenya: Tribal Control in a Pastoral Society* (London:

Routledge & Kegan Paul, 1953), 81. Huntingford's writings on the Nandi include G. W. B. Huntingford, *Nandi Work and Culture*, Colonial Research Studies No. 4 (London: HMSO, 1950); G. W. B. Huntingford and CRV Bell, *East African Background* (London: Longmans, Green and Co., 1950), 17–19, 59–60, 68–70; and several journal articles. For a critical account of his work, including the apt observation that he had very little to say about women—"as the modern commentator would immediately note, unbalanced genderwise as well, Huntingford's account reflecting largely a male view of society"—see J. E. G. Sutton, "Denying History in Colonial Kenya: The Anthropology and Archeology of G. W. B. Huntingford and L. S. B. Leakey," *History in Africa* 33 (2006): 306. Other early accounts of the Nandi include Charles W. Hobley, "Anthropological Studies in Kavirondo and Nandi," *The Journal of the Anthropological Institute of Great Britain and Ireland* 33 (1903): 325–59; and A. C Hollis, *The Nandi, their Language and Folk-lore* (Westport, CT: Negro Universities Press, 1971). The first ethnographies to focus on Nandi women appeared in the late 1970s and 1980s from Myrtle S. Langley, *The Nandi of Kenya: Life Crisis Rituals in a Period of Change* (New York: St Martin's Press, 1979); and Regina S. Oboler, *Women, Power, and Economic Change: The Nandi of Kenya* (Stanford: Stanford University Press, 1985).

52. R. O. Hennings, *African Morning* (London: Chatto and Windus, 1951), 163. Early accounts and histories of the Tugen can be found in Charles W. Hobley, "Notes on the Geography and People of the Baringo District of the East Africa Protectorate," *The Geographical Journal* 28, no. 5 (1906): 471–81; David M. Anderson, "Agriculture and Irrigation at Lake Baringo in the 19th Century," *Azania* 24 (1989): 85–98; David M. Anderson, *Eroding the Commons: The Politics of Ecology in Baringo, Kenya, 1890–1963* (Oxford: James Currey, 2002), 23–47; and David M. Anderson, "The Beginning of Time? Evidence for Catastrophic Drought in Baringo in the Early Nineteenth Century," *Journal of Eastern African Studies* 10, no. 1 (2016): 45–66.

53. Richard Waller, "Pastoral Production in Colonial Kenya: Lessons from the Past?," *African Studies Review* 55, no. 2 (2012): 1–27.

54. Benjamin E. Kipkorir and Joseph Ssennyonga, *A Socio-cultural Profile of Elgeyo-Marakwet District: A Report of the District Socio-Cultural Profiles Project* (Nairobi: Institute of African Studies and the University of Nairobi, 1984), 132. On early Marakwet history, see also Benjamin E. Kipkorir, *The Marakwet of Kenya: A Preliminary Study* (Nairobi: East African Literature Bureau, 1973); and Matthew I. J. Davies and Henrietta L. Moore, "Landscape, Time and Cultural Resilience: A Brief History of Agriculture in Pokot and Marakwet, Kenya," *Journal of Eastern African Studies* 10, no. 1 (2016): 67–87. Henrietta L. Moore's *Space, Text and Gender: An Anthropological Study of the Marakwet of Kenya* (Cambridge: Cambridge University Press, 1986) is the first ethnographic survey of the Marakwet. On

Kalenjin games, see also Jepkorir Rose Chepyator-Thomson, "Traditional Games of Keiyo Children: A Comparison of Pre and Post-Independent Periods in Kenya," *Interchange* 21, no. 2 (1990): 15–25; and Kipchumba Byron and Jepkorir Rose Chepyator-Thomson, "Sports Policy in Kenya: Deconstruction of Colonial and Post-colonial Conditions," *International Journal of Sport Policy and Politics* 7, no. 2 (2015): 302, wherein the authors state: "In the pre-colonial period, Kenyan Africans had their own indigenous sport activities that were part and parcel of people's livelihoods and served as part of the fabric of society."

55. Quoted in Paul Ocobock, *An Uncertain Age: The Politics of Manhood in Kenya* (Athens: Ohio University Press, 2017), 44.

56. Kipkorir, *Marakwet*, 47.

57. Quote in F. B. Welbourn, "Keyo Initiation," *Journal of Religion in Africa* 3, no. 2 (1968): 231. For other early accounts of the Keiyo, see J. A. Massam, *The Cliff Dwellers of Kenya* (London: Seeley, Service & Co. Limited, 1927); and Susan Chebet and Ton Dietz, *Climbing the Cliff: A History of Keiyo* (Eldoret, Kenya: Moi University Press, 2000).

58. Luise White, *The Comforts of Home: Prostitution in Colonial Nairobi* (Chicago: University of Chicago Press, 1991), 31. On livestock exchange in Kalenjin marriage negotiations, see Orchardson, *Kipsigis*, 80 81; Hollis, *Nandi*, 61; Langley, *Nandi*, 74–75; and Kipkorir, *Marakwet*, 49–50.

59. According to Huntingford: "Some of these raids entailed long journeys: the Kony, Suk, and Marakwet are fifty miles from the centre of Nandi, and the Sapei are a hundred miles or more." See his *The Nandi of Kenya*, 81, and pages 76–86. On raiding, see also Massam, *Cliff Dwellers*, 33–40; Kipkorir, *Marakwet*, 35–36; A.T. Matson, "Nandi Traditions on Raiding," in *Hadith* 2, ed. Bethwell A. Ogot (Nairobi: East African Publishing House, 1970); Norman Thomson and Jepkorir Rose Chepyator-Thomson, "Keiyo Cattle Raiding, Kechui Mathematics and Science Education: What do They Have in Common?," *Interchange* 33, no. 1 (2002): 49–83; David M. Anderson, "Stock Theft and Moral Economy in Colonial Kenya," *Africa* 56, no. 4 (1985): 399–416; and Anderson, *Eroding the Commons*, 23–24, 30–37, 42–43. On cattle raiding and Kalenjin running excellence, see Manners, "Kenya's Running Tribe."

60. Manners, "Kenya's Running Tribe," 26.

61. Anderson, "Stock Theft and Moral Economy," 399–400.

62. Quoted in John Manners, "In Search of an Explanation," *The African Running Revolution*, ed. Dave Prokop (Mountain View, CA: World Publications, 1975), 35.

63. Massam, *Cliff Dwellers of Kenya*, 33.

64. Huntingford, *Nandi of Kenya*, 83.

65. A. T. Matson, *Nandi Resistance to British Rule, 1890–1906* (Nairobi: East African Publishing House, 1972), 20.

66. Jack H. Driberg, "The Status of Women Among the Nilotics and Nilo-Hamitics," *Africa* 5, no. 4 (1932): 407, 409. Other accounts of this era confirm a similar division of daily tasks, such as Massam, *Cliff Dwellers*, 86–93; Mervyn W. H. Beech, *The Suk: Their Language and Folklore* (New York: Negro Universities Press, 1969), 17, 33; and Orchardson, *Kipsigis*, 92. On travel undertaken by women in times of scarcity or for marriage, see Hollis, *Nandi*, 15, 62; Massam, *Cliff Dwellers*, 151–60; Orchardson, *Kipsigis*, 73–76; Langley, *Nandi*, 75–76; and Kipkorir, *Marakwet*, 49–51.

67. Orchardson, *Kipsigis*, 78. See also Peristiany, *Social Institutions of the Kipsigis*, 81–82.

68. Langley, *The Nandi of Kenya*, 73. Such unions were not unique to Kalenjin communities. Anthropologist Denise O'Brien in 1977 documented woman-to-woman marriages in more than thirty sub-Saharan African populations, including the Kikuyu and Luo of eastern Africa and the Sotho, Venda, and Zulu of southern Africa. In their survey of the practice, scholars Joseph Carrier and Stephen Murray note that female husbands generally continued to wear female attire, but otherwise they took on the parental, family relations, male prerogatives, and labor roles of men. In her research on the Igbo of southeastern Nigeria, Ifi Amadiume describes female husbands and male daughters as two such arrangements. An Igbo woman became a female husband by accumulating wealth, marrying a wife, and "fathering" their children. A male daughter was designated as such by her father if he had no sons. She was accorded male status and remained unwed while bearing children to continue her father's name. Historian Nwando Achebe observes that wealthy Igbo women acquired wives to enhance their status, such as Ahebi Ugbabe who installed herself as king of her people. Among the Lovedu in southern Africa, queens were barred from taking a male husband and obliged to marry a wife. See Eileen J. Krige, "Woman-Marriage, with Special Reference to the Lovedu–its Significance for the Definition of Marriage," *Africa* 44, no. 1 (1974): 11–37; Denise O'Brien, "Female Husbands in Southern Bantu Societies," in *Sexual Stratification: A Cross-cultural View*, ed. Alice Schlegal (New York: Columbia University Press, 1977), 109–26; R. Jean Cadigan, "Woman-to-Woman Marriage: Practice and Benefits in Sub-Saharan Africa," *Journal of Comparative Family Studies* 29, no. 1 (1989): 89–98; Ifi Amadiume, *Male Daughters, Female Husbands: Gender and Sex in an African Society*, 2nd ed. (London: Zed Books, 1998); Joseph M. Carrier and Stephen O. Murray, "Woman-Woman Marriage in Africa," in *Boy-Wives and Female Husbands: Studies in African Homosexualities*, ed. Stephen O. Murray and Will Roscoe (New York: Palgrave Macmillan, 2008), 255–66; Nwando Achebe, *The Female King of Colonial Nigeria: Ahebi Ugbabe* (Bloomington: Indiana University

Press, 2011).

69. Regina S. Oboler, "Is the Female Husband a Man? Woman/Woman Marriage among the Nandi of Kenya," *Ethnology* 19, no. 1 (1980): 69.

70. Oboler, "Is the Female Husband a Man?" With reference to sexual orientation, Oboler claims that a Nandi female husband was expected to abstain from sexual relations altogether because "if she should conceive, both the issue of inheritance and the dogma that she is a man would be too thoroughly confounded to be withstood." See Oboler, *Women, Power and Economic Change*, 85. Oboler and Orchardson, the latter with reference to the Kipsigis, both emphasize that securing an heir for the family property centrally motivated such unions. Nevertheless, in their study of woman-woman marriages based on interviews with Kikuyu women of central Kenya, scholars Wairimũ Ngarũiya Njambi and William E. O'Brien note other reasons that women entered into such unions, including love, commitment, children, sexual freedom, vulnerability, and empowerment, additional to those that were narrowly economic and instrumental in nature. See Oboler, *Women, Power and Economic Change*; Orchardson, *Kipsigis*; Wairimũ Ngarũiya Njambi and William E. O'Brien, "Revisiting 'Woman-Woman Marriage': Notes on Gĩkũyũ Women," *NWSA Journal* 12, no. 1 (2000): 1–23.

71. Circular Letter, Hon. General Secretary A&ASA, Jeanes School to Provinces, Districts, Schools and Institutions, "African Athletic Sports," 1950 KNA/DC/KSM/1/1/227.

72. Ibid.

73. Anderson, "Development of Athletics," 7.

74. Bale and Sang, *Kenyan Running*, 69.

75. Minutes of a Meeting of the Athletic Council of the Arab and African Sports Association, June 27, 1955, KNA/DC/KSM/1/1/232. On Alexander's life and career, see Maureen M. Smith, "Revisiting South Africa and the Olympic Movement: The Correspondence of Reginald S. Alexander and the International Olympic Committee, 1961–86," *The International Journal of the History of Sport* 23, no. 7 (2006): 1193–216. On his considerable, but ultimately unsuccessful, efforts to host the IOC in Nairobi in 1963, see Michelle M. Sikes, "From Nairobi to Baden-Baden: African Politics, the International Olympic Committee, and Early Efforts to Censure Apartheid South Africa," *The International Journal of the History of Sport* 36, no. 1 (2019): 7–23; and Michelle M. Sikes, "The Enemy of My Enemy Is My Friend? A Clash of Anti-Apartheid Tactics and Targets in the Olympic Movement of the Early 1960s," *The International Journal of the History of Sport*, 37, no. 7 (2020): 520–41.

76. Peggy Northrup competed in the 100- and 400-meters swim events. See "Kenya's Olympic Team Chosen," Press Office Handout No. 825.B, Press Office, Department of Information,

Nairobi, September 17, 1956, KNA/PC/NKU/2/32/15; "Rifle Men in Kenya Olympic Team," Press Office Handout No. 868, Press Office, Department of Information, Nairobi, September 28, 1956, KNA/PC/NKU/2/32/15.

77. Tom Askwith, *Getting My Knees Brown: Day-to-Day Episodes in Colonial Kenya* (Cheltenham, UK: Quorum Technical Services, Ltd., 1996).

78. Anthony Kirk-Greene, "Imperial Administration and the Athletic Imperative: The Case of the District Officer in Africa," in *Sport in Africa: Essays in Social History*, ed. William J. Baker and James A. Mangan (New York: Africana Publishing Company, 1987), 99.

79. Bale and Sang, *Kenyan Running*, 76.

80. Ocobock, *Uncertain Age*, 179.

81. Ibid., 200. On Wamumu, see also Erin Bell, "'A Most Horrifying Maturity in Crime': Age, Gender and Juvenile Delinquency in Colonial Kenya during the Mau Mau Uprising," *Atlantic Studies* 11, no. 4 (2014): 473–90.

82. Ocobock, *Uncertain Age*, 178.

83. "From the Guards to Guarding: Sir Derek Erskine," *Sunday Nation*, August 2, 1970, 31.

84. Anderson, "Development of Athletics," 45.

85. Derek Erskine, President's Report to the KAAA, KNA/DC/KSM/1/1/227.

86. Nyanza Training Centres and Secondary Schools Athletic Association, "Womens [sic] Training Centres June-1958," RVP PC/NKU/3/21/8.

87. Edwin Evans (Secretary), Nyanza Training Centres and Secondary Schools Athletics Association, "Athletics 1958," RVP PC/NKU/3/21/8.

88. Boit to Hextall, December 17, 1959, RVP PC/NKU/3/21/8; Archie Evans to all Provincial Associations, Army, and Kenya Police, "Kenya Decathlon 1959, Kenya Women's Championships 1959," October 31, 1959, RVP PC/NKU/3/21/8; Boit to District Commissioners at Kapsabet, Tambach, and West Suk, the Community Development Officer Baringo, the County District Officer at Nakuru, and African Affairs Officer at Nakuru, "Re: Colony Women Championships and Decathlon," November 23, 1959, Nakuru Sports Association, 1950–1959, RVP PC/NKU/3/21/8.

89. Edwin Evans (Secretary), Nyanza Training Centres and Secondary Schools Athletics Association, "Athletics 1958," RVP PC/NKU/3/21/8. The first women's titles went to Trifa de Souza of Nairobi who won both the 100- and the 220-yards events, Nyanza athletes Mary Aloyo in the 440-yards and Agnes Osundwa in the 80-meters hurdles, and a Nyanza quartet that won the 4x100-yards relay. Nyanza athletes Rose Mokua, Tereza Wambusheri, and Sara Apapur claimed the shot, discus, and javelin titles, respectively. Irene Rybiski of the Coast won the long jump, and Central Province's Mary Namaan finished first in the high jump. See Boit to Hextall, December 17, 1959; and Archie Evans

to all Provincial Associations, "Kenya Women's Championships, 1960," October 31, 1960, both in RVP PC/NKU/3/21/8.

90. At the 1961 Provincial Intermediate Schools competition, three records were set in the discus, javelin, and 220-yards dash and one equaled in the 100-yards, and one new event was contested, the 440-yards. "Nursery For All Nyanza Athletes," *East African Standard*, March 17, 1961, 23. See also "Girls Clip Kenya Times in Nyanza," *East African Standard*, April 11, 1962, 10.

91. "Ten Nyanza Records Go," *East African Standard*, July 28, 1961, 19.

92. "Too Many Athletes So Boys Wait," *East African Standard*, June 19, 1962, 8. See also "Three Records Set by Siriba College Men," *East African Standard*, May 30, 1962, 8.

93. "Les Girls Waited for This Change," *East African Standard*, September 28, 1961, 12.

94. "Chances for Olympic Aspirants," *East African Standard*, May 6, 1960, 28.

95. "Now Nakuru Wants to Stage A.A.A," *East African Standard*, September 14, 1961, 8.

96. Ibid.; "Novice Makes His Mark: Steeplechase 'Find' Strolls to Victory," *East African Standard*, September 11, 1961, 8.

97. Rift Valley Region Sports Association Chairman's Speech of 1961, RVP DC/KPNRIA/18/3.

98. Rift Valley Province Secretary's Report, 1961, RVP DC/KPNRIA/18/3.

99. The meet featured stellar performances by athletes drawn largely from the Coast, Rift Valley, and Nyanza Provinces. A five-woman contingent from the Coast recorded six top-three finishes led by Meldrita Laurent who won the 220-yards and broke her own national record for the 100-yards event. Rhoda Chepngetich of Nyanza set an 80-meters hurdles record and finished second to Laurent in the 100-yards dash before helping to set a Kenya record in the 4x110-yards relay ahead of runner-up Nandi. Rift Valley runners claimed the top-three finishes in the 440-yards event, led by Chepkoech Chuma's record breaking effort. Nandi high jumpers also swept the top-three places led by Chepkirong Birir who set a record of 5 feet, 1.5 inches. See "Standards Highest Yet: Six Records Go at Women's A.A.A. Meeting," *East African Standard*, November 7, 1961, 8.

100. Charles Disney, "No New Stars," *East African Standard*, August 14, 1962, 8. See also "Records Tumble at Rift Sports," *East African Standard*, August 13, 1962, 8.

101. "Teacher Clips Kenya Record," *East African Standard*, August 20, 1962, 8.

102. "Kenya Women's Championships Called Off," *East African Standard*, September 4, 1962, 8.

103. "Athletes on Their Marks," *Daily Nation*, August 9, 1963, 15.

104. Ibid.

105. Archie Evans, "Will These Stars Shine Again?," *Daily Nation*, August 30, 1963, 18.

106. In front of three thousand spectators in Kampala, Kenyan men won seventeen of the twenty events, scoring 123 points to Uganda's forty-four and Tanganyika's eighteen—their

largest-ever winning margin. "Paul Odhiambo Leaps Near World Class," *Daily Nation*, September 2, 1963, 14.

107. Archie Evans, "There's a Bright Future for These New Boys," *Daily Nation*, September 7, 1963, 17.

108. Charles Disney, "Kenya Talent Must be Tapped," *Sunday Nation*, May 16, 1965, 45.

109. Martin Francis, "The Domestication of the Male? Recent Research on Nineteenth and Twentieth Century British Masculinity," *The Historical Journal* 45, no. 3 (2002): 651.

Chapter 2. Nation, Race, Gender, and Athletes' Rights in the Early Independence Era: The Case of Diana Monks

1. "Naftali Temu Shares Glory with Mecser," *East African Standard,* September 4, 1967, 10.

2. "Uganda Girl Pips Diana by Inch," *Daily Nation*, July 23, 1965, 22. On those 1965 games, see Terry Vaios Gitersos, "The Sporting Scramble for Africa: GANEFO, the IOC and the 1965 African Games," *Sport in Society* 14, no. 5 (2011): 645–59; and Pascal Charitas, "A More Flexible Domination: Franco-African Sport Diplomacy during Decolonization, 1945–1966," in *Diplomatic Games: Sport, Statecraft and International Relations since 1945*, ed. Heather L. Dichter and Andrew L. Johns (Lexington: University Press of Kentucky, 2014), 183–214.

3. Jomo Kenyatta, *Facing Mount Kenya: The Tribal Life of the Gikuyu* (London: Mercury Books, Secker and Warburg, 1961); Bethwell A. Ogot and William R. Ochieng', eds., *Decolonization and Independence in Kenya, 1940–93* (London: James Currey, 1995); E. S. Atieno Odhiambo and John Lonsdale, eds., *Mau Mau and Nationhood: Arms, Authority and Narration* (Oxford: James Currey, 2003); David M. Anderson, *Histories of the Hanged: The Dirty War in Kenya and the End of Empire* (New York: W.W. Norton & Company, 2005); Caroline Elkins, *Britain's Gulag: The Brutal End of Empire in Kenya* (London: Jonathan Cape, 2005); Daniel Branch, *Defeating Mau Mau, Creating Kenya: Counterinsurgency, Civil war, and Decolonization* (Cambridge: Cambridge University Press, 2009); and Wunyabari O. Maloba, *Kenyatta and Britain: An Account of Political Transformation, 1929–1963* (Cham, Switzerland: Palgrave Macmillan, 2018).

4. The terms "European," "Asian," and "African" refer to the three-tiered "racial" divisions of Kenyan society; however, these labels obscure the subjective, evolving, and divided nature of these categories, which also encompassed other identities. The Asian community, for example, included a variety of peoples who practiced different religions, spoke separate languages, and divided into castes. See Sana Aiyar, *Indians in Kenya: The*

Politics of Diaspora (Cambridge, MA: Harvard University Press, 2015). For broad histories of Kenya in the years after independence, see Daniel Branch, Nic Cheeseman, and Leigh Gardner, eds., *Our Turn to Eat: Politics in Kenya Since 1950* (Berlin: Lit Verlag, 2010); Daniel Branch, *Kenya: Between Hope and Despair, 1963–2011* (New Haven, CT: Yale University Press, 2011); and Charles Hornsby, *Kenya: A History Since Independence* (London: I.B. Tauris, 2012).

5. The term "Kikuyuization" also emerged reflecting how members of that community came to dominate the upper echelons of government, civil service, and security forces. See Volker Vinnai, "The Creation of an African Civil Service in Kenya," *Verfassung und Recht in Übersee / Law and Politics in Africa, Asia and Latin America* 7, no. 2 (1974): 175–88; and Anaïs Angelo, *Power and the Presidency in Kenya: The Jomo Kenyatta Years* (New York: Cambridge University Press, 2019).

6. Bettina Ng'weno and L Obura Aloo, "Irony of Citizenship: Descent, National Belonging, and Constitutions in the Postcolonial African State," *Law & Society Review* 53, no. 1 (2019): 141–72.

7. Vincent Cable, "The Asians of Kenya," *African Affairs* 68, no. 272 (1969): 223.

8. James Gibbs, "*Uhuru na Kenyatta*: White Settlers and the Symbolism of Kenya's Independence Day Events," *Journal of Imperial and Commonwealth History* 42, no. 3 (2014): 503–29.

9. Hornsby, *Kenya,* 121–22. In 1968, however, the British government betrayed its promise to allow Kenyan Asians with British passports to enter the country when it limited right of entry to those either born in Britain or with at least one of parent or grandparent born there. See Randall Hansen, "The Kenyan Asians, British Politics, and the Commonwealth Immigrants Act, 1968," *The Historical Journal* 42, no. 3 (1999): 809–34.

10. This sport-focused case joins a body of recent works on belonging and citizenship in East African history that respond to Frederick Cooper's 1994 appeal for new histories of African decolonization, including Brennan, *Taifa*; Emma Hunter, *Political Thought and the Public Sphere in Tanzania: Freedom, Democracy and Citizenship in the Era of Decolonization* (New York: Cambridge University Press, 2015); Keren Weitzberg, *We Do Not Have Borders: Greater Somalia and the Predicaments of Belonging in Kenya* (Athens: Ohio University Press, 2017); and Kara Moskowitz, *Seeing Like a Citizen: Decolonization, Development, and the Making of Kenya, 1945–1980* (Athens: Ohio University Press, 2019). That call appears in Frederick Cooper, "Conflict and Connection: Rethinking Colonial African History," *American Historical Review* 99, no. 5 (1994): 1519.

11. "Army Men Steal the Limelight," *East African Standard,* September 4, 1967, 10. See also Norman da Costa, "Temu Races to KAAA Meet Double," *Daily Nation*, September 3, 1967, 23.

12. "Mecser Keen to Run at Kisumu," *East African Standard*, September 5, 1967, 10.

13. "Promising Primary Athletes," *East African Standard*, July 23, 1962, 7.

14. Brian Marsden, "Awards for Schools' Athletes," *Daily Nation*, November 18, 1964, 15.

15. Norman da Costa, "Kenya Ace to Take on World Champions," *Daily Nation*, June 22, 1965, 11; Norman da Costa, "Strong Side Named," *Daily Nation*, June 28, 1965, 15.

16. Gitersos, "Sporting Scramble for Africa," 651.

17. "Girls Make History," *Daily Nation*, July 16, 1965, 14. Monks's mother travelled to the meet in Brazzaville as the chaperone of the two female athletes. Norman da Costa, "Brazzaville Games Squad Named: Gold Grabbers! Kenya Can Land Six Firsts (At Least)," *Daily Nation*, June 29, 1965, 15.

18. Bowers Mugalo, "Kiprugut Will Carry the Colours," *Daily Nation*, July 10, 1965, 9.

19. Photo caption, *Daily Nation*, July 10, 1965, 9.

20. "Uganda Girl Pips Diana by Inch," *Daily Nation*, July 23, 1965, 22.

21. "Kenyans Bid More 'Gold,'" *Daily Nation*, July 24, 1965, 15.

22. "Home with the Loot! Our Triumphant Athletes Return,'" *Daily Nation*, July 27, 1965, 12/13. On Mboya's life and career, see David Goldsworthy, *Tom Mboya: The Man Kenya Wanted to Forget* (Nairobi: Heinemann, 1982); and Edwin Gimode, *Thomas Joseph Mboya: A Biography* (Nairobi: East African Educational Publishers, 1996). His autobiography is Tom Mboya, *Freedom and After* (Nairobi: East African Educational Publishers Ltd., 1986).

23. Photo, *Daily Nation*, July 27, 1965, 13.

24. "Presenting the Athletes of the Year . . . ," *Daily Nation*, June 6, 1966, 1.

25. Monks was selected in her 80-meters hurdles specialty and Stephens in the 100- and 220-yards events after she won both sprints at the 1966 Kenyan national championships. Brian Marsden, "No Shocks in Jamaica Games Squad," *Daily Nation*, July 5, 1966, 15.

26. In Kingston Stephens came sixth in the heats of the 100 yards and eighth in the 220 yards, and Monks finished fifth in the 80-meters hurdles semifinals. Brian Marsden, "Rudisha Loses Deal on Photo," *Daily Nation*, August 13, 1966, 19.

27. "Fastest Mile in Africa Forecast: Keino Expected to Do It If He Is Pushed," *East African Standard*, September 9, 1967, 10.

28. "Mr. Odinga Waits in Vain," *East African Standard*, September 11, 1967, 3. For his autobiography published the same year as this track and field meet, see Oginga Odinga, *Not Yet Uhuru: The Autobiography of Oginga Odinga* (London: Heinemann, 1967). Other accounts of his life include H. Odera Oruka, *Oginga Odinga: His Philosophy and Beliefs* (Nairobi: Initiatives Publishers, 1992); and E. S. Atieno Odhiambo, *Jaramogi Ajuma Oginga Odinga: A Biography* (Nairobi: East African Educational Publishers, 1997).

29. "Minister Praises Standard," *East African Standard*, September 11, 1967, 10. On Grace

Onyango, see Phoebe Musandu, "Drawing from the Wells of Culture: Grace Onyango and the Kenyan Political Scene (1964–1983)," *Wagadu 6: Journal of International Women's Studies* 10, no. 1 (2009): 108–24.

30. "Minister Praises Standard," *East African Standard*, September 11, 1967, 10.

31. "The Best Mile Race in Africa," *East African Standard*, September 12, 1967, 7.

32. "Keino Astonishes the Experts," *East African Standard*, September 11, 1967, 10.

33. "The Best Mile Race in Africa," 7.

34. "Keino Astonishes the Experts," 10.

35. "Schools' Meet Will Wind up 1967 Season," *East African Standard*, September 13, 1967, 16.

36. Rosemary Namusisi won the 80-meters hurdles in a time that was almost a full second slower than what Monks recorded for that event the week before. C. Kabanda of Uganda won the long jump ahead of Stephens in sixteen feet, eight and one-half inches. Monks had won that event the previous week with a jump of seventeen feet, eleven inches, in what was a Kenyan, East African, and stadium record. "Naftali Temu Shares Glory with Mecser," *East African Standard*, September 4, 1967, 10; "Keino Astonishes the Experts," 10.

37. A. S. A Jeneby to all Provincial, County, City, and Municipal Education Officers, Headmasters and Headmistresses of Secondary Schools, Principals of Teacher Training Colleges, and Secretaries of Secondary Schools Sports Councils, "Kenya Schools Invitation Athletic Championships," August 5, 1967, KNA AMP/5/19; and "Uganda Team Wants to Run at K.I.A.," *East African Standard*, September 15, 1967, 24.

38. "Rivalry Among Athletes Reaches Climax," *East African Standard*, September 23, 1967, 10.

39. "Schools' Meet Will Wind up 1967 Season," *East African Standard*, September 13, 1967, 16.

40. "Rivalry Among Athletes Reaches Climax," 10.

41. "Seven Uganda Athletes for K.I.A. Meet," *East African Standard*, September 16, 1967, 10. Chemabwai, who was then in primary school, competed for the KAAA as she did not take part in the Kenya Schools' championships earlier that year. See "Schools' Meet Will Wind up 1967 Season," 16.

42. "Seven Uganda Athletes for K.I.A. Meet," 10.

43. "Uganda Team Wants to Run at K.I.A.," 24.

44. "Seven Uganda Athletes for K.I.A. Meet," *East African Standard*, September 16, 1967, 10; see also "Diana Monks Suspended," *Daily Nation*, September 16, 1967, 23.

45. "Diana Monks Suspended by KAAA," *East African Standard*, September 16, 1967, 10.

46. "Restriction on National Meet Next Year," *East African Standard*, September 23, 1967, 10.

47. For the results of the KAAA/Kenya Schools dual meet, see "Keino Pipped by Temu: Disappointing Race at Schools Meet," *East African Standard*, September 25, 1967, 10.

48. Hezekiah Wepukhulu, "Lydia's Eyes on the Olympics," *East African Standard*, October 25,

1967, 6.

49. Ibid.

50. Ibid.

51. "Game On: The Ace, Lydia Stephens—First Woman from Kenya to Participate in an Olympic Competition," *KBC Sports*, September 2, 2021, https://www.youtube.com/watch?v=OBxzz40YcXw.

52. Stephens's older sister, Elizabeth, competed at the national level before becoming a physical education instructor at Waa Girls School near Mombasa. Hezekiah Wepukhulu, "Lydia's Eyes on the Olympics," *East African Standard,* October 25, 1967, 6.

53. "Game On: The Ace, Lydia Stephens."

54. Ibid.

55. Ibid.

56. Michelle M. Sikes, "Sprinting Past the End of Empire: Seraphino Antao and the Promise of Sport in Kenya, 1960–63," in *Sports in Africa: Past and Present*, ed. Todd Cleveland, Tarminder Kaur, and Gerard Akindes (Athens: Ohio University Press, 2020), 219–32.

57. "Game On: The Ace, Lydia Stephens."

58. "Top Sportswoman Banned from University Team," *East African Standard*, October 26, 1967, 12.

59. Ibid.

60. E. T. Monks, "Suspension of Miss Monks," *East African Standard*, November 1, 1967, 13.

61. Ibid.

62. Abdul V. Hirani, "University's Reply," *East African Standard*, November 1, 1967, 13.

63. "Athletics Ban on Non-Kenyans," *East African Standard*, November 3, 1967, 16.

64. Ibid.

65. American track and field athletes in the early 1970s fought to limit when guests from other nations could compete in US meets in order to prevent South African athletes from competing in American championships; see Michelle M. Sikes and Jacob J. Fredericks, "'It's a Policy Matter, Not a Racial Matter': Athlete Activism and Symbiotic Struggles against Apartheid in US Track and Field of the Early 1970s," *The International Journal of the History of Sport* 39, no. 8–9 (2022): 938–58.

66. R. G. Ngala, "Welcome Message by the Minister for Co-operatives and Social Services," approved by Ngala, August 1967, KNA AMP/5/49.

67. Donald Rothchild, "Kenya's Africanization Program: Priorities of Development and Equity," *American Political Science Review* 64, no. 3 (1970): 738.

68. Maria S. Muller, "The National Policy of Kenyanisation of Trade: Its Impact on a Town in

Kenya," *Canadian Journal of African Studies / Revue Canadienne des Études Africaines* 15, no. 2 (1981): 297; Cable, "Asians of Kenya," 228–29; Hansen, "Kenyan Asians," 817.

69. On this emigration from East African nations, see Aiyar, *Indians in Kenya*; Mahmood Mamdani, *From Citizen to Refugee, Uganda Asians Come to Britain*, 2nd ed. (Cape Town: Pambazuka Press, 2011); and James R. Brennan, *Taifa: Making Nation and Race in Urban Tanzania* (Athens: Ohio University Press, 2012).

70. "Authoritarian Athletics," *East African Standard*, November 3, 1967, 8.

71. "Racialism in Athletics," *East African Standard*, November 7, 1967, 6.

72. "Boycott of Athletics Meetings Proposed," *East African Standard*, November 4, 1967, 10.

73. B. N. Macharia, "Statement Challenged," *East African Standard*, November 7, 1967, 12.

74. Horace Owiti, "Condemned Harshly," *East African Standard*, mailed from Nairobi on November 6, and published on November 7, 1967, 12.

75. P. W. Ndoo, "Condemned Harshly," *East African Standard*, mailed from Nairobi on November 5, and published on November 7, 1967, 12.

76. John Downes, "Ear to the Ground," *East African Standard*, November 10, 1967, 23.

77. Ndoo, "Condemned Harshly."

78. Cyprian Fernandes, "Eight Athletes for Madagascar," *Daily Nation*, February 4, 1967, 23; Norman Da Costa, "Owiti Faces Tough Fight in Madagascar," *Daily Nation*, March 28, 1967, 23; "Top Team for Madagascar," *Daily Nation*, March 29, 1967, 23. The eight selected Kenyan athletes were invited to participate in the Madagascar independence anniversary celebrations track and field meet, which was watched by six cabinet ministers, the British ambassador, and the vice president of the Republic.

79. Aish Jeneby, Manager of the team, "Report of Madagascar Tour of Kenya Athletes-1st April to 8 April 67," April 10, 1967, KNA AMP/5/49.

80. "Athlete's Right of Appeal," *East African Standard*, November 9, 1967, 4.

81. "Racialism in Athletics," *East African Standard*, November 7, 1967, 6.

82. A large body of literature exists on the struggles over South African participation at the 1968 Mexico City Olympics. Discussion can be found in books by Richard Lapchick, *The Politics of Race and International Sport: The Case of South Africa* (Westport, CT: Greenwood Press, 1975); Robert Archer and Antoine Bouillon, *The South African Game: Sport and Racism* (London: Zed Books, 1982); Douglas Booth, *The Race Game: Sport and Politics in South Africa* (London: Frank Cass, 1998); Amy Bass, *Not the Triumph but the Struggle: The 1968 Olympics and the Making of the Black Athlete* (Minneapolis: University of Minnesota Press, 2002); Douglas Hartmann, *Race, Culture, and the Revolt of the Black Athlete: The 1968 Olympic Protests and their Aftermath* (Chicago: University of Chicago

Press, 2003); and Kevin B. Witherspoon, *Before the Eyes of the World: Mexico and the 1968 Olympics* (DeKalb: Northern Illinois University Press, 2008). Articles that delve into aspects of the controversy include Scarlett Cornelissen, "Resolving 'the South Africa Problem': Transnational Activism, Ideology and Race in the Olympic Movement, 1960–91," *International Journal of the History of Sport* 28, no. 1 (2011): 153–67; Dexter Blackman, "African Americans, Pan-Africanism, and the Anti-apartheid Campaign to Expel South Africa from the 1968 Olympics," *Journal of Pan African Studies* 5, no. 3 (2012): 1–25; and Michelle M. Sikes, "Ousting South Africa: Olympic Clashes of 1968," *Acta Academica* 50, no. 2 (2018): 12–33. Discussion of the 1968 suspension of South Africa can also be found in Olympic histories by Allen Guttmann, *The Olympics: A History of the Modern Games* (Urbana: University of Illinois Press, 1992); Richard Espy, *The Politics of the Olympic Games* (Berkeley: University of California Press, 1979); Christopher Hill, *Olympic Politics: Athens to Atlanta 1896–1996* (Manchester: Manchester University Press, 1996), and Alfred Senn, *Power, Politics and the Olympic Games: A History of the Powerbrokers, Events, and Controversies that Shaped the Games* (Champaign, IL: Human Kinetics, 1999).

83. Michelle M. Sikes, "From Nairobi to Baden-Baden: African Politics, the International Olympic Committee, and Early Efforts to Censure Apartheid South Africa," *The International Journal of the History of Sport* 36, no. 1 (2019): 7–23; Michelle M. Sikes, "The Enemy of My Enemy Is My Friend? A Clash of Anti-Apartheid Tactics and Targets in the Olympic Movement of the Early 1960s," *The International Journal of the History of Sport* 37, no. 7 (2020): 520–41.

84. "Racialism in Athletics," *East African Standard*, November 7, 1967, 6.

85. "Call for Inquiry into K.A.A.A.: Games Union to Ask for Mr. Yeda's Resignation," *East African Standard*, November 7, 1967, 12.

86. Ibid.

87. Capitalization in the text. KAAA, "Minutes of the Council Meeting Held on Friday, 23 September 1967 at Gill House, Nairobi 5 p.m.," KNA AMP/5/49.

88. Sulubu Tuva, "Jeneby Shows the Way," *Daily Nation*, November 10, 2003, 34.

89. A. S. A. Jeneby, "Sportsbag: Selection of Kenya Athletes," *East African Standard*, November 11, 1967, 10.

90. Ibid.

91. "Mecser Keen to Run at Kisumu," *East African Standard*, September 5, 1967, 10.

92. "Diverting the Student's Mind from Books," *Daily Nation*, October 12, 1968, 12.

93. "Call for Inquiry into K.A.A.A.: Games Union to Ask for Mr. Yeda's Resignation," *East African Standard*, November 7, 1967, 12.

94. Ibid.

95. J. Ambrose Awuoro Apunda, "Sportsbag: Athlete's View on Suspension," *East African Standard*, November 9, 1967, 10.

96. Ibid.

97. Dissatisfaction with administrative bodies in that country emerged in part from a battle for control of track and field raging between the national governing body of the sport, the Amateur Athletic Union (AAU), and the National Collegiate Athletic Association (NCAA), which controlled college athletics. Battle lines had hardened between the two organizations in the 1960s as both issued threats and allegations and suspended and penalized athletes in their bid for control. On campaigns by American track and field athletes for better treatment and greater control of their competitive opportunities, see Kenny Moore, "The Campaign for Athletes' Rights," *Annals of the American Academy of Political and Social Science* 445 (1979): 59–65; Joseph Turrini, *The End of Amateurism in American Track and Field* (Urbana: University of Illinois Press, 2010); Aaron L. Haberman, "'We're All Professionals Now': Frank Shorter, Deregulation, and the Battle to End 'Shamateurism' in the 1970s," *The International Journal of the History of Sport* 36, no. 15–16 (2019): 1414–32; and Sikes and Fredericks, "It's a Policy Matter, not a Racial Matter." On the acrimonious battles between the AAU and the NCAA, see Howard P. Chudacoff, "AAU v. NCAA: The Bitter Feud That Altered the Structure of American Amateur Sports," *Journal of Sport History* 48, no. 1 (2021): 50–65.

98. Turrini, *End of Amateurism*, 78.

99. In ibid.,79.

100. J. Ambrose Awuoro Apunda, "Sportsbag: Athlete's View on Suspension," *East African Standard*, mailed from Nairobi on November 7, published on November 9, 1967, 10.

101. Ibid.

102. Ibid.

103. Ibid.

104. "Minister Backs Suspension of Miss Monks," *East African Standard*, November 8, 1967, 16; "Minister Supports KAAA," *Daily Nation*, November 8, 1967, 23.

105. Ibid.

106. Kara Moskowitz, "From Multiracialism to Africanization? Race, Politics, and Sport in Decolonizing Kenya," *Journal of Contemporary History* 58, no.1 (2023): 20.

107. "Minister Backs Suspension of Miss Monks," *East African Standard*, November 8, 1967, 16.

108. "Ban Only Applies to Athletics," *East African Standard*, November 9, 1967, 1.

109. "Athlete's Right of Appeal," *East African Standard*, November 9, 1967, 4.

110. "Diana Monks May Appeal Against Ban," *East African Standard*, November 10, 1967, 1.

111. "Diana Monks May Appeal Against Ban," *East African Standard*, November 10, 1967, 1. See

also "Anything but Athletics . . . ," *Daily Nation*, November 10, 1967, 3.

112. "Athlete's Suspension Not Racial: Association Not Prepared to Condone Irresponsible Action," *East African Standard*, November 10, 1967, 24.

113. "Mr Cockar: Example to Others," *East African Standard*, November 10, 1967, 24.

114. Ibid.

115. "Encourage Sportsmen," *East African Standard*, November 10, 1967, 24.

116. Ibid.

117. Jacob Wangatia, "Sportsbag: Deprived of Points," *East African Standard*, November 10, 1967, 24.

118. Quote in Mike Marqusee, *Redemption Song: Muhammad Ali and the Spirit of the Sixties*, 2nd ed. (London: Verso Books, 2005), 214. See also Muhammad Ali with Richard Durham, *The Greatest: My Own Story* (New York: Random House, 1975); Thomas Hauser, *Muhammad Ali: His Life and Times* (New York: Simon & Schuster, 1991); Elliott J. Gorn, ed., *Muhammad Ali: The People's Champ* (Urbana: University of Illinois Press, 1995); Gerald Early, ed., *The Muhammad Ali Reader* (Hopewell, NJ: Ecco Press, 1998); David Remnick, *King of the World: Muhammad Ali and the Rise of an American Hero* (New York: Random House, 1998); and Michael Ezra, *Muhammad Ali: The Making of an Icon* (Philadelphia: Temple University Press, 2009).

119. Jacob Wangatia, "Sportsbag: Deprived of Points," *East African Standard*, November 10, 1967, 24.

120. "Mr. Mbathi: 'Lame Excuse' for Absence," *East African Standard*, November 10, 1967, 24.

121. Ibid.

122. Ibid.

123. Norman da Costa, "Ban on Diana Stays, Says A.A.A," *East African Standard*, December 12, 1967, 31.

124. "Uganda Favourites in Watch Cup Tie," *Daily Nation*, February 22, 1969, 22.

125. "Nairobi's Big Games Squad," *Daily Nation*, December 6, 1967, 27.

126. "Top Runners Again Absent," *East African Standard*, May 27, 1968, 10; "Nakuru Meeting Marred by a Heavy Downpour," *East African Standard*, May 28, 1968, 10.

127. John Underwood, "Lost Laughter," *Sports Illustrated*, September 30, 1968, https://vault.si.com/vault/1968/09/30/lost-laughter.

128. Historian Timothy Parsons has made a similar argument in his study of the Kenya Boy Scout movement. See Timothy H. Parsons, "No More English than the Postal System: The Kenya Boy Scout Movement and the Transfer of Power," *Africa Today* 51, no. 3 (2005): 61–80.

Chapter 3. Precocious Achievement and the Long Run to Inclusion: Marriage, Motherhood, and the Military

1. "Fabulous Maiyo Steals Jamhuri Park Limelight from Elizabeth Chelimo," *Daily Nation*, June 12, 1972, 22.

2. Ibid.

3. "Two Break Africa 1500m. Record," *Sunday Nation*, August 15, 1971, 23.

4. Joshua Okuthe, "Top Performances at Kericho Meet," *Daily Nation*, May 28, 1973, 21.

5. Ibid.

6. Ibid.

7. Peter Moll, "Hoping for a Better Meet," *Daily Nation*, March 11, 1972, 22.

8. Peter Moll, "Six More for Munch: Women Fail to Shine," June 26, 1972, *Daily Nation*, 22. See also Peter Moll, "Adala—Running Back to Happiness," *Daily Nation*, June 22, 1972, 23.

9. Philip Ndoo, "Medals for these Kenya Schoolboys," *Sunday Nation*, August 9, 1970, 37. Ndoo received a track and field scholarship from Eastern New Mexico University after he competed the 1970 Commonwealth Games. He contributed to two national cross-country championships in 1974 and 1974 and won ten All-American honors and two individual titles in the steeplechase and the six-mile event while completing degrees in journalism and economics. Ndoo coached Kenyan teams at the 1978 All Africa Games in Algeria and the 1978 Edmonton Commonwealth games, travelled as an executive officer to the 1984 Los Angeles Olympics, and served on the organizing committee of the 1987 All Africa Games held in Nairobi. In 2005 after battling threat cancer he passed away at the age of fifty-eight. See Hezekiah Wepukhulu, "Philip Ndoo's Untold Story of the Olympic Movement in Kenya," *The East African*, February 14–20, 2005, 8; "Hall of Honors: Philip Ndoo," Eastern New Mexico Athletics, https://goeasternathletics.com/honors/hall-of-honors/philip-ndoo/91.

10. Philip Ndoo, "Women: Plenty but Usually Wasted Talent," *Daily Nation*, August 16, 1986, 22.

11. Philip Ndoo, "Onyambu Survives the Fading Bug," *Daily Nation,* September 16, 1986, 29.

12. "Golden Day for Kenya," *Daily Nation*, January 30, 1974, 24; Norman da Costa, "Kenya's Heroes Delayed in NZ," *Daily Nation*, February 4, 1974, 1.

13. Gishinga Njoroge, "Women's Best Chance Since Mexican Debut," *Daily Nation*, March 4, 1992, 25.

14. For statistics on Kenyan Olympic participation, see Olympedia, http://www.olympedia.org/.

15. Mike Boit, "Why do Kenyan Girls Drop Out?," *Weekly Review*, August 19, 1988, 45.

16. Philip Ndoo, "Kenya Schools and Colleges Championships: Memorable Climax," *Daily Nation*, August 11, 1979, 20.

17. "The 13 Year Old Who's Training for the Olympics: Justina Goes for Gold," *Drum* (East African Edition), October 1981, 49–50.

18. "A New Star Is Born," *Sports Review*, May 1982, 41.

19. "13 Year Old Who's Training for the Olympics."

20. "Olympics Games '84: Here I Come [Justina Chepchirchir]," *True Love*, December 1983, 17–18.

21. Bale and Sang, *Kenyan Running*, 112.

22. "Mukhora's Plans for Athletics," *Daily Nation*, April 11, 1968, 23.

23. Thomas Rajula, "Meet the First Female Athlete to Represent Kenya at the Olympic Games," *Sunday Nation*, April 18, 2021, 6–7; Tecla Chemabwai, interview with author, Eldoret, Kenya, January 20, 2010.

24. From 1964 to 1985, Kenyan students followed a 7-4-2-3 system: seven years of primary education, four years of lower secondary school (Forms 1–4), two years of upper secondary school (Forms 5–6), and three years of university education. In 1985 the Kenyan government introduced an 8-4-4 system of education, which entailed eight years of primary school education, four years of secondary school, and four years of university. Maurice N. Amutabi, "Political Interference in the Running of Education in Post-independence Kenya: A Critical Retrospection," *International Journal of Educational Development* 23, no. 2 (2003): 127–44.

25. Joseph Nyanoti, "Temu: The Man Who Beat the World at Its Own Game," *Sunday Times*, October 13, 1991, 8.

26. Bruce Tulloh, "Second to None in Natural Ability," *Daily Nation*, June 14, 1973, 22.

27. Walter Abmayr, *Track and Field Best Performances: Kenya 1987* (Nairobi: ATFS, 1988), 26.

28. Thomas Rajula, "Meet the First Female Athlete to Represent Kenya at the Olympic Games," *Sunday Nation*, April 18, 2021, 6–7.

29. "Dutchwoman Kiplagat Seeks First New York Marathon," *Daily Nation*, October 5, 2005, 55.

30. Elias Makori, "At Home in Iten and Holland: Long-Distance Runner's Training Camp in Kenya Breeding New Stars," *Sunday Nation*, August 15, 2004, 2.

31. Makori, "At Home in Iten and Holland," 2.

32. Sydney O. Hall, "The Role of Physical Education and Sport in the Nation-building Process in Kenya" (PhD diss., Ohio State University, 1973), 101.

33. On the history of education in Kenya, see John E. Anderson, *The Struggle for the School: The Interaction of Missionary, Colonial Government and Nationalist Enterprise in the Development of Formal Education in Kenya* (London: Longman, 1970); James R. Sheffield,

Education in Kenya: An Historical Study (New York: Teachers College Press, 1973); Sorobea N. Bogonko, *A History of Modern Education in Kenya (1895–1991)* (Nairobi: Evans Brothers, 1992); Tabitha Kanogo, *African Womanhood in Colonial Kenya: 1900–1950* (Oxford: James Currey, 2005), Chapter 7: Girls Are Frogs; Girls, Missions and Education"; Oliver W. Furley, "The Struggle for Transformation in Education in Kenya Since Independence," *East African Journal* 9, no. 8 (1972): 23–27.

34. Mikiko Nishimura and Takashi Yamano, "Emerging Private Education in Africa: Determinants of School Choice in Rural Kenya," *World Development* 43 (2013): 266–75. President Kenyatta in December 1973 decreed that education should be free for the first four years of primary school. President Moi in 1978 extended this policy to cover years five to seven. Kenyatta's announcement triggered an influx of students into schools, many of which were unprepared to accommodate such numbers, resulting in the recruitment of untrained teachers and large class sizes. For a critical perspective on these and other policy changes, see Maurice N. Amutabi, "Political Interference: Political Interference in the Running of Education in Post-independence Kenya: A Critical Retrospection," *International Journal of Educational Development* 23, no. 2 (2003): 127–44; and Daniel N. Sifuna, "Increasing Access and Participation of Pastoralist Communities in Primary Education in Kenya," *International Review of Education* 51, no. 5–6 (2005): 499–516.

35. George S. Eshiwani, *Implementing Educational Policies in Kenya*, World Bank Discussion Papers no. 85. Africa Technical Department Series (Washington, DC: World Bank, 1990), 22.

36. World Bank, *Kenya: The Role of Women in Economic Development: A World Bank Country Study* (Washington, DC: World Bank, 1989), 35, 37.

37. Sydney O. Hall, "The Role of Physical Education and Sport in the Nation-building Process in Kenya" (PhD diss., Ohio State University, 1973), 119. On gender and education in Kenya, see Mutindi M. Kiluva-Ndunda, *Women's Agency and Educational Policy: The Experiences of the Women of Kilome, Kenya* (Albany: State University of New York Press, 2001); and Fibian Lukalo, *Mothers and Schooling: Poverty, Gender and Educational Decision-Making in Rural Kenya* (London: Routledge, 2021).

38. In Toby Tanser, *Train Hard, Win Easy: The Kenyan Way*, 2nd ed. (Mountain View, CA: Tafnews Press, 2001), 61.

39. In 1985, 35 percent of students enrolled in these top schools were girls. World Bank, *Kenya: The Role of Women in Economic Development: A World Bank Country Study* (Washington, DC: World Bank, 1989), 37.

40. Philip Ndoo, "The Kenyan Success," in *The African Running Revolution*, ed. Dave Prokop (Mountain View, CA: World Publishers, 1975), 55.

41. Bale and Sang, *Kenyan Running*, 116.

42. On Batchelor, see Michelle M. Sikes, "Sprinting Past the End of Empire: Seraphino Antao and the Promise of Sport in Kenya, 1960–63," in *Sports in Africa: Past and Present*, ed. Todd Cleveland, Tarminder Kaur, and Gerard Akindes (Athens: Ohio University Press, 2020), 219–32. On Whitfield, see Kevin B. Witherspoon, "'An Outstanding Representative of America': Mal Whitfield and America's Black Sports Ambassadors in Africa," in *Defending the American Way of Life: Sport, Culture, and the Cold War*, ed. Toby C. Rider and Kevin B. Witherspoon (Fayetteville: University of Arkansas Press, 2018), 129–40. On Velzian, see Cyprian Fernandes, "Kenya Olympic Hero Says Thanks to Coach: Velzian Tops-Kiprugut," *Daily Nation*, December 22, 1964, 23; "Olympic Prospects on Show at Nakuru Meet," *Daily Nation*, July 15, 1967, 23; Philip Ndoo, "University Games Open Today at Nairobi," *Daily Nation*, December 13, 975, 23; John Bale and Joe Sang, *Kenyan Running: Movement Culture, Geography and Global Change* (London: Frank Cass, 1996), 112; and Kara Moskowitz, "From Multiracialism to Africanization? Race, Politics, and Sport in Decolonizing Kenya," *Journal of Contemporary History* 53, no. 1 (2023): 134; and Martin Kane, "A Very Welcome Redcoat," *Sports Illustrated*, December 19, 1966, https://vault.si.com/vault/1966/12/19/a-very-welcome-redcoat; and John Underwood, "Lost Laughter, *Sports Illustrated*, September 30, 1968, https://vault.si.com/vault/1968/09/30/lost-laughter.

43. "ASAK Elections," *Weekly Review*, May 13, 1988, 36.

44. Peter Moll, "Rift Schools Off Today," *Daily Nation*, August 8, 1973, 31.

45. Ibid.

46. "Schools Still Seeking Cash," *Daily Nation*, January 25, 1973, 22.

47. "Still Short of Target," *Daily Nation*, June 27, 1973, 30; Joshua Okuthe, "Schools' Tour Needs Sponsors," *Daily Nation*, January 16, 1973, 22; "Local Sports," *Daily Nation*, February 2, 1973, 31; "Tour of Europe Will be Valuable Experience," *Daily Nation*, June 15, 1973, 35.

48. "Sporting Envoys," *Daily Nation*, July 21, 1973, 7.

49. "Rift Whizz Kids Set Fast Pace," *Daily Nation*, July 16, 1973, 26.

50. "Sacred Music from Bluffton Is Here Sunday," *Orrville Courier-Crescent* (Ohio), April 20, 1967, 2.

51. "Bluffton Graduates Busy with Summer Activities," *The Lima News* (Ohio), August 3, 1967, 2; Harold Miller, "Ank de Vlas: A Life Devoted to Kenya's Runners and Students," *Canadian Mennonite* 19, no. 1, January 2, 2013. See also Joseph Kiprop and John Koskey Chang'ach, "A History of Kapsabet Girls' High School, Nandi County, Kenya, 1960–1979," *Asia Pacific Journal of Education, Arts and Sciences* 3, no. 1 (2016): 10–20.

52. Toby Tanser, *More Fire: How to Run the Kenyan Way* (Yardley, PA: Westholme Publishing, 2008), 50. See also Bale and Sang, *Kenyan Running*, 115.

53. "Singore in Rift Victory," *Daily Nation*, March 15, 1972, 35.

54. "Rift Valley Boys Win Again," *Daily Nation*, August 23, 1973, 23.

55. "Kenyans in Contention for Final Medal Haul," *Daily Nation*, August 18, 1985, 26; Ochieng' Angela, "Kenya Staging of Games Gets Praise," *Daily Nation*, August 15, 1987, 23.

56. "Tall Order for a 14-Year-Old," *Weekly Review*, June 21, 1991, 46.

57. Eric Odanga, "Barsosio: A Gold Medalist at 19!" *Young Nation*, October 19, 1997, 8.

58. Philip Ndoo, "Onyambu Survives the Fading Bug," *Daily Nation*, September 16, 1986, 29.

59. "Presents Pour in for 'Toto' Elizabeth," *Daily Nation*, May 5, 1979, 23; Philip Ndoo, "Tiny Elizabeth Steals the Show . . . As Atuti Sets African Record," *Daily Nation*, June 21, 1979, 28; Amrik Singh, "Thomson's Chance to Avenge Defeat, *Daily Nation*, June 27, 1979, 30; Elijah Ochieng Achoch, "Tiny Onyambu Delighted Us," *Daily Nation*, July 14, 1979, 21; "Onyambu Receives More Honours," *Daily Nation*, July 18, 1979, 39; Philip Ndoo, "Future Stars on Parade Tomorrow," *Daily Nation*, August 4, 1979, 22; Richard Tomkins, "Elizabeth Onyambu: Recognition Follows Sensational Victories," *Daily Nation*, September 1, 1979, 20; "Onyambu Gets Her Award," *Daily Nation*, August 21, 1979, 18.

60. George Obiero, "Kenya: In Pursuit of Gold Medals," *Standard*, July 6, 1979, 36.

61. "Onyambu in Kenya Squad to Mexico," *Daily Nation*, August 24, 1979, 34.

62. Ndoo, "Onyambu Survives," 29.

63. Ibid.

64. Walter Abmayr, *Track and Field Best Performances: Kenya 1982* (Nairobi: ATFS, 1983), 59.

65. Rose Tata-Muya, interview with author, Nairobi, Kenya, February 19, 2011.

66. In Tanser, *More Fire*, 51.

67. Joshua Okuthe, "Top Performances at Kericho Meet," *Daily Nation*, May 28, 1973, 21; "Good Reply," *Daily Nation*, February 27, 1974, 22.

68. "Guinness Award," *Daily Nation*, July 10, 1973, 27; "Fast Run by Sabina Chebichi in 1,500m," *Daily Nation*, November 17, 1973, 26; "Kenya Finish as Top Athletics Nation in the Commonwealth," *Nation Sport*, February 3, 1974, 1; "Kenya's Latest Track Wonder . . . Sabina," *Daily Nation*, February 8, 1974, 30; "Chance for Young Ones to Show Their Class," *Daily Nation*, August 9, 1974, 20.

69. "Kenya's Latest Track Wonder . . . Sabina," *Daily Nation*, February 8, 1974, 30.

70. Ibid.

71. Pekka Rinne, "The Ills Plaguing Kenya Athletics," *Daily Nation*, April 7, 1976, 20.

72. Philip Ndoo, "Two Break Africa 1500m Record," *Daily Nation*, August 15, 1971, 21; "Cherono for Munich," *Daily Nation,* March 20, 1972, 23.

73. "Fabulous Maiyo Steals Jamhuri Park Limelight from Elizabeth Chelimo," *Daily Nation*, June 12, 1972, 22.

74. "Kenyan Steeplechase Pioneer Lives Life of Squalor," *Reuters*, February 28, 2004, 19.

75. In Tanser, *More Fire*, 57.

76. Tecla Chemabwai, interview with author, Eldoret, Kenya, January 20, 2010.

77. "A True Heroine on Track and Off," *Daily Nation*, March 21, 1992, 15.

78. "Rose Tata Muya: Seventeen Years as a Hurdler," *True Love*, April 1991, 10–11, 20.

79. "Looking at Women's Problems," *Weekly Review*, May 29, 1987, 71.

80. Tim Alex, "Allocated Funds Lying Idle," *Weekly Review*, September 14, 1990, 30–31.

81. In Tanser, *More Fire*, 68.

82. Regina S. Oboler, *Women, Power, and Economic Change: The Nandi of Kenya* (Stanford: Stanford University Press, 1985), 210, 235. She calculates that 1.3 percent of men's time was spent on these tasks.

83. Henrietta L. Moore, *Space, Text and Gender: An Anthropological Study of the Marakwet of Kenya* (Cambridge: Cambridge University Press, 1986); Bruce Roberts, "Livestock Production, Age and Gender Among the Keiyo of Kenya," *Human Ecology* 24, no. 2 (1996): 215–30.

84. World Bank, *Kenya: The Role of Women in Economic Development: A World Bank Country Study* (Washington, DC: World Bank, 1989), xiii-xiv.

85. P. Ogorno, "Working Woman's Double Shift," *Standard,* March 14, 1989.

86. Mike Boit, "Why Do Kenyan Girls Drop Out?," *Weekly Review*, August 19, 1988, 45.

87. Elias Makori, "Iten Camp Major Boost to Kenyan Women's Talent," *Daily Nation*, November 9, 2000, 49.

88. In Tanser, *More Fire,* 47.

89. Tecla Chemabwai, interview with author, Eldoret, Kenya, January 20, 2010.

90. "Agnes' Determination Pays Off," *Drum* (East African Edition), July 1982, 34. On Rose Nyaguthii, see Ndoo, "Ng'eno's Last Hope Shattered," *Daily Nation*, July 29, 1972, 23.

91. Hezekiah Wepukhulu, "Eyes on Olympics for Mother of Six," *East African Standard,* August 7, 1968, 6.

92. "Chris Sets New Record in 20-Km. Walk," *Daily Nation*, May 20, 1968, 4.

93. "David Kuria Wins Walking Marathon," *Daily Nation*, July 8, 1968, 19.

94. Hezekiah Wepukhulu, "Eyes on Olympics for Mother of Six," *East African Standard,* August 7, 1968, 6.

95. Frank Murphy, *The Silence of Great Distance: Women Running Long* (Kansas City: Windsprint Press, 2000), 225.

96. "Thomson Leaves for Studies," *Daily Nation*, September 20, 1979, 26; "Rose Thomson," Celebrating Wisconsin's Black History, Wisconsin Badgers Legends, University of Wisconsin, https://uwbadgers.com/sports/2015/8/21/GEN_20140101838.aspx.

97. Maureen Otire, "Meet the Running Mother Mrs. Rose Thomson," *Daily Nation*, December 17, 1977, 21. Chepyator-Thomson herself recounted some of these events in Jepkorir Rose Chepyator-Thomson, "African Women Run for Change: Challenges and Achievements in Sports," in *African Women and Globalization: Dawn of the 21ˢᵗ Century*, ed. Jepkorir Rose Chepyator-Thomson (Trenton, NJ: Africa World Press, 2005), 239–58.

98. Maureen Otire, "Meet the Running Mother Mrs. Rose Thomson," *Daily Nation*, December 17, 1977, 21.

99. Ibid.

100. Philip Ndoo, "Not Easy Selecting a Chaperone," *Daily Nation*, April 28, 1978, 35.

101. "Alice, the Policewoman Who's Always on the Run . . . ," *Trust*, September 1976, 14.

102. "Competition Mature in Schools," *Sports Review*, January/February 1983, 17.

103. "Posts' Girls Looks to 1984," *Sportsworld*, July 1980, 6.

104. "Joyce Is All Set for the Games," *True Love*, January 1987, 10–11. See also "East and Central African Championships," GBR Athletics, http://www.gbrathletics.com/ic/ecafc.htm.

105. Colm O'Connell, interview with author, Iten, Kenya, January 15, 2010.

106. In Tanser, *More Fire*, 60; "Tata Qualified for Games," *Nation Sport*, December 9, 1973, 1.

107. "Rose Tata Muya: Seventeen Years as a Hurdler," *True Love*, April 1991, 10–11, 20.

108. Tim Alex, "Seven New Records Set," *Weekly Review*, July 13, 1990, 38.

109. "Rose Tata Muya," 10–11, 20.

110. Mary Chemweno, interview with author, Eldoret, Kenya, January 12, 2010.

111. "Chemweno and Kevin Honoured," *Daily Nation*, March 15, 1978, 30.

112. "Dusseldorf," *Daily Nation*, August 26, 1980, 31.

113. Stephen Ongaro, "Ikhoni Is the Top Sportsman," *Daily Nation*, April 24, 1981, 35.

114. Mary Chemweno, interview with author, Eldoret, Kenya, January 12, 2010.

115. Amrik Singh, "Pair Dominate Track Meet," *Daily Nation*, November 9, 1981, 19; "Kipchoge, Temu to Feature in Nairobi 'Veterans Meet,'" *Daily Nation*, January 21, 1993, 29.

116. D. Agudah, "Corporal Ruth Waithera," *Daily Nation*, December 3, 1977, 28.

117. "Waithera and Tata Set Track Records," *Daily Nation,* April 22, 1979, 30.

118. Ruth Waithera, interview with author, Nairobi, Kenya, February 18, 2011.

119. Ibid.

120. Patricia A. Vertinsky, *The Eternally Wounded Woman: Women, Doctors and Exercise in the Late Nineteenth Century* (Manchester: Manchester University Press, 1990); Kathleen McCrone, *Playing the Game: Sport and the Physical Emancipation of English Women, 1870–1914* (London: Routledge, 1988); Susan Cahn, *Coming on Strong: Gender and Sexuality in Twentieth-Century Women's Sport* (New York: Free Press, 1994); Jennifer Hargreaves, *Sporting Females: Critical Issues in the History and Sociology of Women's Sports*

(London: Routledge, 1994).

121. Ruth Waithera, interview with author, Nairobi, Kenya, February 18, 2011.

122. Ibid.

123. Kenda Mutongi, *Worries of the Heart: Widows, Family, and Community in Kenya* (Chicago: University of Chicago Press, 2007). See also Edwins Laban Moogi Gwako, "Widow Inheritance among the Maragoli of Western Kenya," *Journal of Anthropological Research* 54, no. 2 (1998): 173–98.

124. Ruth Waithera, interview with author, Nairobi, Kenya, February 18, 2011.

125. Ibid.

126. Baker N. Maggwa, Japheth K. Mathi, Susan Mbugua, and David J. Hunter, "Validity of Contraceptive Histories in a Rural Community in Kenya," *International Journal of Epidemiology* 22, no. 4 (1993): 692.

127. Oboler, *Women, Power and Economic Change*, 71.

128. For an elaboration of related ideas, see Derek R. Peterson, *Ethnic Patriotism and the East African Revival: A History of Dissent, c. 1935–1972* (Cambridge: Cambridge University Press, 2012), 1–36.

129. Kanogo, *African Womanhood*, 231. For work on "deviant" women in Africa history, see, for instance, Dorothy L. Hodgson and Sheryl A. McCurdy, eds., *"Wicked" Women and the Reconfiguration of Gender in Africa* (Portsmouth, NH: Heinemann, 2001).

130. Gabrielle Lynch, *I Say to You: Ethnic Politics and the Kalenjin in Kenya* (Chicago: Chicago University Press, 2007); Timothy H. Parsons, *The African Rank and File: Social Implications of Colonial Military Service in the King's African Rifles, 1902–1964* (Portsmouth, UK: Heinemann, 1999). See also Myles Osborne, *Ethnicity and Empire in Kenya: Loyalty and Martial Race among the Kamba, c. 1800 to the Present* (New York: Cambridge University Press, 2014).

131. Ruth Waithera, interview with author, Nairobi, Kenya, February 18, 2011.

132. Ibid.

133. Philip Ndoo, "Corporal Ruth Waithera," *Daily Nation*, December 3, 1977, 28.

134. Ruth Waithera, interview with author, Nairobi, Kenya, February 18, 2011.

135. Peter Moll, "Girl Wonder," *Nation Sport*, June 20, 1971, 22; Peter Moll, "Adala—Running Back to Happiness," *Daily Nation*, June 22, 1972, 23.

136. Philip Ndoo, "Corporal Ruth Waithera," *Daily Nation*, December 3, 1977, 28.

137. Ibid.

138. Harry Werre Silas, "The Year of Farce and Fuss," *Daily Nation*, December 24, 1977, 29.

139. Ruth Waithera, interview with author, Nairobi, Kenya, February 18, 2011.

140. "Athletics Meeting Switched to Nyeri," *Daily Nation*, May 21, 1977, 22; Philip Ndoo, "10

Olympians on Parade at Nyeri Meet Today," *Daily Nation,* May 28, 1977, 23; "Ng'eno Free to Run on One Condition," *Daily Nation*, June 3, 1977, 31.

141. "Singh Says It Was Just Bad Luck," *Daily Nation*, August 20, 1977, 23; J. Mucheru, "Mucheru Wins Top Award," *The Standard*, December 10, 1978, 21.

142. Ruth Waithera, interview with author, Nairobi, Kenya, February 18, 2011.

143. Ibid.

144. Claire C. Robertson, *Trouble Showed the Way: Women, Men, and Trade in the Nairobi Area, 1890–1990* (Bloomington: Indiana University Press, 1997); Kanogo, *African Womanhood*; Luise White, *The Comforts of Home: Prostitution in Colonial Nairobi* (Chicago: University of Chicago Press, 1990); Jane Bujra, "Women 'Entrepreneurs' of Early Nairobi," *Canadian Journal of African Studies* 9, no. 2 (1975): 213–34; Bodil F. Frederiksen, "African Women and their Colonisation of Nairobi: Representations and Realities," *Azania: Archaeological Research in Africa* 36–37, no. 1 (2001): 223–34.

145. Peterson, *Ethnic Patriotism.*

146. Philip Ndoo, "Corporal Ruth Waithera," *Daily Nation*, December 3, 1977, 28.

147. Ibid.

148. Ruth Waithera, interview with author, Nairobi, Kenya, February 18, 2011.

149. Philip Ndoo, "Corporal Ruth Waithera," 28.

150. "The University of Arizona Sports Hall of Fame by Induction Year," Arizona Wildcats, University of Arizona Athletics, https://arizonawildcats.com/sports/2015/9/5/209273862. aspx.

151. Ruth Waithera, interview with author, Nairobi, Kenya, February 18, 2011.

152. Ibid.

153. Francis Noronha, *Kipchoge of Kenya* (Nakuru, Kenya: Elimu Publishers, 1970), 48.

154. "Kenyan Steeplechase Pioneer Lives Life of Squalor," *Reuters*, February 28, 2004, 19.

Chapter 4. The World Beckons: Kenya, Title IX, and the Expansion of Women's Track and Field

1. "A Rising Star Sets Sights on Olympics," *East African Standard*, December 15, 1967, 25. Accounts of her age at the time of 1968 Mexico City Olympics vary from as young as twelve to thirteen or fourteen years old. Chemabwai has also reported that Kenyan officials referred to her age as eighteen so that she could obtain a passport to travel to Mexico. See Pete Herrera, "UNM's Chemabwai Seeks Olympic Gold," *Albuquerque Journal*, June 3, 1982, F8; Thomas Rajula, "Meet the First Female Athlete to Represent Kenya in

Olympics," *Sunday Nation*, April 18, 2021, 6–7; and Tecla Chemabwai, interview with author, Eldoret, Kenya, January 20, 2010.

2. At the final pre-Olympic Kenyan time trials held at an altitude of 8000 feet, Chemabwai won the quarter mile with a time of 55.5, one of her fastest times of the season. Norman da Costa, "Temu Proves Clarke's Time Not Good Enough," September 26, 1968, *Daily Nation*, 23.

3. Oyamo Beauttah, "Tecla Chemabwai: Meet the Pioneer Kenyan Female Olympian, Her Illustrious Career and Her Current Investments," *Who Owns Kenya*, July 9, 2022, https://whownskenya.com/index.php/2022/07/09/tecla-chemabwai-meet-the-pioneer-female-olympian-her-illustrious-career-and-her-current-investments/.

4. In 1976 Kenya was one of twenty-eight nations to withdraw from the Montreal Olympics in protest of New Zealand's continued sporting ties with apartheid South Africa, and in 1980, Kenya supported the United States–led boycott of the Moscow games. See Nicholas Sarantakes, *Dropping the Torch: Jimmy Carter, the Olympic Boycott, and the Cold War* (New York: Cambridge University Press, 2011); and Courtney Mason, "The Bridge to Change: The 1976 Montreal Olympic Games, South African Apartheid Policy, and the Olympic Boycott Paradigm," in *Onward to the Olympics : Historical Perspectives on the Olympic Games*, ed. Gerald P. Schaus and Stephen R. Wenn (Waterloo, Ont.: Wilfrid Laurier University Press, 2007), 283–96.

5. Ruth Waithera competed at 200 and 400 meters, Selina Chirchir at 800 meters, Justina Chepchirchir at 1500 meters, Hellen Kimaiyo at 3000 meters, and Mary Wagaki in the marathon, as indicated in "Kenya," Olympedia, http://www.olympedia.org/countries/KEN. Injuries prevented Elizabeth Chelimo from competing at the 1972 Munich games and kept Lydia Stephens from racing the 200 meters at the 1968 Olympics, though she did compete in the 100 meters. Rose Tata-Muya earned a berth on the 1984 Kenyan Olympic team, and she travelled to Los Angeles, but she was unable to compete in the 400 meters hurdles.

6. Gishinga Njoroge, "A True Heroine on Track and Off," *Daily Nation*, March 21, 1992, 16.

7. In Jaime Schultz, "Going the Distance: The Road to the 1984 Olympic Women's Marathon," *The International Journal of the History of Sport* 32, no. 1 (2015): 76.

8. Scholars contend that one, possibly two, women ran the marathon course unofficially at the 1896 games. See Schultz, "Going the Distance," 73.

9. In Allen Guttmann, *Women's Sports: A History* (New York: Columbia University Press, 1991), 163.

10. In Richard Holt, *Sport and The British: A Modern History* (Oxford: Oxford University Press, 1989), 129–30.

11. Gymnastics was added on a demonstration basis in 1908. Sheila Mitchell, "Women's Participation in the Olympic Games, 1900–1926," *Journal of Sport History* 4, no. 2 (1977): 212, 217, 225. On these early Olympic games, see Mark Dyreson, *Making the American Team: Sport, Culture, and the Olympic Experience* (Urbana: University of Illinois Press, 1998); and on the 1904 games, Mark Dyreson, "The Playing of Progress: American Athletic Nationalism and the St. Louis Olympics of 1904," *Gateway Heritage* 14 (1993), 4–23, and David Lunt and Mark Dyreson, "The 1904 Olympic Games: Triumph or Nadir?," in *The Palgrave Handbook of Olympic Studies*, ed. Stephen Wagg and Helen Lenskyj (London: Palgrave/Macmillan, 2012), 44–59. On the gendered history of figure skating, see Mary Louise Adams, *Artistic Impressions: Figure Skating, Masculinity, and the Limits of Sport* (Toronto: University of Toronto Press, 2011). Sailing at the 1908 London games was not divided by sex, and one woman took part, as noted in Lindsay Parks Pieper, *Sex Testing: Gender Policing in Women's Sports* (Urbana: University of Illinois Press, 2016), 190.

12. Mark Dyreson, "Icons of Liberty or Objects of Desire? American Women Olympians and the Politics of Consumption," *Journal of Contemporary History* 38, no. 3 (2003): 435–60; Linda Borish, "'The Cradle of American Champions, Women Champions . . . Swim Champions': Charlotte Epstein, Gender and Jewish Identity, and the Physical Emancipation of Women in Aquatic Sports," *The International Journal of the History of Sport* 21, no. 2 (2004): 197–235; Lisa Bier, *Fighting the Current: The Rise of American Women's Swimming, 1870–1926* (Jefferson, NC: McFarland & Company, 2011).

13. Jörg Krieger, Michele Krech, and Lindsay Parks Pieper, "'Our Sport': The Fight for Control of Women's International Athletics," *The International Journal of the History of Sport* 37, no. 5–6 (2020): 451.

14. Bruce Kidd, "Another World Is Possible': Recapturing Alternative Olympic Histories, Imagining Different Games," *Sport in Society* 16 no. 4 (2013): 503–14.

15. Mary H. Leigh and Thérèse M. Bonin, "The Pioneering Role of Madame Alice Milliat and the FSFI in Establishing International Trade and Field Competition for Women," *Journal of Sport History* 4, no. 1 (1977): 72–83; Thierry Terret, "From Alice Milliat to Marie-Thérèse Eyquem: Revisiting Women's Sport in France (1920s–1960s)," *The International Journal of the History of Sport* 27, no. 7 (2010): 1154–72.

16. Leigh and Bonin, "Pioneering Role of Madame Alice," 78.

17. On the 1928 Amsterdam 800-meters race, see Colleen English, "'Beyond Women's Powers of Endurance': The 1928 800-Meter and Women's Olympic Track and Field in the Context of the United States," *Sport History Review* 50, no. 2 (2019): 187–204; Dyreson, "Icons of Liberty," 455–56; Guttmann, *Women's Sports*, 169; and Pieper, *Sex Testing*, 18.

18. Helen Lenskyj, *Out of Bounds: Women, Sport and Sexuality* (Toronto: Women's Press,

1986), 17–54; Patricia A. Vertinsky, *The Eternally Wounded Woman: Woman, Doctors, and Exercise in the Late Nineteenth Century* (Manchester: Manchester University Press, 1990); Susan K. Cahn, *Coming on Strong: Gender and Sexuality in Twentieth-Century Women's Sport* (New York: Free Press, 1994), 7–30; Jennifer Hargreaves, *Sporting Females: Critical Issues in the History and Sociology of Women's Sports* (London: Routledge, 1994), 42–111; Collette Dowling, *The Frailty Myth: Women Approaching Physical Equality* (New York: Random House, 2000).

19. Guttmann, *Women's Sports*, 154–55.

20. In Lynne Robinson, "'Tripping Daintily into the Arena': A Social History of English Women's Athletics 1921–1960" (PhD diss., University of Warwick, 1996), 215.

21. Cahn, *Coming on Strong*, 83–109, 140–84; Lenskyj, *Out of Bounds*, 95–108, 127–38; Mary Jo Festle, *Playing Nice: Politics and Apologies in Women's Sports* (New York: Columbia University Press, 1996), 75–104; Martha H. Verbrugge, *Active Bodies: A History of Women's Physical Education in Twentieth-Century America* (New York: Oxford University Press, 2012), 102–52; Schultz, *Qualifying Times*, 73–102.

22. Jaime Schultz, *Women's Sports: What Everyone Needs to Know* (Oxford: Oxford University Press, 2018), 20.

23. Cahn, *Coming on Strong*, 110–12, 131–32; Cat M. Ariail, *Passing the Baton: Black Women Track Stars and American Identity* (Urbana: University of Illinois Press, 2020), 13.

24. Frank Murphy, *The Silence of Great Distance: Women Running Long* (Kansas City: Windsprint Press, 2000), 44–46.

25. Cahn, *Coming on Strong*, 246.

26. Guttmann, *Women's Sports*, 204.

27. David Maraniss, *Rome 1960: The Olympics that Changed the World* (New York: Simon & Schuster, 2008).

28. In Schultz, "Going the Distance," 73–74.

29. Ibid., 74.

30. For her own account of the race, see Kathrine Switzer, *Marathon Woman: Running the Race to Revolutionize Women's Sports* (New York: Carroll & Graf, 2007). See also Laura Chase, "Beyond Boston and Kathrine Switzer: Women's Participation in Distance Running," in *Endurance Running: A Socio-Cultural Examination*, ed. William Bridel, Pirkko Markula, and Jim Denison (London: Routledge, 2016), 61–75. On American women's long-distance running of this era, see Jaime Schultz, "Breaking into the Marathon: Women's Distance Running as Political Activism," *Frontiers: A Journal of Women Studies* 40, no. 2 (2019): 1–26.

31. Schultz, "Going the Distance," 74; Jacqueline Hansen, "The Women's Marathon

Movement," *Marathon & Beyond* 16, no. 1 (January/February 2012): 1–2.

32. Christopher Merrett, "Race, Gender and Political Dissent in the Comrades Marathon, 1921–1981," *South African Historical Journal* 59, no. 1 (2007): 251–54. See also Christopher Merrett, "Perpetual Outsiders: Women in Athletics and Road Running in South Africa," in *Routledge Handbook of Sport, Gender and Sexuality*, ed. Jennifer Hargreaves and Eric Anderson (London: Routledge, 2014), 139–48.

33. "The World Oldest Woman Marathon Bräunlingen," AIMS—Association of International Marathons and Road Races, http://aimsworldrunning.org/documents/2012_congress/2012.5_michael-schwar_schwarzwald-marathon.pdf.

34. On the 1970s running boom, see Pamela Cooper, "The 'Visible Hand' on the Footrace: Fred Lebow and the Marketing of the Marathon," *Journal of Sport History* 19, no. 3 (1992): 244–56; Ron Rubin, *Anything for a T-Shirt: Fred Lebow and the New York City Marathon, the World's Greatest Footrace* (Syracuse, NY: Syracuse University Press, 2004); Darcy C. Plymire, "Positive Addiction: Running and Human Potential in the 1970s," *Journal of Sport History* 31, no. 3 (2004): 297–315; Aaron L. Haberman, "Thousands of Solitary Runners Come Together: Individualism and Communitarianism in the 1970s Running Boom," *Journal of Sport History* 44, no. 1 (2017): 35–49; Aaron L. Haberman, "Escape & Pursuit: Contrasting Visions of the 1970s Long-Distance Running Boom in American Popular Culture," *Sport History Review* 48, no. 1 (2017): 1–17; Roger Robinson, *When Running Made History* (Syracuse, NY: Syracuse University Press, 2018); Aaron L. Haberman, "'We're All Professionals Now': Frank Shorter, Deregulation, and the Battle to End 'Shamateurism,' in the 1970s," *The International Journal of the History of Sport* 36, no. 15–16 (2019): 1414–32; Jörg Krieger and April Henning, "Who Governs a Movement? The IAAF and Road-Running: Historical and Contemporary Considerations," *Journal of Sport History* 47, no. 1 (2020): 59–75.

35. Schultz, "Going the Distance," 78.

36. Amanda Edwards, "Why Sport? The Development of Sport as a Policy Issue in Title IX of the Education Amendments of 1972," *Journal of Policy History* 22, no. 3 (2010): 306.

37. Susan Ware, *Game, Set Match: Billie Jean King and the Revolution in Women's Sports* (Chapel Hill: University of North Carolina Press, 2011), 9.

38. On second wave feminism, see Ruth Rosen, *The World Split Open: How the Modern Women's Movement Changed America* (New York: Viking, 2000); Estelle Freedman, *No Turning Back: The History of Feminism and the Future of Women* (New York: Ballantine, 2002); Sara M. Evans, *Tidal Wave: How Women Changed America at Century's End* (New York: Free Press, 2003); Benita Roth, *Separate Roads to Feminism: Black, Chicana, and White Feminist Movements in America's Second Wave* (Cambridge: Cambridge University

Press, 2004); Stephanie Gilmore, ed., *Feminist Coalitions: Historical Perspectives on Second-Wave Feminism in the United States* (Urbana: University of Illinois Press, 2008); Gail Collins, *When Everything Changed: The Amazing Journey of American Women from 1960 to the Present* (New York: Little, Brown and Company, 2009); and Carol Giardina, *Freedom for Women: Forging the Women's Liberation Movement, 1953–1970* (Gainesville: University Press of Florida, 2010).

39. Quoted in Edwards, "Why Sport," 304.

40. Cahn, *Coming on Strong*, 252; Ware, *Game, Set Match*; Selena Roberts, *A Necessary Spectacle: Billie Jean King, Bobby Riggs, and the Tennis Match that Leveled the Game* (New York: Crown Publishers, 2005); and Jaime Schultz, "The Physical Activism of Billie Jean King," in *Myths and Milestones in the History of Sport*, ed. Stephen Wagg (Palgrave Macmillan: London, 2011), 203–23. For her own writing, see Billie Jean King with Frank Deford, *Billie Jean* (New York: Viking Press, 1982); Billie Jean King with Cynthia Starr, *We Have Come a Long Way: The Story of Women's Tennis* (New York: Regina Ryan, 1988); and Billie Jean King with Christine Brennan, *Pressure Is a Privilege: Lessons I've Learned from Life and the Battle of the Sexes* (New York: LifeTime Media, 2008).

41. Joseph Turrini, "'It Was Communism Versus the Free World': The USA-USSR Dual Track Meet Series and the Development of Track and Field in the United States, 1958–1985," *Journal of Sport History* 28, no. 3 (2001): 427–71.

42. On Soviet promotion of women's athletics, see Pieper, *Sex Testing*, 118–19; and Murphy, *Silence of Great Distance*, 104–5.

43. John F. Kennedy, "The Soft American," *Sports Illustrated*, December 26, 1960, 15–16; John F. Kennedy, "The Vigor We Need," *Sports Illustrated*, July 16, 1962, 12–15. On the American Cold War campaign for physical fitness, see Robert L. Griswold, "The 'Flabby American,' the Body and the Cold War," in *A Shared Experience: Men, Women and the History of Gender*, ed. Laura McCall and Donald Yacovone (New York: New York University Press, 1998), 323–47.

44. Murphy, *Silence of Great Distance*, 101 to 103 on women's track and field at the Munich Olympic games, 104 to 129 for women's middle distance running in the Soviet Union from the early 1970s to the mid-1980s, and 129 to 130 on women and doping in track and field history. For other accounts of the systematic regimes of banned performance enhancing substances later discovered, see John Hoberman, *Testosterone Dreams: Rejuvenation, Aphrodisia, Doping* (Berkeley: University of California Press, 2005); Paul Dimeo, *A History of Drug Use in Sport 1876–1976: Beyond Good and Evil* (New York: Routledge, 2007); and Thomas M. Hunt, *Drug Games: The International Olympic Committee and the Politics of Doping, 1960–2008* (Austin: University of Texas Press, 2011).

45. In Murphy, *Silence of Great Distance*, 149. See also Pieper, *Sex Testing*, 109–10, 127–29.

46. Cahn, *Coming on Strong*, 112. For the most comprehensive historical account of Black American track women, see Ariail, *Passing the Baton*. On Wilma Rudolph's life and career, see Maureen M. Smith, *Wilma Rudolph: A Biography* (Westport, CT: Greenwood Press, 2006); Wayne Wilson, "Wilma Rudolph: The Making of an Olympic Icon," in *Out of the Shadows: A Biographical History of African American Athletes*, ed. David K. Wiggins (Fayetteville: University of Arkansas Press, 2006), 207–22; Aram Goudsouzian, "Wilma Rudolph (1940–1994): Running for Freedom," in *Tennessee Women: Their Lives and Times*, ed. Sarah Wilkerson Freeman and Beverly Greene Bond (Athens: University of Georgia Press, 2009), 305–32; Jennifer H. Lansbury, *Spectacular Leap: Black Women Athletes in Twentieth-Century America* (Fayetteville: University of Arkansas Press, 2014), 110–34; Rita Liberti and Maureen M. Smith, *(Re)presenting Wilma Rudolph* (Syracuse: Syracuse University Press, 2015); Cat M. Ariail, "'One of the Greatest Ambassadors that the United States Has Ever Sent Abroad': Wilma Rudolph, American Athletic Icon for the Cold War and Civil Rights Movement," in *Defending the American Way of Life: Sport, Politics, and the Cold War*, ed. Toby C. Rider and Kevin B. Witherspoon (Fayetteville: University of Arkansas Press, 2018), 141–54. On Wyomia Tyus, see Lansbury, *Spectacular Leap*, 135–62; Wyomia Tyus and Elizabeth Terzakis, *Tigerbelle: The Wyomia Tyus Story* (Brooklyn, NY: Akashic Books, 2018); and Rita Liberti and Mary G. McDonald, "Back on Track: Wyomia Tyus, Breaking Historical Silences, and the Sporting Activist Legacies of 1968," *The International Journal of the History of Sport* 36, no. 9–10 (2019): 796–811. See also Cindy H. Gissendanner, "African American Women Olympians: The Impact of Race, Gender, and Class Ideologies, 1932–1968," *Research Quarterly for Exercise and Sport* 67, no. 2 (1996): 172–82; and Cahn, *Coming on Strong*, 110–39.

47. In postponing its decision about the women's marathon, the IOC invoked an often-ignored rule that at least twenty-five countries should practice a sport before including it on the program, while the Los Angeles Olympic Organizing Committee argued that adding the women's marathon be too costly. Schultz, "Going the Distance," 81–82.

48. Ibid., 83.

49. The women's 3000-meters steeplechase was not included until the 2008 Beijing Olympics, marking the first time in more than one hundred years of Olympic history that women and men competed in the same events on the track. On the roads, however, men continued to contest the 50-kilometer race walk, an event without female equivalent. To bring the programs fully into alignment, the IOC declared its intention to replace the 50-kilometer race with a mixed-team racewalking event at the 2024 games. See Ken Belson, "50-kilometer Racewalking Strides off the Olympic Stage," *New York Times*, August

5, 2021, https://www.nytimes.com/2021/08/05/sports/olympics/racewalking-olympics.
html.

50. A. Parker, "All Roads Lead to Afraha Stadium," *Daily Nation*, June 19, 1981, 31; Johnny Pewa, "Two Records Tumble," *Daily Nation*, May 3, 1981, 25.

51. In Megan Chawansky, "Getting the Girl: Female Athletes' Narratives of the Recruiting Process" (PhD diss., Ohio State University, 2008), 22.

52. In Cahn, *Coming on Strong,* 250.

53. On Title IX, see Linda Jean Carpenter and R. Vivian Acosta, *Title IX* (Champaign, IL: Human Kinetics, 2005); Welch Suggs, *A Place on the Team: The Triumph and Tragedy of Title IX* (Princeton: Princeton University Press, 2005); Nancy Hogshead-Makar and Andrew Zimbalist, eds., *Equal Play: Title IX and Social Change* (Philadelphia: Temple University Press, 2007); Mary Jo. Festle, *Playing Nice: Politics and Apologies in Women's Sports* (New York: Columbia University Press, 1996), 105–290; Sarah K. Fields, *Female Gladiators: Gender, Law, and Contact Sport in America* (Urbana: University of Illinois Press, 2005); Ying Wushanley, *Playing Nice and Losing: The Struggle for Control of Women's Intercollegiate Athletics, 1960–2000* (Syracuse: Syracuse University Press, 2004), 47–162; Guttmann, *Women's Sports*, 207–66; and Cahn, *Coming on Strong*, 254–79.

54. Nancy Hogshead-Makar and Andrew Zimbalist, "Staking a Claim: The First Decade: Introduction," in *Equal Play: Title IX and Social Change*, ed. Nancy Hogshead-Makar and Andrew Zimbalist (Philadelphia: Temple University Press, 2007), 50.

55. For these and other statistics on women's participation, see Carpenter and Acosta, *Title IX*, 168–69; and Cahn, *Coming on Strong*, 246, 259.

56. "Title XI Fact Sheet: The Battle for Gender Equity in Athletics in Colleges and Universities," National Women's Law Center, http://www.nwlc.org/sites/default/files/pdfs/battle_for_gender_equity_in_college_athletics.pdf; Beau Dure, "50 Years of Title IX: The US Law that Attempted to Make Sports Equal," *The Guardian*, June 23, 2022, https://www.theguardian.com/sport/2022/jun/23/50-years-of-title-ix-the-us-law-that-attempted-to-make-sports-equal.

57. Victoria Jackson, "Title IX and the Big Time: Women's Intercollegiate Athletics at the University of North Carolina at Chapel Hill, 1950–1992" (PhD diss., Arizona State University, 2015), 53.

58. Catharine R. Stimpson, "Dereliction, Due Process, and Decorum: The Crises of Title IX," *Signs* 47, no. 2 (2022): 265.

59. On the incremental progression of Title IX through Congress and the executive branch and the regulatory challenges it faced, see Andrew Fishel and Janice Pottker, *National Politics and Sex Discrimination in Education* (Lexington, MA: Lexington Books, 1977); and

Deborah L. Brake, *Getting in the Game: Title IX and the Women's Sports Revolution* (New York: New York University Press, 2010).

60. Louise Mead Tricard, *American Women's Track and Field, 1981–2000: A History* (Jefferson, NC: McFarland & Company, 2008), 107. Ohio State University had been an early leader in women's intercollegiate athletics when it organized the inaugural women's golf national championships in 1941. See Cahn, *Coming on Strong*, 248; and Ronald A. Smith, *The Myth of the Amateur: A History of College Athletic Scholarships* (Austin: University of Texas Press, 2021), 160–62.

61. Murphy, *Silence of Great Distance*, 228.

62. Ibid.; Cahn, *Coming on Strong*, 256–57.

63. Its full elaboration in the NCAA rules appeared as bylaw 4-1-(f)-(2). See John Manners, "Foreign Invasion," *Sports Illustrated*, June 24, 1974, 35.

64. J. Conrad, "Coaches Bemoan Foreign Flood," *Eugene Register-Guard*, June 12, 1974, 9.

65. John Manners, "African Recruiting Boom," in *The African Running Revolution*, ed. Dave Prokop (Mountain View, CA: World Publications, 1975), 6.

66. John Bale, *The Brawn Drain: Foreign Student-Athletes in American Universities* (Urbana: University of Illinois Press, 1991), 79. For other accounts of Kenyan athletes competing for US universities, see John Bale and Joe Sang, *Kenyan Running: Kenyan Running (Movement Culture, Geography, and Global Change* (London: Frank Cass, 1996), 122–26; and Jenny Lee and Thomas Opia, "Coming to America: Challenges and Difficulties Faced by African Student Athletes," *Sport, Education and Society* 16, no. 5 (2011): 629–44. On the international movement of Kenyan athletes between 1998 and 2007, see Wycliffe W. Simiyu Njororai, "Global Inequality and Athlete Labour Migration from Kenya," *Leisure/Loisir* 34, no. 4 (2010): 443–61.

67. "Track Is Main Attraction: Foreign College Athletics Becoming More Common," *New York Times*, March 16, 1977, 7B.

68. Gail Rosemblum, "NCAA Ruling to Bring in Women Opens Up a Recruiting Controversy," *Albuquerque Journal*, February 15, 1981, F1.

69. Pat Kailer, "Women's Intercollegiate Athletics Launched on New Program at UNM," *Albuquerque Journal*, September 9, 1973, A21.

70. Manners, "African Recruiting Boom," 64. The first Kenyan athlete to compete for an American university was Stephen Makora in the early 1960s, although he came not on a sport scholarship but through a fellowship to study agricultural economics at Cornell University. The Kenyan press acclaimed his achievements, noting that although in the United States he was known as Stephen Machooka, at home he used the surname Makora. See "Kisii Athlete Goes West and Makes Good," *East African Standard*, September

9, 1961, 19.

71. Manners, "African Recruiting Boom," 64.

72. Bale and Sang, *Kenyan Running*, 125.

73. Walter Abmayr, *Track and Field Best Performances, 1982* (Nairobi: ATFS, 1983).

74. On Whitfield's life and career, see Kevin B. Witherspoon, "'An Outstanding Representative of America': Mal Whitfield and America's Black Sports Ambassadors in Africa," in *Defending the American Way of Life: Sport, Culture, and the Cold War*, ed. Toby C. Rider and Kevin B. Witherspoon (Fayetteville: University of Arkansas Press, 2018), 129–40. On his role in connecting athletes with Washington State, see Howard F. Stidwill, "Motives Toward Track and Field Competition of Foreign and Domestic Grant-in-Aid Student-Athletes in NCAA Division I Colleges and Universities" (PhD diss., Oregon State University, 1984), 21.

75. Norman Da Costa, "US Coaches to Put Foot Down on African Athletes," *Daily Nation*, December 19, 1973, 29; "Coaches Poll Shows Support: NCAA to Study Possible Ban on Foreign Track, Field Stars," *The Observer*, June 8, 1974, B7; John Manners, "Foreign Invasion," *Sports Illustrated*, June 24, 1974, 35.

76. Gordon Monson, "Track," *Los Angeles Times*, May 24, 1986, 21. See also "Last Call for 31-Year-Old," *Sports Illustrated*, July 28, 1980, 7. For an examination of an extraordinary Kenyan athlete who navigated these dynamics, see Michelle M. Sikes, "'Rebel' on the Run: Kenyan Gambles on Intercollegiate Athletics, Apartheid Sport, and US Road Racing of the 1980s—The Case of Samson Obwocha," *The International Journal of the History of Sport* 39, no. 8–9 (2022): 959–86.

77. In Manners, "African Recruiting Boom," 69.

78. In Stidwill, "Motives Toward Track and Field Competition," 32.

79. Ibid.

80. Bale, *Brawn Drain*, 90.

81. "The Way It Was," *South End Review* (Chicago), January 2, 1975, 6. See also "Chemabwai for States' University," *Daily Nation*, April 28, 1973, 22; and "Track," *Chicago Tribune*, February 26, 1974, sec. 3, pg. 3.

82. Thomas Rajula, "Meet the First Female Athlete to Represent Kenya in Olympics," *Sunday Nation*, April 18, 2021, 6. Similar recollections were shared in an interview with the author. Tecla Chembawai, interview with author, Eldoret, Kenya, January 20, 2010.

83. "Naftali Temu Shares Glory with Mecser," *East African Standard,* September 4, 1967, 10; "Keino Astonishes the Experts," *East African Standard*, September 11, 1967, 10; "Schools' Meet Will Wind up 1967 Season," *East African Standard*, September 13, 1967, 16.

84. Thomas Rajula, "Meet the First Female Athlete to Represent Kenya in Olympics," *Sunday*

Nation, April 18, 2021, 6.

85. Ibid.

86. "Track and Field," *The Bangor Daily News* (Bangor, Maine), November 19, 1973, 26.

87. Tecla Chemabwai, interview with author, Eldoret, Kenya, January 20, 2010.

88. Ibid.

89. Philip Ndoo, "Tecla Chemabwai: The Kenya Star who Plans to Keep on Running, Coaching," *Daily Nation*, December 10, 1977, 25. See also "Chemabwai for States' University," *Daily Nation*, April 28, 1973, 22.

90. Tecla Chemabwai, interview with author, Eldoret, Kenya, January 20, 2010.

91. Rick Wright, "Estes Was Linchpin in UNM's Reach for Sports Equality," *Albuquerque Journal*, June 23, 2022, https://www.abqjournal.com/2510873/estes-was-linchpin-in-unms-reach-for-sports-equality.html.

92. Philip Ndoo, "Tecla Chemabwai: The Kenya Star who Plans to Keep on Running, Coaching," *Daily Nation*, December 10, 1977, 25.

93. University of New Mexico Board of Regents, "University of New Mexico Board of Regents Minutes for May 18, 1980," https://digitalrepository.unm.edu/bor_minutes/878.

94. Tecla Chemabwai, interview with author, Eldoret, Kenya, January 20, 2010; Thomas Rajula, "Meet the First Female Athlete to Represent Kenya in Olympics," *Sunday Nation*, April 18, 2021, 7.

95. W. A. Walei, "Tata Looks Back in Wonder," *The Standard*, March 7, 1992, 22.

96. Barrack Otieno, "K.A.A.A. Calendar of Events," *The Standard*, January 15, 1980, 16.

97. Joshua Okuthe, "Brooke Bond Pour 60,000 into Kenya AAA Coffers," *Daily Nation*, January 15, 1976, 22.

98. 1959 Annual Report Elgeyo-Marakwet, KNA DC/ELG/1/7.

99. Joshua Okuthe, "Kisii Meeting a Disappointment," *Daily Nation*, October 8, 1973, 22.

100. "Kisii Athletics Meet Switched to Kisumu," *Daily Nation*, February 13, 1976, 31.

101. "Money Pinch Delays Kericho Track Renovation," *Daily Nation*, March 31, 1976, 26; "Kericho Meet to be Held on Grass Track," *Daily Nation*, April 7, 1976, 27.

102. Joshua Okuthe, "High Performances Expected at Kapsabet," *Daily Nation*, April 24, 1976, 18; "Rono Stars at Kapsabet," *Daily Nation*, April 26, 1976, 15. At that meet the following year, the press warned that the Kapsabet meet had "hit a snag! Sections of the stadium walls have collapsed as a result of rains in the area!" Joshua Okuthe, "Storms Could Hit Tea Run Meet," *Daily Nation*, February 16, 1977, 27.

103. Roy Gachugi, "Athletes Thrill Capacity Crowd," *Daily Nation*, May 24, 1980, 20.

104. "Two Records Fall as 10 Qualify for Club Games," *Daily Nation*, April 10, 1978, 18.

105. Walter Abmayr, *Track and Field Best Performances: Kenya 1982* (Nairobi: ATFS

publication, 1983), 3.

106. Bruce Tulloh, "Second to None in Natural Ability . . . ," *Daily Nation*, June 14, 1973, 22.

107. "Courage not Competition," *Sunday Nation*, August 24, 1969, 43.

108. Ibid.

109. Peter Moll, "Munich Girls," *Daily Nation*, August 11, 1971.

110. Chege Kariuki, "Women Athletes," *Standard*, April 29, 1989, 13.

111. "Yet Another Kenyan Hits Olympic Mark," *Daily Nation*, April 27, 1976, 19.

112. "Kilili Morris Complete Double at Nairobi Meeting," *Daily Nation*, May 17, 1976, 15.

113. Joshua Okuthe, "More Overseas Meets for Kenya's Top Athletes," *Daily Nation*, May 5, 1976, 31; "Paul Mose Storms Back to Form," *Daily Nation*, May 10, 1976, 14.

114. Johnny Pewa, "Soccer Fans Turn out to Give Athletes Morale," *Daily Nation*, August 3, 1985, 21.

Chapter 5. I Have a Whole Battalion that Depends on Me: Professionals, Patrons, and Pioneers of Women's Running in Kenya

1. Jere Longman, "A Runner's Victory Is Cultural as Well," *New York Times*, April 16, 1995, 8. Estimates at the time equated her prize money winnings to KShs 2.5 million.

2. On amateurism in track and field, see Joseph Turrini, *The End of Amateurism in American Track and Field* (Urbana: University of Illinois Press, 2010); Austin Duckworth, Thomas M. Hunt, and Jan Todd, "Cold Hard Cash: Commercialization, Politics, and Amateurism in United States Track and Field," *Sport in History* 38, no. 2 (2018): 145–63; Aaron Haberman, "'We're All Professionals Now': Frank Shorter, Deregulation, and the Battle to End 'Shamateurism,' in the 1970s," *The International Journal of the History of Sport* 36, no. 15–16 (2019): 1414–32; April Henning and Jörg Krieger, "Dropping the Amateur: The International Association of Athletics Federations and the Turn Towards Professionalism," *Sport History Review* 51, no. 1 (2020): 64–83; Jörg Krieger, *Power and Politics in World Athletics: A Critical History* (London: Routledge, 2021); Michelle M. Sikes and Jacob J. Fredericks, "'It's a Policy Matter, Not a Racial Matter': Athlete Activism and Symbiotic Struggles against Apartheid in US Track and Field of the Early 1970s," *The International Journal of the History of Sport* 39, no. 8–9 (2022): 938–58; and Michelle M. Sikes, A 'Rebel' on the Run: Kenyan Gambles on Intercollegiate Athletics, Apartheid Sport, and US Road Racing of the 1980s—The Case of Samson Obwocha," *The International Journal of the History of Sport* 39, no. 8–9 (2022): 959–86.

3. John Lonsdale, "Moral Ethnicity and Political Tribalism," in *Inventions and Boundaries:*

Historical and Anthropological Approaches to the Study of Ethnicity and Nationalism, ed. Preben Kaarsholm and Jan Hultin (Denmark: Institute for Development Studies, Roskilde University, 1994), 131–50. See also Jan Bender Shetler, *Claiming Civic Virtue Gendered Network Memory in the Mara Region, Tanzania* (Madison: University of Wisconsin Press, 2019).

4. Walter Abmayr, *Africa Track and Field: 4th All-Africa-Games Nairobi/Kenya 1987* (Nairobi: ATFS, 1987), 35.

5. "Athletics: Starring Roles for Ondiek, Kitur," *Weekly Review*, May 6, 1988, 37.

6. Paul Muhoho, "Field Day for Viewers," *Daily Nation*, August 13, 1987, 22.

7. "The 4th All-Africa Games: Athletics: Alight with Power and Drama: Kenyans' Performance in Track Events Lives up to Old Expectations," *Weekly Review*, August 14, 1987, 34–36.

8. Tom Mshindi, "Food Prices Double," *Daily Nation*, August 13, 1987, 5.

9. "In Mombasa It Was All Cheers for Kenya," *Daily Nation*, August 13, 1987, 5; Paul Muhoho, "Field Day for TV Viewers," *Daily Nation*, August 13, 1987, 22.

10. Peter Shard, "Track Stars, Boxers, and Gor Mahia Keep Kenya in Limelight," *Daily Nation*, December 28, 1987, 22; Leah Malot, interview with author, Eldoret, Kenya, January 24, 2011.

11. "Kenya Continues to Pile Up Gold Medals," *Daily Nation*, August 10, 1987, 1.

12. Ochieng' Angela, "Kenya Increases her Medal Tally," *Daily Nation*, August 12, 1987, 23.

13. Hezekiah Wepukhulu, "Medal Prospects Look Good for 'Super Team,'" *Daily Nation*, August 20, 1988, 13.

14. "Women Runners Still Get a Raw KAAA Deal," *Daily Nation*, August 16, 1993, 15.

15. John Nene, "Kenyans Set to Lead Africa's Onslaught," *Daily Nation*, March 17, 1997, 13.

16. Quoted in Martin Polley, "'The Amateur Rules': Amateurism and Professionalism in Post-War British Athletics," in *Amateurs and Professionals in Post-war British Sport*, ed. Adrian Smith and Dilwyn Porter (London: Frank Cass, 2000), 87. See also Theresa Walton, "Steve Prefontaine: From Rebel with a Cause to Hero with a Swoosh," *Sociology of Sport Journal* 21, no. 1 (2004): 61–83; and Krieger, *Power and Politics in World Athletics*, 121.

17. See Turrini, *The End of Amateurism*, on the US context and Krieger, *Power and Politics in World Athletics*, especially chapter 9 on how the IAAF replaced amateurism with professionalism between 1981 and 2000.

18. Krieger, *Power and Politics in World Athletics*, 163–64; John Velzian, "Editorial Obituary—Primo Nebiolo," *IAAF Bulletin*, Special Issue, December (Nairobi: Regional Development Centre, 1999), 2.

19. Bernd Frick, Joachim Prinz, and Frank Tolsdorf, "*Citius, Altius, Fortius*: The Production of

World Records in the Running and Technical Disciplines in Track and Field," in *Handbook on the Economics of Sport*, ed. Wladimir Andreff and Stefan Szymanski (Cheltenham, UK: Edward Elgar, 2006), 351.

20. "Nebiolo Given a Fifth Term," *The Standard*, August 4, 1995, 29.

21. Omolo Okoth, "IAAF to Discuss Another Circuit," *The Standard*, November 11, 1993, 30.

22. Ibid.

23. "Richest Year of Mobil Grand Prix," *The Standard*, November 13, 1993, 21.

24. Joe Oloo, "Reebok to Sponsor," *The Standard*, February 13, 1993, 20.

25. Chege Kariuki, "Foreigners for Ngong," *The Standard*, February 26, 1993, 42.

26. "Women Runners Still Get a Raw KAAA Deal," *Daily Nation*, August 16, 1993, 15; Peter Njenga, "Ngotho Smashes Seven-year Record," *Daily Nation*, July 11, 1991, 25.

27. Sulubu Tuva, "Trials a Forum," *The Standard*, July 20, 1993, 27.

28. Frick et al., "Citius, Altius, Fortius," 351.

29. Ibid.

30. Krieger, *Power and Politics in World Athletics*, 166.

31. Dann O'Werre, "Money Power," *The Standard*, July 14, 1997, 31; Omolo Okoth, "Rewarding Performers," *The Standard*, March 31, 1997, 29.

32. "Ondieki's Final Kick Best in the World," *The Standard*, July 17, 1993, 21.

33. Reuters, "IAAF Chief Rules," *The Standard*, January 24, 1993, 21.

34. Omolo Okoth, "Rewarding," 29; "Boost for the KAAA," *The Standard*, August 28, 1993, 20.

35. Omolo Okoth, "Rewarding Performers," *The Standard*, March 31, 1997, 29.

36. "Cash Award to Replace Car," *The Standard*, January 14, 1997, 30.

37. Elias Makori, "NOCK Opt for Nike Deal," *The Standard*, January 7, 1993, 27.

38. Joe Oloo, "Reebok to Sponsor," *The Standard*, February 13, 1993, 20.

39. Elias Makori, "NOCK Opt for Nike Deal," *The Standard*, January 7, 1993, 27.

40. Ibid.

41. Joe Oloo, "Boost for the KAAA But . . . ," *The Standard*, August 28, 1993, 20.

42. Ochieng Angela, "KAAA Seek Shs 17.1m," *The Standard*, December 20, 1993, 23.

43. Oloo, "Boost for the KAAΛ," 20.

44. Peter Njenga, "Kenyan Athletes off to Cape Town Today," *Daily Nation*, March 21, 1996, 38; "New Man Takes over from Muchoki as Coach," *Daily Nation*, March 13, 1996, 39.

45. Eric Odanga, "Little Known Runner Becomes a Heroine," *Daily Nation*, July 30, 1996, 39.

46. "Konga's Success Hailed," *Daily Nation*, July 30, 1996, 39.

47. "Prize Money Distributions by Year" (2009), Association of Road Racing Statisticians, https://www.arrs.run/PM_ByYr.htm.

48. "Track & Field News Rankings," Track and Field News, www.trackandfieldnews.com/

rankings.

49. "Prize Money Distributions by Year (2013)," Association of Road Racing Statisticians, https://www.arrs.run/PM_ByYr.htm.

50. "Tegla Loroupe—Princess of Perkau," *The Standard*, November 20, 2005.

51. D. Macharia, "Kenyan Athletics Starts Now," *Daily Nation*, April 21, 2007, 24.

52. In E. Cheserek, "Why Iten Camps Are Loved by Many Athletes," *The Standard*, January 5, 2011, 19.

53. Martin Keino, interview with author, Eldoret, Kenya, January 18, 2011.

54. "Mozambique Has a Star to Count On," *The Standard*, June 19, 1993, 21.

55. Tuva, "Star-studded Team," 3.

56. Omolo Okoth, "Sporting Giant," *The Standard*, December 12, 1993, XV.

57. Charles Owino, "Where Are Women in Kenya?," *The Standard*, August 21, 1995, 4.

58. "Athlete Profile: Tegla Loroupe," World Athletics, https://worldathletics.org/athletes/kenya/tegla-loroupe-14289238.

59. "Loroupe Victorious at IAAF/VSZ World Half Marathon Championships, while Romania Takes Team Title," IAAF report, World Athletics, October 4, 1997, https://worldathletics.org/news/report/loroupe-ken-victorious-in-iaafvsz-world-half.

60. Quoted in "Anthem Moves Athlete to Tears," *Daily Nation*, April 19, 2000, 39. See also "Loroupe Beats Heat to Win New York Mini-Marathon," *Daily Nation*, June 12, 2000, 32; Jere Longman, "82 Pounds of Steel; Girded by Past Struggles, Loroupe Runs for Kenyan Gold," *New York Times*, August 13, 2000, 11.

61. Liz Gitonga, "On the Mark for Community," *Sunday Nation*, July 18, 2004, 3; Peter Njenga, "Among the Top in Kenya's Roll of World Conquerors," *Sunday Nation*, July 18, 2004, 3.

62. Jeffrey Gettleman, "A Kenyan Runner Seeks Peace for her Corner of the World," *New York Times*, November 18, 2006, A4.

63. Gitonga, "On the Mark for Community," 3.

64. Jere Longman, "82 Pounds of Steel," 11; Lori Shontz, "The Pioneers Who Led the Way," *Post-Gazette* (Pittsburgh), May 6, 2002, https://old.post-gazette.com/sports/other/20020506kenya0506p2.asp.

65. Gettleman, "A Kenyan Runner Seeks Peace," A4.

66. Gitonga, "On the Mark for Community," 3.

67. Ibid.

68. Pat Butcher, "The Daintiest Record Breaker: Athletics: Kenya's Tegla Loroupe has Overcome Heavy Odds on Her Way to Becoming a World-Beater," *Financial Times*, October 9, 1999, 22.

69. Longman, "82 Pounds of Steel," 11.

70. Ibid.

71. "Lorupe: No Running Career," *Daily Nation*, November 12, 1994, 25.

72. Njenga, "Among the Top in Kenya's Roll of World Conquerors," 3; Omolo Okoth, "Track Officials Dropped," *The Standard*, March 14, 1989, 26; Chege Kariuki, "Preps for the Norway Tussle," *The Standard*, February 27, 1989, 21; "Ngugi Does It Again!," *The Standard*, March 20, 1989, 1.

73. D. Lewis, "Tegla—I Am All Woman," *Mirror*, April 17, 2000, 41.

74. Susan Cahn, *Coming on Strong: Gender and Sexuality in Women's Sport* (New York: Free Press, 1994); Jaime Schultz, "Going the Distance: The Road to the 1984 Olympic Women's Marathon," *The International Journal of the History of Sport* 32, no. 1 (2015): 72–88; Jaime Schultz, "Breaking into the Marathon: Women's Distance Running as Political Activism." *Frontiers: A Journal of Women Studies* 40, no. 2 (2019): 1–26; Cat M. Ariail, *Passing the Baton: Black Women Track Stars and American Identity* (Urbana: University of Illinois Press, 2020).

75. Gettleman, "A Kenyan Runner Seeks Peace," A4.

76. Gitonga, "On the Mark for Community," 3.

77. Ibid.

78. Sulubu Tuva, "Star-Studded Team Stands Real Chance of a Great Performance," *Saturday Nation*, August 14, 2004, 3; Liz Gitonga, "Star Athlete's Stunning Dress for Special Occasions," *Sunday Nation*, July 18, 2004, 3.

79. Gitonga, "On the Mark for Community," 3.

80. Ibid.

81. "Kenyan Star in Sydney," *Sunday Nation*, September 24, 2000, 3.

82. John Lonsdale, "Anti-colonial Nationalism and Patriotism in sub-Saharan Africa," in *The Oxford Handbook on the History of Nationalism*, ed. John Breuilly (Oxford: Oxford University Press, 2013), 325.

83. Ibid., 325.

84. Dennis Mabuka, "How Kenyan Athletes Have Invested Their Money," *Management*, December 2011–January 2012, 28. For the website of the Tegla Loroupe Peace Foundation, see https://teglapeace.org/.

85. Fred Awori, "Running for Peace in West Pokot," *Daily Nation*, December 23, 2005, 12.

86. On North Rift Valley conflicts, see Dave Eaton, "The Business of Peace: Raiding and Peace Work Along the Kenya-Uganda Border (Part I)," *African Affairs* 107, no. 426 (2008): 89–110; Dave Eaton, "The Business of Peace: Raiding and Peace Work Along the Kenya-Uganda Border (Part II)," *African Affairs* 107, no. 427 (2008): 243–59.

87. Gitonga, "On the Mark for Community," 3.

88. Sulubu Tuva, "Hats Off Visionary Loroupe," *Daily Nation*, November 18, 2006, 34.

89. Ibid.

90. Gitonga, "On the Mark for Community," 3.

91. Awori, "Running for Peace in West Pokot," 12.

92. Ottavio Castellini, "Tegla Loroupe Race for Peace," no. 1, *IAAF Magazine*, April 2004.

93. S. Lorge, "She Can Make It Three; Loroupe Eyes Third Victory," *Reuters News*, November 2, 1996; Shontz, "The Pioneers Who Led the Way."

94. Nic Cheeseman, "Kenya Since 2002: The More Things Change the More They Stay the Same," in *Turning Points in African Democracy*, ed. Lindsay Whitfield and Raufu Mustapha (Suffolk, UK: James Currey, 2009), 94–113.

95. Lonsdale, "Moral Ethnicity and Political Tribalism," 149.

96. Elias Makori, "Kenya Comes Together to Celebrate Jelimo's Triumphant Homecoming," World Athletics, September 18, 2008, https://worldathletics.org/news/news/kenya-comes-together-to-celebrate-jelimos-tri.

97. "Pamela Jelimo Is the 2008 Golden Girl of Athletics," February 3, 2009, extract from IAAF 2008 Yearbook, World Athletics, https://worldathletics.org/news/news/pamela-jelimo-is-the-2008-golden-girl-of-athl.

98. Eric Odanga, "Ndereba: The Marathon Queen," *Daily Nation*, October 3, 2003, 2; "Anthem Moves Athlete to Tears," 39.

99. "Ndereba Rewarded for Paris Victory, *Daily Nation*, September 17, 2003, 51; Lori Shontz, "Crazy Catherine, on Top of the World," *Post-Gazette* (Pittsburgh), May 7, 2002, https://old.post-gazette.com/sports/other/20020507kenya0507p3.asp.

100. Lori Shontz, "Looking Toward a New Kenya," *Post-Gazette* (Pittsburgh), May 9, 2002, https://old.post-gazette.com/sports/other/20020509kenyaa0509p2.asp.

101. "Athletics: Kenya Still Has the Best Record from Africa," *The Nation,* August 23, 2003, 2–3.

102. Ng'ang'a Mbugua, *Catherine Ndereba: The Marathon Queen* (Nairobi: Sasa Sema Publications, 2008).

103. Omolo Okoth, "Cheruiyot One to Beat in Durham," *The Standard*, March 20, 1995, 5. Rose Cheruiyot, interview with author, Eldoret, Kenya, January 14, 2010.

104. Jane Perlez, "African Women Reach Starting Line," *New York Times*, July 1, 1992, B10. Susan Sirma, interview with author, Iten, Kenya, January 23, 2011.

105. Lornah Kiplagat Sports Academy, Business Plan, 2009, in possession of the author.

106. Elias Makori, "At Home in Iten and Holland: Long-distance Runner's Training Camp in Kenya Breeding New Stars," *Sunday Nation*, August 15, 2004, 2–3; "Dutchwoman Kiplagat Seeks First New York Marathon Win," *Daily Nation*, October 5, 2005, 55.

107. Monica Cheruiyot, interview with author, Iten, Kenya, April 9, 2011.

108. Eunice Jelimo, interview with author, Iten, Kenya, April 16, 2011.

109. Jackie Lebo, "The Things Runners Have Built," originally printed mid-2007, reprinted in 2008 by MarathonGuide.com, http://www.marathonguide.com/news/exclusives/EldoretKenyaAthletesTraining.cfm.

110. Michelle M. Sikes, "Running for Peace and Development in Kenya's Rift Valley," *Peace Review* 32, no. 4 (2020): 480–87.

111. Patrick Sang, interview with author, Eldoret, Kenya, January 24, 2011.

112. Mabuka, "How Kenyan Athletes Have Invested Their Money," 28.

113. Ruth Waithera, interview with author, Nairobi, Kenya, February 18, 2011.

114. Leah Malot, interview with author, Eldoret, Kenya, January 24, 2011.

115. Tecla Chembawai, interview with author, Eldoret, Kenya, January 31, 2011.

116. Rose Tata-Muya, interview with author, Nairobi, Kenya, February 19, 2011.

117. Tecla Chemabwai, interview with author, Eldoret, Kenya, January 31, 2011.

118. Ruth Waithera, interview with author, Nairobi, Kenya, February 18, 2011.

119. Tecla Chemabwai, interview with author, Eldoret, Kenya, January 31, 2011.

120. Ruth Waithera, interview with author, Nairobi, Kenya, February 18, 2011.

121. Tecla Chemabwai, interview with author, Eldoret, Kenya, January 31, 2011.

122. Ruth Waithera, interview with author, Nairobi, Kenya, February 18, 2011.

123. Susan Sirma, interview with author, Iten, Kenya, January 14, 2010.

124. Margaret Muret, interview with author, Iten, Kenya, April 1, 2011.

125. "So . . . Gothenburg?," *The Standard*, August 21, 1995, 2.

126. Vincent Onywera, Robert Scott, Michael Boit, and Yannis Pitsiladis, "Demographic Characteristics of Elite Kenyan Endurance Runners," *Journal of Sports Sciences* 24, no. 4 (2006): 420.

127. See, for instance, Alan Klein, *Sugarball: The American Game, the Dominican Dream* (New Haven: Yale University Press, 2001); Louis Moore, *I Fight for a Living: Boxing and the Battle for Black Manhood, 1880–1915* (Urbana: University of Illinois Press, 2007); Darcy Frey, *The Last Shot: City Streets, Basketball Dreams* (New York: Mariner Books, 1994); and Paul Darby, James Esson and Christian Ungruhe, *African Football Migration: Aspirations, Experiences and Trajectories* (Manchester: Manchester University Press, 2022).

128. "Treat Prize Money as 'Confidential', Lorupe," *East African Standard*, May 5, 1997, 31.

129. "Bittersweet Return for Olympic Star: Success brings Unwelcome Attention for 18-Year-Old Runner with $1m in the Bank," *The Guardian*, http://www.guardian.co.uk/world/2008/oct/04/kenya.olympicsandthemedia.

130. "Bittersweet Return for Olympic Star."

131. Ann Jepkosgei, interview with author, February 9, 2011.

Conclusion

1. Eric J. Hobsbawm, *The Age of Empire, 1875–1914* (New York: Vintage Books, 1989), 216.

2. Taylor Dutch, "How Kenyan Women Runners Are Responding to Agnes Tirop's Death," *Runner's World*, November 3, 2021, https://www.runnersworld.com/runners-stories/a38137912/agnes-tirop-death-kenyan-runners-respond/.

3. Molly McElwee, "One Woman's Mission to End Abuse in Kenyan Athletes," *The Telegraph*, October 28, 2022, https://www.telegraph.co.uk/athletics/2022/10/28/one-womans-mission-end-abuse-kenyan-athletics/?utm_content=women+sport&utm_medium=Social&utm_campaign=Echobox&utm_source=Twitter%23Echobox%3D1666951811.

4. Martha Saavedra, "Sport," in *A Companion to Gender Studies*, ed. Philomena Essed, Audrey Kobayashi, and David Theo Goldberg (London: Blackwell Publishing, 2005), 438.

5. Tom Cunningham, "'These Our Games'—Sport and the Church of Scotland Mission to Kenya, c. 1907–1937," *History in Africa* 43 (2016): 263.

6. Todd Cleveland, Tarminder Kaur, and Gerard Akindes, "Introduction: More Than Just Games," in *Sports in Africa: Past and Present*, ed. Todd Cleveland, Tarminder Kaur, and Gerard Akindes (Athens: Ohio University Press, 2020), 7.

7. Bea Vidacs, "Through the Prism of Sports: Why Should Africanists Study Sports?," *Afrika Spectrum* 41, no. 3 (2006): 331.

8. "Konga's 'Golden' Moment for Kenya," *Daily Nation*, July 30, 1996, 1.

9. Victor Sicle, "Athletes Carry the Hopes of a Nation to London Games," *Daily Nation*, July 26, 2012, Olympic Games 2012 special, pg. U.

Bibliography

Abmayr, Walter. *Africa Track and Field: 4th All-Africa-Games Nairobi/Kenya 1987*. Nairobi: ATFS, 1987.

———. *Track and Field Best Performances: Kenya 1982*. Nairobi: ATFS, 1983.

———. *Track & Field Best Performances: Kenya 1984*. Nairobi: ATFS, 1985.

———. *Track and Field Best Performances: Kenya 1987*. Nairobi: ATFS, 1988.

Achebe, Nwando. *Farmers, Traders, Warriors, and Kings: Female Power and Authority in Northern Igboland, 1900–1960*. Portsmouth, NH: Heinemann, 2005.

———. *The Female King of Colonial Nigeria: Ahebi Ugbabe*. Bloomington: Indiana University Press, 2011.

———. *Female Monarchs and Merchant Queens in Africa*. Athens: Ohio University Press, 2020.

Adams, Mary Louise. *Artistic Impressions: Figure Skating, Masculinity, and the Limits of Sport*. Toronto: University of Toronto Press, 2011.

Aiyar, Sana. *Indians in Kenya: The Politics of Diaspora*. Cambridge, MA: Harvard University Press, 2015.

Akyeampong, Emmanuel. "Bukom and the Social History of Boxing in Accra: Warfare and Citizenship in Precolonial Ga Society." *The International Journal of African Historical Studies* 35, no. 1 (2002): 39–60.

Akyeampong, Emmanuel, and Charles Ambler. "Leisure in African History: An Introduction." *The International Journal of African Historical Studies* 35, no. 1 (2002): 1–16.

Alegi, Peter. *African Soccerscapes: How a Continent Changed the World's Game*. Athens: Ohio University Press, 2010.

———. *Laduma! Soccer, Politics and Society in South Africa, from its Origins to 2010*. 2nd ed. Scottsville, South Africa: University of KwaZulu-Natal Press, 2010.

Ali, Muhammad, with Richard Durham. *The Greatest: My Own Story*. New York: Random House, 1975.

Amadiume, Ifi. *Male Daughters, Female Husbands: Gender and Sex in an African Society*, 2nd ed. London: Zed Books, 1998.

Amutabi, Maurice N. "Political Interference in the Running of Education in Post-independence Kenya: A Critical Retrospection." *International Journal of Educational Development* 23, no. 2 (2003): 127–44.

Anderson, David M. "Agriculture and Irrigation at Lake Baringo in the 19th Century." *Azania* 24 (1989): 85–98.

———. "The Beginning of Time? Evidence for Catastrophic Drought in Baringo in the Early Nineteenth Century." *Journal of Eastern African Studies* 10, no. 1 (2016): 45–66.

———. *Eroding the Commons: The Politics of Ecology in Baringo, Kenya, 1890–1963*. Oxford: James Currey, 2002.

———. *Histories of the Hanged: The Dirty War in Kenya and the End of Empire*. New York: W.W. Norton & Company, 2005.

———. "Stock Theft and Moral Economy in Colonial Kenya." *Africa* 56, no. 4 (1985): 399–416.

Anderson, John E. *The Struggle for the School: The Interaction of Missionary, Colonial Government and Nationalist Enterprise in the Development of Formal Education in Kenya*. London: Longman, 1970.

Anderson, Malcolm. "The Development of Athletics in 1950s Kenya: Order or Leisure?" Master's thesis, Oxford University, 2008.

Angelo, Anaïs. *Power and the Presidency in Kenya: The Jomo Kenyatta Years*. New York: Cambridge University Press, 2019.

Archer, Robert, and Antoine Bouillon. *The South African Game: Sport and Racism*. London: Zed Books, 1982.

Ariail, Cat M. "'One of the Greatest Ambassadors that the United States Has Ever Sent Abroad': Wilma Rudolph, American Athletic Icon for the Cold War and Civil Rights Movement." In *Defending the American Way of Life: Sport, Politics, and the Cold War*, edited by Toby C. Rider and Kevin B. Witherspoon, 141–54. Fayetteville: University of Arkansas Press, 2018.

———. *Passing the Baton: Black Women Track Stars and American Identity*. Urbana: University of Illinois Press, 2020.

Armstrong, Gary. "The Global Footballer and the Local War-zone: George Weah and Transnational Networks in Liberia, West Africa." *Global Networks* 7, no. 2 (2007): 230–47.

Armstrong, Gary, and Richard Giulianotti, eds. *Football in Africa: Conflict, Conciliation, and Community*. Basingstoke: Palgrave Macmillan, 2004.

Askwith, Tom. *Getting My Knees Brown: Day-to-Day Episodes in Colonial Kenya*. Cheltenham: Quorum Technical Services, 1996.

Ayuk, Augustine E., ed. *Football (Soccer) in Africa: Origins, Contributions, and Contradictions*. Cham, Switzerland: Palgrave Macmillan, 2022.

Baker, William J. *Playing with God: Religion and Modern Sport*. Cambridge, MA: Harvard University Press, 2007.

Bale, John. *The Brawn Drain: Foreign Student-Athletes in American Universities*. Urbana: University of Illinois Press, 1991.

———. "Kenyan Running before the 1968 Mexico Olympics." In *East African Running: Towards a Cross-Disciplinary Perspective*, edited by Yannis Pitsiladis, John Bale, Craig Sharp, and Tim Noakes, 11–23. Abingdon: Routledge, 2007.

———. "Lassitude and Latitude: Observations on Sport and Environmental Determinism." *International Review for the Sociology of Sport* 37, no.2 (2002): 147–58.

Bale, John, and Joe Sang. *Kenyan Running: Movement Culture, Geography, and Global Change*. London: Frank Cass, 1996.

Baller, Susann, and Martha Saavedra. "La Politique du Football en Afrique: Mobilisations et Trajectoires." *Politique Africaine* 118 (2010): 5–21.

Barber, Karin. "Popular Arts in Africa." *African Studies Review* 30, no. 3 (1987): 1–75.

Bass, Amy. *Not the Triumph but the Struggle: The 1968 Olympics and the Making of the Black Athlete*. Minneapolis: University of Minnesota Press, 2002.

Bauer, Gretchen, and Hannah Britton, eds. *Women in African Parliaments*. Boulder, CO: Lynne Rienner, 2006.

Beech, Mervyn W. H. *The Suk: Their Language and Folklore*. New York: Negro Universities Press, 1969.

Bell, Erin. "'A Most Horrifying Maturity in Crime': Age, Gender and Juvenile Delinquency in Colonial Kenya during the Mau Mau Uprising." *Atlantic Studies* 11, no. 4 (2014): 473–90.

Berman, Bruce. *Control and Crisis in Colonial Kenya: The Dialectic of Domination*. London: James Currey, 1990.

Berman, Bruce, and John Lonsdale. "Coping with the Contradictions: The Development of the Colonial State in Kenya, 1895–1914." In *Unhappy Valley: Conflict in Kenya and Africa*, Book 1: State and Class, edited by Bruce Berman and John Lonsdale, 77–100. London: James

Currey, 1992.

———. *Unhappy Valley: Conflict in Kenya and Africa*, Book 1: State and Class. London: James Currey, 1992.

Bier, Lisa. *Fighting the Current: The Rise of American Women's Swimming, 1870–1926*. Jefferson, NC: McFarland & Company, 2011.

Birley, Derek. *Sport and the Making of Britain*. Manchester: Manchester University Press, 1993.

Blackman, Dexter. "African Americans, Pan-Africanism, and the Anti-apartheid Campaign to Expel South Africa from the 1968 Olympics." *Journal of Pan African Studies* 5, no. 3 (2012): 1–25.

Blaschke, Anne M. "Running the Cold War: Gender, Race, and Track in Cultural Diplomacy, 1955–1975." *Diplomatic History* 40, no. 5 (2016): 826–44.

Bloomfield, Steve. *Africa United: How Football Explains Africa*. New York: Harper Perennial, 2010.

Bogonko, Sorobea N. *A History of Modern Education in Kenya (1895–1991)*. Nairobi: Evans Brothers, 1992.

Bolsmann, Chris, and Andrew Parker. "Soccer, South Africa and Celebrity Status: Mark Fish, Popular Culture and the Post-apartheid State." *Soccer & Society* 8, no. 1 (2007): 109–24.

Booth, Douglas. *The Race Game: Sport and Politics in South Africa*. London: Frank Cass, 1998.

Borenstein, Hannah. "Labouring Athletes, Labouring Mothers: Ethiopian Women Athletes' Bodies at Work." In *Sport, Migration, and Gender in the Neoliberal Age*, edited by Niko Besnier, Domenica Gisella Calabrò, and Daniel Guinness, 65–82. London: Routledge, 2021.

Borish, Linda. "'The Cradle of American Champions, Women Champions . . . Swim Champions': Charlotte Epstein, Gender and Jewish Identity, and the Physical Emancipation of Women in Aquatic Sports." *The International Journal of the History of Sport* 21, no. 2 (2004): 197–235.

Brake, Deborah L. *Getting in the Game: Title IX and the Women's Sports Revolution*. New York: New York University Press, 2010.

Branch, Daniel. *Defeating Mau Mau, Creating Kenya: Counterinsurgency, Civil War, and Decolonization*. Cambridge: Cambridge University Press, 2009.

———. *Kenya: Between Hope and Despair, 1963–2011*. New Haven, CT: Yale University Press, 2011.

Branch, Daniel, and Nic Cheeseman. "Democratization, Sequencing and State Failure in Africa: Lessons from Kenya." *African Affairs* 108, no. 430 (2008): 1–26.

Branch, Daniel, Nic Cheeseman, and Leigh Gardner, eds. *Our Turn to Eat: Politics in Kenya Since 1950*. Berlin: Lit Verlag, 2010.

Brennan, James R. *Taifa: Making Nation and Race in Urban Tanzania*. Athens: Ohio University Press, 2012.

Bromber, Katrin. *Sports and Modernity in Late Imperial Ethiopia*. Suffolk, UK: James Currey, 2022.

———. "The Stadium and the City: Sports Infrastructure in Late Imperial Ethiopia and Beyond." *Cadernos de Estudos Africanos* 32, no. 1 (2016): 53–72.

Bujra, Jane. "Women 'Entrepreneurs' of Early Nairobi." *Canadian Journal of African Studies* 9, no. 2 (1975): 213–34.

Byron, Kipchumba, and Jepkorir Rose Chepyator-Thomson. "Sports Policy in Kenya: Deconstruction of Colonial and Post-colonial Conditions." *International Journal of Sport Policy and Politics* 7, no. 2 (2015): 301–13.

Cable, Vincent. "The Asians of Kenya." *African Affairs* 68, no. 272 (1969): 218–31.

Cadigan, R. Jean. "Woman-to-Woman Marriage: Practices and Benefits in Sub-Saharan Africa." *Journal of Comparative Family Studies* 29, no. 1 (1998): 89–98.

Caesar, Ed. *Two Hours: The Quest to Run the Impossible Marathon*. New York: Simon & Schuster, 2015.

Cahn, Susan K. *Coming on Strong: Gender and Sexuality in Twentieth-Century Women's Sport*. New York: Free Press, 1994.

Carotenuto, Matthew. "Grappling with the Past: Wrestling and Performative Identity in Kenya." *The International Journal of the History of Sport* 30, no. 16 (2013): 1889–902.

Carpenter, Florence, and Jean-Pierre Lefevre. "The Modern Olympic Movement, Women's Sport and the Social Order during the Inter-war Period." *The International Journal of the History of Sport* 23, no. 7 (2006): 1112–27.

Carpenter, Linda Jean, and R. Vivian Acosta. *Title IX*. Champaign, IL: Human Kinetics, 2005.

Carrier, Joseph M., and Stephen O. Murray. "Woman-Woman Marriage in Africa." In *Boy-Wives and Female Husbands: Studies in African Homosexualities*, edited by Stephen O. Murray and Will Roscoe, 255–66. New York: Palgrave Macmillan, 2008.

Carter, Neil. "From Knox to Dyson: Coaching, Amateurism and British Athletics, 1912–1947." *Sport in History* 30, no. 1 (2010): 55–81.

Catsam, Derek C. *Flashpoint: How a Little-Known Sporting Event Fueled America's Anti-Apartheid Movement*. Lamham, MD: Rowman & Littlefield, 2021.

Chandler, Timothy J. L. "Emergent Athleticism: Games in Two English Public Schools, 1800–60." *The International Journal of the History of Sport* 5, no. 3 (1988): 312–30.

Chapman, Michael, ed. *The Drum Decade: Stories from the 1950s*. Pietermaritzburg: University of KwaZulu-Natal Press, 1989.

Charitas, Pascal. "A More Flexible Domination: Franco-African Sport Diplomacy during

Decolonization, 1945–1966." In *Diplomatic Games: Sport, Statecraft and International Relations since 1945*, edited by Heather L. Dichter and Andrew L. Johns, 183–214. Lexington: University Press of Kentucky, 2014.

Chase, Laura. "Beyond Boston and Kathrine Switzer: Women's Participation in Distance Running." In *Endurance Running: A Socio-Cultural Examination*, edited by William Bridel, Pirkko Markula, and Jim Denison, 61–75. London: Routledge, 2016.

Chawansky, Megan. "Getting the Girl: Female Athletes' Narratives of the Recruiting Process." PhD diss., Ohio State University, 2008.

Chebet, Susan, and Ton Dietz. *Climbing the Cliff: A History of Keiyo*. Eldoret, Kenya: Moi University Press, 2000.

Cheeseman, Nic. "Kenya Since 2002: The More Things Change the More They Stay the Same." In *Turning Points in African Democracy*, edited by Lindsay Whitfield and Raufu Mustapha, 94–113. Suffolk, UK: James Currey, 2009.

Chepyator-Thomson, Jepkorir Rose. "African Women Run for Change: Challenges and Achievements in Sports." In *African Women and Globalization: Dawn of the 21st Century*, edited by Jepkorir Rose Chepyator-Thomson, 239–58. Trenton, NJ: Africa World Press, 2005.

———. "Traditional Games of Keiyo Children: A Comparison of Pre- and Post-Independent Periods in Kenya." *Interchange* 21, no. 2 (1990): 15–25.

Chipande, Hikabwa D. "The Structural Adjustment of Football in Zambia: Politics, Decline and Dispersal, 1991–1994." *The International Journal of the History of Sport* 33, no. 15 (2016): 1847–65.

Christensen, Dirk L., Gerrit Van Hall, and Leif Hambraeus. "Food and Macronutrient Intake of Male Adolescent Kalenjin Runners in Kenya." *British Journal of Nutrition* 88, no. 6 (2002): 711–17.

Chudacoff, Howard P. "AAU v. NCAA: The Bitter Feud That Altered the Structure of American Amateur Sports." *Journal of Sport History* 48, no. 1 (2021): 50–65.

Clayton, Anthony. "Sport and African Soldiers: The Military Diffusion of Western Sport throughout sub-Saharan Africa." In *Sport in Africa: Essays in Social History*, edited by William J. Baker and James A. Mangan, 114–37. New York: Africana Publishing Company, 1987.

Clayton, Anthony, and Donald C. Savage. *Government and Labour in Kenya, 1895–1963*. London: Frank Cass, 1974.

Cleophas, Francois, ed. *Exploring Decolonising Themes in SA Sport History: Issues and Challenges*. Stellenbosch, South Africa: Sun Press, 2018.

———. "A Historical Social Overview of Athletics in 19th Century Cape Colony, South Africa:

Sport History." *African Journal for Physical Health Education, Recreation and Dance* 20, no. 2 (2014): 585–92.

Cleveland, Todd. *Following the Ball: The Migration of African Soccer Players across the Portuguese Colonial Empire, 1949–1975.* Athens: Ohio University Press, 2017.

Cleveland, Todd, Tarminder Kaur, and Gerard Akindes, eds. *Sports in Africa: Past and Present.* Athens: Ohio University Press, 2020.

Clowes, Lindsay. "To Be a Man: Changing Constructions of Manhood in *Drum* Magazine, 1951–1965." In *African Masculinities: Men in Africa from the Late Nineteenth Century to the Present*, edited by Lahoucine Ouzgane and Robert Morrell, 89–108. New York/Scottsville, South Africa: Palgrave Macmillan/University of Kwa-Zulu-Natal Press, 2005.

Collins, Gail. *When Everything Changed: The Amazing Journey of American Women from 1960 to the Present.* New York: Little, Brown and Company, 2009.

Collins, Tony. *Rugby's Great Split: Class, Culture and the Origins of Rugby League Football*, 2nd ed. London: Routledge, 2006.

Cooper, Frederick. "Conflict and Connection: Rethinking Colonial African History." *American Historical Review* 99, no. 5 (1994): 1516–45.

Cooper, Pamela. "The 'Visible Hand' on the Footrace: Fred Lebow and the Marketing of the Marathon." *Journal of Sport History* 19, no. 3 (1992): 244–56.

Cornelissen, Scarlett. "Resolving 'the South Africa Problem'. Transnational Activism, Ideology and Race in the Olympic Movement, 1960–91." *International Journal of the History of Sport* 28, no. 1 (2011): 153–67.

Crawley, Michael. *Out of Thin Air: Running Wisdom and Magic from Above the Clouds in Ethiopia.* London: Bloomsbury, 2021.

Crump, Jeremy. "Athletics." In *Sport in Britain: A Social History*, edited by Tony Mason, 44–77. Cambridge: Cambridge University Press, 1989.

Cunningham, Tom. "'These Our Games'—Sport and the Church of Scotland Mission to Kenya, c. 1907–1937." *History in Africa* 43 (2016): 259–88.

Darby, Paul. "'Let Us Rally Around the Flag': Football, Nation-building, and Pan-Africanism in Kwame Nkrumah's Ghana." *The Journal of African History* 54, no. 2 (2013): 221–46.

———. "Politics, Resistance and Patronage: The African Boycott of the 1966 World Cup and its Ramification." *Soccer & Society* 20, no. 7–8 (2019): 936–47.

Darby, Paul, James Esson, and Christian Ungruhe. *African Football Migration: Aspirations, Experiences and Trajectories.* Manchester: Manchester University Press, 2022.

Davies, Matthew I. J., and Henrietta L. Moore. "Landscape, Time and Cultural Resilience: A Brief History of Agriculture in Pokot and Marakwet, Kenya." *Journal of Eastern African Studies* 10, no. 1 (2016): 67–87.

Decker, Alicia. *In Idi Amin's Shadow: Women, Gender, and Militarism in Uganda*. Athens: Ohio University Press, 2014.

de Smedt, Johan. "'No Raila, No Peace!' Big Man Politics and Election Violence at the Kibera Grassroots." *African Affairs* 108, no. 433 (2009): 581–98.

Dimeo, Paul. *A History of Drug Use in Sport 1876–1976: Beyond Good and Evil*. New York: Routledge, 2007.

Domingos, Nuno. *Football and Colonialism: Body and Popular Culture in Urban Mozambique*. Athens: Ohio University Press, 2017.

Dowling, Collette. *The Frailty Myth: Women Approaching Physical Equality*. New York: Random House, 2000.

Driberg, Jack H. "The Status of Women Among the Nilotics and Nilo-Hamitics." *Africa* 5, no. 4 (1932): 404–21.

Driver, Dorothy. "*Drum* Magazine (1951–9) and the Spatial Configurations of Gender." In *Text, Theory, Space: Land, Literature and History in South Africa and Australia*, edited by Kate Darian-Smith, Liz Gunner, and Sarah Nuttall, 227–38. London: Routledge, 1996.

Dubinsky, Itamar. *Entrepreneurial Goals: Development and Africapitalism in Ghanaian Soccer Academies*. Madison: University of Wisconsin Press, 2022.

Duckworth, Austin, Thomas M. Hunt, and Jan Todd. "Cold Hard Cash: Commercialization, Politics, and Amateurism in United States Track and Field." *Sport in History* 38, no. 2 (2018): 145–63.

Dunzendorfer, Jan. "The Early Days of Boxing in Accra: A Sport Is Taking Root (1920–1940)." *The International Journal of the History of Sport* 28, no. 15 (2011): 2142–58.

Dyreson, Mark. "Icons of Liberty or Objects of Desire? American Women Olympians and the Politics of Consumption." *Journal of Contemporary History* 38, no. 3 (2003): 435–60.

———. *Making the American Team: Sport, Culture, and the Olympic Experience*. Urbana: University of Illinois Press, 1998.

———. "Nature by Design: American Ideas about Sport, Energy, Evolution and Republics." *Journal of Sport History* 26, no. 3 (1999): 447–70.

———. "The Playing of Progress: American Athletic Nationalism and the St. Louis Olympics of 1904." *Gateway Heritage* 14 (1993): 4–23.

———. "Sport." In *New Dictionary of the History of Ideas*, vol. 5, edited by Maryanne Cline, 2246–50. New York: Charles Scribner's Sons, 2004.

Early, Gerald, ed. *The Muhammad Ali Reader*. Hopewell, NJ: Ecco Press, 1998.

Eaton, Dave. "The Business of Peace: Raiding and Peace Work Along the Kenya-Uganda Border (Part I)." *African Affairs* 107, no. 426 (2008): 89–110.

———. "The Business of Peace: Raiding and Peace Work Along the Kenya-Uganda Border

(Part II)." *African Affairs* 107, no. 427 (2008): 243–59.

Edwards, Amanda. "Why Sport? The Development of Sport as a Policy Issue in Title IX of the Education Amendments of 1972." *Journal of Policy History* 22, no. 3 (2010): 300–336.

Elias, Norbert, and Eric Dunning, eds. *Quest for Excitement: Sport and Leisure in the Civilizing Process*. Oxford: Blackwell, 1986.

Elkins, Caroline. *Britain's Gulag: The Brutal End of Empire in Kenya*. London: Jonathan Cape, 2005.

Engh, Mari Haugaa. "Tackling Femininity: The Heterosexual Paradigm and Women's Soccer in South Africa." *The International Journal of the History of Sport* 28, no. 1 (2011): 137–52.

Engh, Mari Haugaa, and Cheryl Potgieter. "Hetero-sexing the Athlete: Public and Popular Discourses on Sexuality and Women's Sport in South Africa." *Acta Academica* 50, no. 2 (2018): 34–51.

English, Colleen. "'Beyond Women's Powers of Endurance': The 1928 800-Meter and Women's Olympic Track and Field in the Context of the United States." *Sport History Review* 50, no. 2 (2019): 187–204.

Eshiwani, George S. *Implementing Educational Policies in Kenya*. World Bank Discussion Papers no. 85: Africa Technical Department Series. Washington, DC: World Bank, 1990.

Espy, Richard. *The Politics of the Olympic Games*. Berkeley: University of California Press, 1979.

Evans, Sara M. *Tidal Wave: How Women Changed America at Century's End*. New York: Free Press, 2003.

Ezra, Michael. *Muhammad Ali: The Making of an Icon*. Philadelphia: Temple University Press, 2009.

Fair, Laura. "Ngoma Reverberations: Swahili Music Culture and the Making of Football Aesthetics in Early Twentieth-Century Zanzibar." In *Football in Africa: Conflict, Conciliation and Community*, edited by Gary Armstrong and Richard Giulianotti, 103–11. Houndmills, UK: Palgrave Macmillan, 2004.

———. *Pastimes and Politics: Culture, Community, and Identity in Post-Abolition Urban Zanzibar, 1890–1945*. Athens: Ohio University Press, 2001.

Festle, Mary Jo. *Playing Nice: Politics and Apologies in Women's Sports*. New York: Columbia University Press, 1996.

Fields, Sarah K. *Female Gladiators: Gender, Law, and Contact Sport in America*. Urbana: University of Illinois Press, 2005.

Finn, Adharanand. *Running with the Kenyans: Discovering the Secrets of the Fastest People on Earth*. London: Faber and Faber, 2012.

Fishel, Andrew, and Janice Pottker. *National Politics and Sex Discrimination in Education*. Lexington, MA: Lexington Books, 1977.

Francis, Martin. "The Domestication of the Male? Recent Research on Nineteenth and Twentieth Century British Masculinity." *The Historical Journal* 45, no. 3 (2002): 637–52.

Frederiksen, Bodil F. "African Women and their Colonisation of Nairobi: Representations and Realities." *Azania: Archaeological Research in Africa* 36–37, no. 1 (2001): 223–34.

Freedman, Estelle. *No Turning Back: The History of Feminism and the Future of Women*. New York: Ballantine, 2002.

Frey, Darcy. *The Last Shot: City Streets, Basketball Dreams*. New York: Mariner Books, 1994.

Frick, Bernd, Joachim Prinz, and Frank Tolsdorf. "*Citius, Altius, Fortius*: The Production of World Records in the Running and Technical Disciplines in Track and Field." In *Handbook on the Economics of Sport*, edited by Wladimir Andreff and Stefan Szymanski, 349–63. Cheltenham, UK: Edward Elgar, 2006.

Fridy, Kevin S., and Victor Brobbey. "Win the Match and Vote for Me: The Politicisation of Ghana's Accra Hearts of Oak and Kumasi Asante Kotoko Football Clubs." *Journal of Modern African Studies* 47, no. 1 (2009): 19–39.

Furley, Oliver W. "The Struggle for Transformation in Education in Kenya Since Independence." *East African Journal* 9, no. 8 (1972): 23–27.

Gennaro, Michael. "'The Cause Is a Worthy One, So Come along with Your Sixpence and Enjoy Yourselves with One Hour of Lusty Sport': Sport in Lagos, Nigeria during WWII." *Journal of African Military History* 4, no. 1–2 (2020): 41–65.

Gennaro, Michael J., and Saheed Aderinto, eds. *Sports in African History: Politics, and Identity Formation*. London: Routledge, 2019.

Giardina, Carol. *Freedom for Women: Forging the Women's Liberation Movement, 1953–1970*. Gainesville: University Press of Florida, 2010.

Gibbs, James. "*Uhuru na Kenyatta*: White Settlers and the Symbolism of Kenya's Independence Day Events." *Journal of Imperial and Commonwealth History* 42, no. 3 (2014): 503–29.

Gilmore, Stephanie, ed. *Feminist Coalitions: Historical Perspectives on Second-Wave Feminism in the United States*. Urbana: University of Illinois Press, 2008.

Gimode, Edwin. *Thomas Joseph Mboya: A Biography*. Nairobi: East African Educational Publishers, 1996.

Gissendanner, Cindy H. "African American Women Olympians: The Impact of Race, Gender, and Class Ideologies, 1932–1968." *Research Quarterly for Exercise and Sport* 67, no. 2 (1996): 172–82.

Goetz, Anne Marie, and Shireen Hassim, eds. *No Shortcuts to Power: African Women in Politics and Policy Making*. New York: Zed Books, 2003.

Goldsworthy, David. *Tom Mboya: The Man Kenya Wanted to Forget*. Nairobi: Heinemann, 1982.

Gorn, Elliott J., ed. *Muhammad Ali: The People's Champ*. Urbana: University of Illinois Press, 1995.

Goudsouzian, Aram. "Wilma Rudolph (1940–1994): Running for Freedom." In *Tennessee Women: Their Lives and Times*, edited by Sarah Wilkerson Freeman and Beverly Greene Bond, 305–32. Athens: University of Georgia Press, 2009.

Griswold, Robert L. "The 'Flabby American,' the Body and the Cold War." In *A Shared Experience: Men, Women and the History of Gender*, edited by Laura McCall and Donald Yacovone, 323–47. New York: New York University Press, 1998.

Guttmann, Allen. *From Ritual to Record: The Nature of Modern Sports*, 2nd ed. New York: Columbia University Press, 2004.

———. *Games and Empires: Modern Sports and Cultural Imperialism*. New York: Columbia University Press, 1994.

———. *The Olympics: A History of the Modern Games*. Urbana: University of Illinois Press, 1992.

———. *Women's Sports: A History.* New York: Columbia University Press, 1991.

Guyer, Jane. "Household and Community in African Studies." *African Studies Review* 24, no. 2/3 (1981): 87–137.

Gwako, Edwins Laban Moogi. "Widow Inheritance among the Maragoli of Western Kenya." *Journal of Anthropological Research* 54, no. 2 (1998): 173–98.

Haberman, Aaron L. "Escape & Pursuit: Contrasting Visions of the 1970s Long-Distance Running Boom in American Popular Culture." *Sport History Review* 48, no. 1 (2017): 1–17.

———. "Thousands of Solitary Runners Come Together: Individualism and Communitarianism in the 1970s Running Boom." *Journal of Sport History* 44, no. 1 (2017): 35–49.

———. "'We're All Professionals Now': Frank Shorter, Deregulation, and the Battle to End 'Shamateurism' in the 1970s." *The International Journal of the History of Sport* 36, no. 15–16 (2019): 1414–32.

Hain, Peter, and André Odendaal. *Pitch Battles: Sport, Racism and Resistance*. Lanham, MD: Rowman & Littlefield, 2021.

Hall, Sydney O. "The Role of Physical Education and Sport in the Nation-building Process in Kenya." PhD diss., Ohio State University, 1973.

Halladay, Eric. *Rowing in England: A Social History: The Amateur Debate*. Manchester: Manchester University Press, 1990.

Hansen, Jacqueline. "The Women's Marathon Movement." *Marathon & Beyond* 16, no. 1 (January/February 2012): 1–17.

Hansen, Randall. "The Kenyan Asians, British Politics, and the Commonwealth Immigrants Act, 1968." *The Historical Journal* 42, no. 3 (1999): 809–34.

Hargreaves, Jennifer. *Heroines of Sport: The Politics of Difference and Identity*. London:

Routledge, 2000.

———. *Sporting Females: Critical Issues in the History and Sociology of Women's Sports.* London: Routledge, 1994.

Hartmann, Douglas. *Race, Culture, and the Revolt of the Black Athlete: The 1968 Olympic Protests and their Aftermath.* Chicago: University of Chicago Press, 2003.

Hauser, Thomas. *Muhammad Ali: His Life and Times.* New York: Simon & Schuster, 1991.

Henning, April, and Jörg Krieger. "Dropping the Amateur: The International Association of Athletics Federations and the Turn Towards Professionalism." *Sport History Review* 51, no. 1 (2020): 64–83.

Hennings, R. O. *African Morning.* London: Chatto and Windus, 1951.

Hill, Christopher. *Olympic Politics: Athens to Atlanta 1896–1996.* Manchester: Manchester University Press, 1996.

Hill, M. F. *Permanent Way: The Story of the Kenya and Uganda Railway*, 2nd ed. Nairobi: East African Railways and Harbours, 1961.

Hoberman, John. *Testosterone Dreams: Rejuvenation, Aphrodisia, Doping.* Berkeley: University of California Press, 2005.

Hobley, Charles W. "Anthropological Studies in Kavirondo and Nandi." *The Journal of the Anthropological Institute of Great Britain and Ireland* 33 (1903): 325–59.

———. "Notes on the Geography and People of the Baringo District of the East Africa Protectorate." *The Geographical Journal* 28, no. 5 (1906): 471–81.

Hobsbawm, Eric J. *Age of Empire, 1875–1914.* New York: Vintage Books, 1989.

———. *Industry and Empire: The Birth of the Industrial Revolution, from 1750 to the Present Day*, 2nd ed. London: Penguin Group, 1999.

Hodgson, Dorothy L. "Pastoralism, Patriarchy and History: Changing Gender Relations among Maasai in Tanganyika, 1890–1940." *The Journal of African History* 40, no. 1 (1999): 42.

Hodgson, Dorothy L., and Sheryl A. McCurdy, eds. *"Wicked" Women and the Reconfiguration of Gender in Africa.* Portsmouth, NH: Heinemann, 2001.

Hogshead-Makar, Nancy, and Andrew Zimbalist, eds. *Equal Play: Title IX and Social Change.* Philadelphia: Temple University Press, 2007.

———. "Staking a Claim: The First Decade: Introduction." In *Equal Play: Title IX and Social Change*, edited by Nancy Hogshead-Makar and Andrew Zimbalist, 49–55. Philadelphia: Temple University Press, 2007.

Hokkanen, Markku. "'Christ and the Imperial Games Fields' in South-Central Africa—Sport and the Scottish Missionaries in Malawi, 1880–1914: Utilitarian Compromise." *The International Journal of the History of Sport* 22, no. 4 (2005): 745–69.

Hollis, A. C. *The Nandi, their Language and Folk-lore.* Westport, CT: Negro Universities Press, 1971.

Holt, Richard. *Sport and the British: A Modern History*. Oxford: Oxford University Press, 1989.

Hornsby, Charles. *Kenya: A History Since Independence*. London: I.B. Tauris, 2012.

Huggins, Mike. *The Victorians and Sport*. London: Bloomsbury Academic, 2004.

Hughes, Thomas. *Tom Brown's School Days*. Oxford: Oxford University Press, 1999.

Hunt, Thomas M. *Drug Games: The International Olympic Committee and the Politics of Doping, 1960–2008*. Austin: University of Texas Press, 2011.

Hunter, Emma. *Political Thought and the Public Sphere in Tanzania: Freedom, Democracy and Citizenship in the Era of Decolonization*. New York: Cambridge University Press, 2015.

Huntingford, G. W. B. *The Nandi of Kenya: Tribal Control in a Pastoral Society*. London: Routledge & Kegan Paul, Ltd., 1953.

———. *Nandi Work and Culture*, Colonial Research Studies No. 4. London: HMSO, 1950.

Huntingford, G. W. B., and C. R. V. Bell. *East African Background*. London: Longmans, Green and Co., 1950.

International Amateur Athletic Federation. *IAAF: 80 Years for Athletics*. Monaco: IAAF, 1992.

Jackson, Victoria. "Title IX and the Big Time: Women's Intercollegiate Athletics at the University of North Carolina at Chapel Hill, 1950–1992." PhD diss., Arizona State University, 2015.

Jeffreys, Kevin. "Lord Burghley, *Chariots of Fire* and the Gentleman Amateur in British Athletics." *Sport in History* 33, no. 4 (2013), 445–64.

Jones, Bill. *The Ghost Runner: The Tragedy of the Man They Couldn't Stop, The True Story of John Tarrant*. Edinburgh: Mainstream Publishing Company, 2011.

Jones, Denise E. M. "In Pursuit of Empowerment: Sensei Nellie Kleinsmidt, Race and Gender Challenges." In *Freeing the Female Body: Inspirational Icons*, edited by James A. Mangan and Fan Hong, 219–36. London: Frank Cass, 2001.

———. "Women and Sport in South Africa: Shaped by History and Shaping Sporting History." In *Sport and Women: Social Issues in International Perspective*, edited by Ilse Hartmann-Tews and Gertrud Pfister, 130–44. London: Routledge, 2003.

Judah, Tim. *Bikila: Ethiopia's Barefoot Olympian*. London: Reportage Press, 2008.

Kanogo, Tabitha. *African Womanhood in Colonial Kenya: 1900–1950*. Oxford: James Currey, 2005.

Kenyatta, Jomo. *Facing Mount Kenya: The Tribal Life of the Gikuyu*. London: Mercury Books, Secker and Warburg, 1961.

Kettel, Bonnie. "The Commoditization of Women in Tugen (Kenya) Social Organization." In *Women and Class in Africa*, edited by Claire Robertson and Iris Berger, 45–61. New York, 1986.

Kidd, Bruce. "Another World Is Possible': Recapturing Alternative Olympic Histories, Imagining

Different Games." *Sport in Society* 16, no. 4 (2013): 503–14.

———. "Muscular Christianity and Value-Centred Sport: The Legacy of Tom Brown in Canada." *Sport in Society* 16, no. 4 (2013): 405–15.

Kiluva-Ndunda, Mutindi M. *Women's Agency and Educational Policy: The Experiences of the Women of Kilome, Kenya*. Albany: State University of New York Press, 2001.

King, Billie Jean, with Christine Brennan. *Pressure Is a Privilege: Lessons I've Learned from Life and the Battle of the Sexes*. New York: LifeTime Media, 2008.

King, Billie Jean, with Frank Deford. *Billie Jean*. New York: Viking Press, 1982.

King, Billie Jean, with Cynthia Starr. *We Have Come a Long Way: The Story of Women's Tennis*. New York: Regina Ryan, 1988.

Kipkorir, Benjamin E. *The Marakwet of Kenya: A Preliminary Study*. Nairobi: East African Literature Bureau, 1973.

Kipkorir, Benjamin E., and Joseph Ssennyonga. *A Socio-cultural Profile of Elgeyo-Marakwet District: A Report of the District Socio-Cultural Profiles Project*. Nairobi: Institute of African Studies and the University of Nairobi, 1984.

Kiprop, Joseph, and John Koskey Chang'ach. "A History of Kapsabet Girls' High School, Nandi County, Kenya, 1960–1979." *Asia Pacific Journal of Education, Arts and Sciences* 3, no. 1 (2016): 10–20.

Kirk-Greene, Anthony. "Imperial Administration and the Athletic Imperative: The Case of the District Officer in Africa." In *Sport in Africa: Essays in Social History*, edited by William Baker and James Mangan, 81–113. New York: Africana Publishing Company, 1987.

Kitching, Gavin N. *Class and Economic Change in Kenya: The Making of an African Petite-Bourgeoisie, 1905–1970*. New Haven, CT: Yale University Press, 1980.

Klein, Alan. *Sugarball: The American Game, the Dominican Dream*. New Haven, CT: Yale University Press, 2001.

Kovač, Uroš. *The Precarity of Masculinity: Football, Pentecostalism, and Transnational Aspirations in Cameroon*. New York: Berghahn Books, 2022.

Krieger, Jörg. *Power and Politics in World Athletics: A Critical History*. London: Routledge, 2021.

Krieger, Jörg, and April Henning. "Who Governs a Movement? The IAAF and Road-Running: Historical and Contemporary Considerations." *Journal of Sport History* 47, no. 1 (2020): 59–75.

Krieger, Jörg, Michele Krech, and Lindsay Parks Pieper. "'Our Sport': The Fight for Control of Women's International Athletics." *The International Journal of the History of Sport* 37, no. 5–6 (2020): 451–72.

Krige, Eileen J. "Woman-Marriage, with Special Reference to the Lovedu–its Significance for the Definition of Marriage." *Africa* 44, no. 1 (1974): 11–37.

Kyle, Keith. *The Politics of the Independence of Kenya*. New York: St. Martin's Press, 1999.

Lake, Robert. *A Social History of Tennis in Britain*. London: Routledge, 2014.

Lang'at, S. C. "Some Aspects of Kipsigis History before 1914." In *Ngano: Studies in Traditional and Modern East African History*, edited by Brian G. McIntosh, 73–94. Nairobi: East African Publishing House, 1969.

Langley, Myrtle S. *The Nandi of Kenya: Life Crisis Rituals in a Period of Change*. New York: St Martin's Press, 1979.

Lansbury, Jennifer H. *Spectacular Leap: Black Women Athletes in Twentieth-Century America*. Fayetteville: University of Arkansas Press, 2014.

Lapchick, Richard. *The Politics of Race and International Sport: The Case of South Africa*. Westport, CT: Greenwood Press, 1975.

Larsen, Henrik. "Kenyan Dominance in Distance Running." *Comparative Biochemistry and Physiology Part A: Molecular and Integrative Physiology* 136, no. 1 (2003): 161–70.

Lee, Jenny, and Thomas Opia. "Coming to America: Challenges and Difficulties Faced by African Student Athletes." *Sport, Education and Society* 16, no. 5 (2011): 629–44.

Leigh, Mary H., and Thérèse M. Bonin. "The Pioneering Role of Madame Alice Milliat and the FSFI in Establishing International Trade and Field Competition for Women." *Journal of Sport History* 4, no. 1 (1977): 72–83.

Lenskyj, Helen. *Out of Bounds: Women, Sport and Sexuality*. Toronto: Women's Press, 1986.

Leseth, Anne. "The Use of *Juju* in Football: Sports and Witchcraft in Tanzania." In *Entering the Field: New Perspectives on World Football*, edited by Gary Armstrong and Richard Giulianotti, 159–74. Oxford: Berg, 1997.

Levine, Peter. *Ellis Island to Ebbets Field: Sport and the American Jewish Experience*. New York: Oxford University Press, 1992.

Lewis, Joanna. *Empire State-Building: War and Welfare in Kenya, 1925–52*. Oxford: James Currey, 2000.

Liberti, Rita, and Mary G. McDonald. "Back on Track: Wyomia Tyus, Breaking Historical Silences, and the Sporting Activist Legacies of 1968." *The International Journal of the History of Sport* 36, no. 9–10 (2019): 796–811.

Liberti, Rita, and Maureen M. Smith. *(Re)presenting Wilma Rudolph*. Syracuse, NY: Syracuse University Press, 2015.

Llewellyn, Matthew P. "'The Best Distance Runner the World Has Ever Produced': Hannes Kolehmainen and the Modernisation of British Athletics." *The International Journal of the History of Sport* 29, no. 7 (2012): 1016–34.

———. *Rule Britannia: Nationalism, Identity and the Modern Olympic Games*. London: Routledge, 2012.

Llewellyn, Matthew P., and John Gleaves. *The Rise and Fall of Olympic Amateurism*. Urbana: University of Illinois Press, 2016.

Lonsdale, John. "Anti-colonial Nationalism and Patriotism in sub-Saharan Africa." In *The Oxford Handbook on the History of Nationalism*, edited by John Breuilly, 318–37. Oxford: Oxford University Press, 2013.

———. "The Conquest State of Kenya, 1895–1905." In *Unhappy Valley: Conflict in Kenya and Africa, Book One: State and Class*, edited by Bruce Berman and John Lonsdale, 13–44. Athens, OH: Ohio University Press, 1992.

———. "Moral Ethnicity and Political Tribalism." In *Inventions and Boundaries: Historical and Anthropological Approaches to the Study of Ethnicity and Nationalism*, edited by Preben Kaarsholm and Jan Hultin, 131–50. Denmark: Institute for Development Studies, Roskilde University, 1994.

———. "The Politics of Conquest: The British in Western Kenya, 1894–1908." In *Unhappy Valley: Conflict in Kenya and Africa, Book One: State and Class*, edited by Bruce Berman and John Lonsdale, 45–74. Athens, OH: Ohio University Press, 1992.

Lovesey, Peter. *The Official Centenary History of the Amateur Athletic Association*. Enfield, UK: Guinness Superlatives, 1979.

Lowerson, John. *Sport and the English Middle Classes 1870–1914*. Manchester: Manchester University Press, 1995.

Lukalo, Fibian. *Mothers and Schooling: Poverty, Gender and Educational Decision-Making in Rural Kenya*. London: Routledge, 2021.

Lunt, David, and Mark Dyreson. "The 1904 Olympic Games: Triumph or Nadir?" In *The Palgrave Handbook of Olympic Studies*, edited by Stephen Wagg and Helen Lenskyj, 44–59. London: Palgrave/Macmillan, 2012.

Lynch, Gabrielle. *I Say to You: Ethnic Politics and the Kalenjin in Kenya*. Chicago: Chicago University Press, 2007.

———. "Moi: The Making of an African 'Big-Man.'" *Journal of East African Studies* 2, no. 1 (2008): 18–43.

MacAloon, John J., ed. *Muscular Christianity and the Colonial and Post-Colonial Worlds*. London: Routledge, 2009.

Maggwa, Baker N., Japheth K. Mathi, Susan Mbugua, and David J. Hunter. "Validity of Contraceptive Histories in a Rural Community in Kenya." *International Journal of Epidemiology* 22, no. 4 (1993): 692–97.

Maloba, Wunyabari O. *Kenyatta and Britain: An Account of Political Transformation, 1929–1963*. Cham, Switzerland: Palgrave Macmillan, 2018.

Mamdani, Mahmood. *From Citizen to Refugee, Uganda Asians Come to Britain*. 2nd ed. Cape

Town: Pambazuka Press, 2011.

Mandle, Jay R., and Joan D. Mandle. *Grass Roots Commitment: Basketball and Society in Trinidad and Tobago.* Parkersburg, IA: Caribbean Books, 1988.

Mandle, William. "Games People Played: Cricket and Football in England and Victoria in the Late Nineteenth Century." *Historical Studies* 15, no. 60 (1973): 511–35.

Mangan, James A. *Athleticism in the Victorian and Edwardian Public Schools: The Emergence and Consolidation of an Educational Ideology.* Cambridge: Cambridge University Press, 1981.

———. "Britain's Chief Spiritual Export: Imperial Sport as Moral Metaphor, Political Symbol and Cultural Bond." *The International Journal of the History of Sport* 27, no. 1–2 (2010): 328–36.

———, ed. *The Cultural Bond: Sport, Empire, Society.* Abingdon: Routledge, 1992.

———. "Ethics and Ethnocentricity: Imperial Education in British Tropical Africa." In *Sport in Africa: Essays in Social History*, edited by William J. Baker and James A. Mangan, 138–71. New York: Africana Publishing Company, 1987.

———. *The Games Ethic and Imperialism: Aspects of the Diffusion of an Ideal.* New York: Viking, 1986.

Manners, John. "African Recruiting Boom." In *The African Running Revolution*, edited by Dave Prokop, 62–69. Mountain View, CA: World Publications, 1975.

———. "In Search of an Explanation." *The African Running Revolution*, edited by Dave Prokop, 26–39. Mountain View, CA: World Publications, 1975.

———. "Kenya's Running Tribe." *The Sports Historian* 17, no. 2 (1997): 14–27.

———. "Raiders from the Rift Valley: Cattle Raiding and Distance Running in East Africa." In *East African Running: Towards a Cross-Disciplinary Perspective*, edited by Yannis Pitsiladis, John Bale, Craig Sharp, and Tim Noakes, 40–50. Abingdon, UK: Routledge, 2007.

Maraniss, David. *Rome 1960: The Olympics that Changed the World.* New York: Simon & Schuster, 2008.

Marqusee, Mike. *Redemption Song: Muhammad Ali and the Spirit of the Sixties.* 2nd ed. London: Verso Books, 2005.

Martin, Phyllis M. *Leisure and Society in Colonial Brazzaville.* Cambridge: Cambridge University Press, 1995.

Mason, Courtney. "The Bridge to Change: The 1976 Montreal Olympic Games, South African Apartheid Policy, and the Olympic Boycott Paradigm." In *Onward to the Olympics: Historical Perspectives on the Olympic Games*, edited by Gerald P. Schaus and Stephen R. Wenn, 283–96. Waterloo, Ontario: Wilfrid Laurier University Press, 2007.

Mason, Tony. *Association Football and English Society, 1863–1915.* Brighton, UK: Branch Line, 1982.

Massam, J. A. *The Cliff Dwellers of Kenya*. London: Seeley, Service & Co. Limited, 1927.

Massao, Prisca, and Kari Fasting. "Women and Sport in Tanzania." In *Sport and Women: Social Issues in International Perspective*, edited by Ilse Hartmann-Tews and Gertrud Pfister, 124–25. London: Routledge, 2003.

Matson, A. T. *Nandi Resistance to British Rule, 1890–1906*. Nairobi: East African Publishing House, 1972.

———. "Nandi Traditions on Raiding." In *Hadith* 2, edited by Bethwell A. Ogot, 61–78. Nairobi: East African Publishing House, 1970.

Maxon, Robert. *Struggle for Kenya: The Loss and Reassertion of Imperial Initiative, 1912–1923*. Rutherford, NJ: Farleigh Dickinson University Press, 1993.

Mboya, Tom. *Freedom and After*. Nairobi: East African Educational Publishers Ltd., 1986.

Mbugua, Ng'ang'a. *Catherine Ndereba: The Marathon Queen*. Nairobi: Sasa Sema Publications, 2008.

McCrone, Kathleen. *Playing the Game: Sport and the Physical Emancipation of English Women, 1870–1914*. London: Routledge, 1988.

Médard, Jean-François. "Charles Njonjo: The Portrait of a 'Big Man' in Kenya." In *Neopatrimonialism in Africa and Beyond*, edited by Daniel C. Bach and Mamoudou Gazibo, 58–78. Abingdon, UK: Routledge, 2012.

Meier, Marianne, and Martha Saavedra. "Esther Phiri and the Moutawakel Effect in Zambia: An Analysis of the Use of Female Role Models in Sport-for-Development." *Sport in Society* 12, no. 9 (2009): 1158–76.

Merrett, Christopher. "Perpetual Outsiders: Women in Athletics and Road Running in South Africa." In *Routledge Handbook of Sport, Gender and Sexuality*, edited by Jennifer Hargreaves and Eric Anderson, 139–48. London: Routledge, 2014.

———. "Race, Gender and Political Dissent in the Comrades Marathon, 1921–1981." *South African Historical Journal* 59, no. 1 (2007): 242–60.

Mitchell, Sheila. "Women's Participation in the Olympic Games, 1900–1926." *Journal of Sport History* 4, no. 2 (1977): 208–28.

Moore, Henrietta L. *Space, Text and Gender: An Anthropological Study of the Marakwet of Kenya*. Cambridge: Cambridge University Press, 1986.

Moore, Kenny. "The Campaign for Athletes' Rights." *Annals of the American Academy of Political and Social Science* 445 (1979): 59–65.

Moore, Louis. *I Fight for a Living: Boxing and the Battle for Black Manhood, 1880–1915*. Urbana: University of Illinois Press, 2007.

Moskowitz, Kara. "From Multiracialism to Africanization? Race, Politics, and Sport in Decolonizing Kenya." *Journal of Contemporary History* 58, no. 1 (2022): 115–35.

———. *Seeing Like a Citizen: Decolonization, Development, and the Making of Kenya, 1945–1980*. Athens: Ohio University Press, 2019.

Muller, Maria S. "The National Policy of Kenyanisation of Trade: Its Impact on a Town in Kenya." *Canadian Journal of African Studies / Revue Canadienne des Études Africaines* 15, no. 2 (1981): 293–301.

Murphy, Frank. *The Silence of Great Distance: Women Running Long*. Kansas City: Windsprint Press, 2000.

Musandu, Phoebe. "Drawing from the Wells of Culture: Grace Onyango and the Kenyan Political Scene (1964–1983)." *Wagadu 6: Journal of International Women's Studies* 10, no. 1 (2009): 108–24.

Mutongi, Kenda. *Worries of the Heart: Widows, Family, and Community in Kenya*. Chicago: University of Chicago Press, 2007.

Mwanzi, Henry A. *A History of the Kipsigis*. Nairobi: East African Literature Bureau, 1977.

Nauright, John. "Masculinity, Muscular Islam and Popular Culture: 'Coloured' Rugby Cultural Symbolism in Working-Class Cape Town c. 1930–70." *The International Journal of the History of Sport* 14, no. 1 (1997): 184–90.

Ndee, Hamad. "Western Influences on Sport in Tanzania: British Middle-Class Educationalists, Missionaries and the Diffusion of Adapted Athleticism." *International Journal of the History of Sport* 27, no. 5 (2010): 905–36.

Ndoo, Philip. "The Kenyan Success." In *The African Running Revolution*, edited by Dave Prokop, 49–57. Mountain View, CA: World Publishers, 1975.

Ng'weno, Bettina, and L Obura Aloo. "Irony of Citizenship: Descent, National Belonging, and Constitutions in the Postcolonial African State." *Law & Society Review* 53, no. 1 (2019): 141–72.

Njambi, Wairimũ Ngarũiya, and William E. O'Brien. "Revisiting 'Woman-Woman Marriage': Notes on Gĩkũyũ Women." *NWSA Journal* 12, no. 1 (2000): 1–23.

Nicolas, Claire. "From Handball Courts to Ministries: The Cousins of Côte d'Ivoire." In *Histories of Women's Work in Global Sport: A Man's World?*, edited by Georgia Cervin and Claire Nicolas, 217–44. Cham, Switzerland: Palgrave Macmillan, 2019.

Nishimura, Mikiko, and Takashi Yamano. "Emerging Private Education in Africa: Determinants of School Choice in Rural Kenya." *World Development* 43 (2013): 266–75.

Njororai, Wycliffe W. Simiyu. "Colonial Legacy, Minorities and Association Football in Kenya." *Soccer & Society* 10, no. 6 (2009): 866–82.

———. "Global Inequality and Athlete Labour Migration from Kenya." *Leisure/Loisir* 34, no. 4 (2010): 443–61.

———. "Players of African Descent Representing European National Football Teams: A

Double-edged Sword." *Soccer & Society* 22, no. 4 (2021): 411–28.

Noronha, Francis. *Kipchoge of Kenya.* Nakuru, Kenya: Elimu Publishers, 1970.

Nteere, Jacob S. "A Comparative Assessment of the Central Organizations for Amateur Sport in England and Kenya." PhD diss., University of Manchester, 1990.

O'Brien, Denise. "Female Husbands in Southern Bantu Societies." In *Sexual Stratification: A Cross-cultural View*, edited by Alice Schlegal, 109–26. New York: Columbia University Press, 1977.

Obbo, Christine. "Dominant Male Ideology and Female Options: Three East African Case Studies." *Africa* 46, no. 4 (1976): 371–89.

Oboler, Regina S. "Is the Female Husband a Man? Woman/Woman Marriage among the Nandi of Kenya." *Ethnology* 19, no. 1 (1980): 69–88.

———. *Women, Power, and Economic Change: The Nandi of Kenya.* Stanford: Stanford University Press, 1985.

Ocobock, Paul. *An Uncertain Age: The Politics of Manhood in Kenya.* Athens: Ohio University Press, 2017.

Odendaal, André. "'Neither Cricketers nor Ladies': Towards a History of Women and Cricket in South Africa, 1860s–2000s." *The International Journal of the History of Sport* 28, no. 1 (2011): 115–36.

———. "South Africa's Black Victorians: Sport and Society in South Africa in the Nineteenth Century." In *Pleasure, Profit, Proselytism: British Culture and Sport at Home and Abroad 1700–1914*, edited by James A. Mangan, 193–214. London: Frank Cass, 1988.

———. *The Story of an African Game: Black Cricketers and the Unmasking of One of Cricket's Greatest Myths, South Africa, 1850–2003.* Cape Town, South Africa: David Philip, 2003.

Odhiambo, E. S. Atieno, *Jaramogi Ajuma Oginga Odinga: A Biography.* Nairobi: East African Educational Publishers, 1997.

Odhiambo, E. S. Atieno, and John Lonsdale, eds. *Mau Mau and Nationhood: Arms, Authority and Narration.* Oxford: James Currey, 2003.

Odhiambo, Tom. "The Black Female Body as a 'Consumer and a Consumable' in Current *Drum* and *True Love* Magazines in South Africa." *African Studies* 67, no. 1 (2008): 71–80.

Odinga, Oginga. *Not Yet Uhuru: The Autobiography of Oginga Odinga.* London: Heinemann, 1967.

Ogonda, R. T. "Transport and Communications in the Colonial Economy." In *An Economic History of Kenya*, edited by William R. Ochieng' and Robert M. Maxon, 129–47. Nairobi: East African Educational Publishers, 1992.

Ogot, Bethwell A., and William R. Ochieng', eds. *Decolonization and Independence in Kenya, 1940–93.* London: James Currey, 1995.

Onwumechili, Chuka, ed. *Africa's Elite Football: Structure, Politics, and Everyday Challenges.* New York: Routledge, 2020.

Onywera, Vincent, Robert A. Scott, Michael K. Boit, and Yannis P. Pitsiladis. "Demographic Characteristics of Elite Kenyan Endurance Runners." *Journal of Sports Sciences* 24, no. 4 (2006): 415–22.

Orchardson, Ian Q. *The Kipsigis* [original manuscript of 1929–1937 abridged, edited and partially re-written posthumously by A. T. Matson]. Kampala: East African Literature Bureau, 1961.

———. "Some Traits of the Kipsigis in Relation to their Contact with Europeans." *Africa* 4, no. 4 (1931): 466–74.

Oruka, Odera H. *Oginga Odinga: His Philosophy and Beliefs.* Nairobi: Initiatives Publishers, 1992.

Osborne, Myles. *Ethnicity and Empire in Kenya: Loyalty and Martial Race among the Kamba, c. 1800 to the Present.* New York: Cambridge University Press, 2014.

Owen, Caleb E. "Lands of Leisure: Recreation, Space, and the Struggle for Urban Kenya, 1900–2000." PhD diss., Michigan State University, 2016.

Parpart, Jane L., and Kathleen A. Staudt, eds. *Women and the State in Africa.* Boulder, CO: Reinner, 1989.

Parsons, Timothy H. *The African Rank and File: Social Implications of Colonial Military Service in the King's African Rifles, 1902–1964.* Portsmouth: Heinemann, 1999.

———. "No More English than the Postal System: The Kenya Boy Scout Movement and the Transfer of Power." *Africa Today* 51, no. 3 (2005): 61–80.

Pelak, Cynthia F. "Local-Global Processes: Linking Globalization, Democratization, and the Development of Women's Football in South Africa." *Afrika Spectrum* 41, no. 3 (2006): 371–92.

———. "Negotiating Gender/Race/Class Constraints in the New South Africa: A Case Study of Women's Soccer." *International Review for the Sociology of Sport* 40, no. 1 (2005): 53–70.

———. "Women and Gender in South Africa Soccer: A Brief History." *Soccer and Society* 11, no. 2 (2010): 63–78.

Peristiany, John G. *The Social Institutions of the Kipsigis.* New York: Humanities Press, 1964.

Peterson, Derek R. *Ethnic Patriotism and the East African Revival: A History of Dissent, c. 1935–1972.* Cambridge: Cambridge University Press, 2012.

Pieper, Lindsay Parks. *Sex Testing: Gender Policing in Women's Sports.* Urbana: University of Illinois Press, 2016.

Plymire, Darcy C. "Positive Addiction: Running and Human Potential in the 1970s." *Journal of Sport History* 31, no. 3 (2004): 297–315.

Polley, Martin. "'The Amateur Rules': Amateurism and Professionalism in Post-War British Athletics." In *Amateurs and Professionals in Post-War British Sport*, edited by Adrian Smith and Dilwyn Porter, 81–114. London: Frank Cass, 2000.

Presley, Cora Ann. *Kikuyu Women, the Mau Mau Rebellion, and Social Change in Kenya*. Abingdon, UK: Routledge, 2018.

Prokop, Dave, ed. *The African Running Revolution*. Mountain View, CA: Runner's World Magazine, 1975.

Putney, Clifford. *Muscular Christianity: Manhood and Sports in Protestant America, 1880–1920*. Cambridge, MA: Harvard University Press, 2003.

Rambali, Paul. *Barefoot Runner: The Life of Marathon Champion Abebe Bikila*. London: Serpent's Tail, 2006.

Ranger, Terence. "Pugilism and Pathology: African Boxing and the Black Urban Experience in Southern Rhodesia." In *Sport in Africa: Essays in Social History*, edited by William J. Baker and James A. Mangan, 196–213. New York: Africana Publishing Company, 1987.

Reid, Richard. "Past and Presentism: The 'Precolonial' and the Foreshortening of African History." *The Journal of African History* 52, no. 2 (2011): 135–55.

Remnick, David. *King of the World: Muhammad Ali and the Rise of an American Hero*. New York: Random House, 1998.

Roberts, Bruce. "Livestock Production, Age and Gender Among the Keiyo of Kenya." *Human Ecology* 24, no. 2 (1996): 215–30.

Roberts, Selena. *A Necessary Spectacle: Billie Jean King, Bobby Riggs, and the Tennis Match that Leveled the Game*. New York: Crown Publishers, 2005.

Robertson, Claire C. *Trouble Showed the Way: Women, Men, and Trade in the Nairobi Area, 1890–1990*. Bloomington: Indiana University Press, 1997.

Robinson, Lynne. "'Tripping Daintily into the Arena': A Social History of English Women's Athletics 1921–1960." PhD diss., University of Warwick, 1996.

Robinson, Roger. *When Running Made History*. Syracuse, NY: Syracuse University Press, 2018.

Rosbrook-Thompson, James, and Gary Armstrong. "Fields and Visions: The 'African Personality' and Ghanaian Soccer." *Du Bois Review* 7, no. 2 (2010): 293–314.

Rosen, Ruth. *The World Split Open: How the Modern Women's Movement Changed America*. New York: Viking, 2000.

Roth, Benita. *Separate Roads to Feminism: Black, Chicana, and White Feminist Movements in America's Second Wave*. Cambridge: Cambridge University Press, 2004.

Rothchild, Donald. "Kenya's Africanization Program: Priorities of Development and Equity." *American Political Science Review* 64, no. 3 (1970): 737–53.

Rubin, Joshua D. *Animated by Uncertainty: Rugby and the Performance of History in South*

Africa. Ann Arbor: University of Michigan Press, 2021.

Rubin, Ron. *Anything for a T-Shirt: Fred Lebow and the New York City Marathon, the World's Greatest Footrace*. Syracuse, NY: Syracuse University Press, 2004.

Saavedra, Martha. "Football Feminine—Development of the African Game: Senegal, Nigeria and South Africa." *Soccer and Society* 4, no. 2–3 (2003): 225–53.

———. "Sport." In *A Companion to Gender Studies*, edited by Philomena Essed, Audrey Kobayashi, and David Theo Goldberg, 437–54. London: Blackwell Publishing, 2005.

Saltin, Bengt, H. Larsen, N. Terrados, J. Bangsbo, T. Bak, C. K. Kim, J. Svedenhag, and C. J. Rolf. "Aerobic Exercise Capacity at Sea Level and at Altitude in Kenyan Boys, Junior and Senior Runners Compared with Scandinavian Runners." *Scandinavian Journal of Medical Science and Sports* 5, no. 4 (1995): 209–21.

Sarantakes, Nicholas. *Dropping the Torch: Jimmy Carter, the Olympic Boycott, and the Cold War*. New York: Cambridge University Press, 2011.

Schmidt, Nancy J. "Jack H. Driberg: A Humanistic Anthropologist before His Time." *Anthropologica* 31, no. 2 (1989): 179–94.

Schultz, Jaime. "Breaking into the Marathon: Women's Distance Running as Political Activism." *Frontiers: A Journal of Women Studies* 40, no. 2 (2019): 1–26.

———. "Going the Distance: The Road to the 1984 Olympic Women's Marathon." *The International Journal of the History of Sport* 32, no. 1 (2015): 72–88.

———. *Qualifying Times: Points of Change in U.S. Women's Sport*. Urbana: University of Illinois Press, 2014.

———. "The Physical Activism of Billie Jean King." In *Myths and Milestones in the History of Sport*, edited by Stephen Wagg, 203–23. London: Palgrave Macmillan, 2011.

———. *Women's Sports: What Everyone Needs to Know*. Oxford: Oxford University Press, 2018.

Scott, Robert, and Yannis P. Pitsiladis. "Genotypes and Distance Running: Clues from Africa." *Sports Medicine* 37, no. 4–5 (2007): 424–27.

Semley, Lorelle. "When We Discovered Gender: A Retrospective on Ifi Amadiume's Male Daughters, Female Husbands: Gender and Sex in an African Society." *Journal of West African History* 3, no. 2 (2017): 117–23.

Senn, Alfred. *Power, Politics and the Olympic Games: A History of the Powerbrokers, Events, and Controversies that Shaped the Games*. Champaign, IL: Human Kinetics, 1999.

Shadle, Brett L. *"Girl Cases": Marriage and Colonialism in Gusiiland, Kenya, 1890–1970*. Portsmouth, NH: Heinemann, 2006.

———. *The Souls of White Folk: White Settlers in Kenya, 1900s–1920s*. Manchester: Manchester University Press, 2015.

Sharp, Craig, and John Bale. "Introduction." In *East African Running: Toward a*

Cross-Disciplinary Perspective, edited by Yannis Pitsiladis, John Bale, Craig Sharp, and Tim Noakes, 1–8. Abingdon, UK: Routledge, 2007.

Sheffield, James R. *Education in Kenya: An Historical Study*. New York: Teachers College Press, 1973.

Sheldon, Kathleen. *African Women: Early History to the 21st Century*. Bloomington: Indiana University Press, 2017.

Shetler, Jan Bender. *Claiming Civic Virtue: Gendered Network Memory in the Mara Region, Tanzania*. Madison: University of Wisconsin Press, 2019.

Sifuna, Daniel N. "Increasing Access and Participation of Pastoralist Communities in Primary Education in Kenya." *International Review of Education* 51, no. 5–6 (2005): 499–516.

Sikes, Michelle M. "The Enemy of My Enemy Is My Friend? A Clash of Anti-Apartheid Tactics and Targets in the Olympic Movement of the Early 1960s." *The International Journal of the History of Sport* 37, no. 7 (2020): 520–41.

———. "From Nairobi to Baden-Baden: African Politics, the International Olympic Committee, and Early Efforts to Censure Apartheid South Africa." *The International Journal of the History of Sport* 36, no. 1 (2019): 7–23.

———. "Ousting South Africa: Olympic Clashes of 1968." *Acta Academica* 50, no. 2 (2018): 12–33.

———. "'Rebel' on the Run: Kenyan Gambles on Intercollegiate Athletics, Apartheid Sport, and US Road Racing of the 1980s—The Case of Samson Obwocha." *The International Journal of the History of Sport* 39, no. 8–9 (2022): 959–86.

———. "Running for Peace and Development in Kenya's Rift Valley." *Peace Review* 32, no. 4 (2020): 480–87.

———. "Sprinting Past the End of Empire: Seraphino Antao and the Promise of Sport in Kenya, 1960–63." In *Sports in Africa: Past and Present*, edited by Todd Cleveland, Tarminder Kaur, and Gerard Akindes, 219–32. Athens: Ohio University Press, 2020.

Sikes, Michelle M., and Jacob J. Fredericks. "'It's a Policy Matter, Not a Racial Matter': Athlete Activism and Symbiotic Struggles against Apartheid in US Track and Field of the Early 1970s." *The International Journal of the History of Sport* 39, no. 8–9 (2022): 938–58.

Sikes, Michelle M., Toby C. Rider, and Matthew P. Llewellyn, eds. *Sport and Apartheid South Africa: Histories of Politics, Power and Protest*. London: Routledge, 2022.

Skillen, Fiona. *Women, Sport and Modernity in Interwar Britain*. Oxford: Peter Lang, 2013.

Smith, Maureen M. "Revisiting South Africa and the Olympic Movement: The Correspondence of Reginald S. Alexander and the International Olympic Committee, 1961–86." *The International Journal of the History of Sport* 23, no. 7 (2006): 1193–216.

———. *Wilma Rudolph: A Biography*. Westport, CT: Greenwood Press, 2006.

Smith, Ronald A. *The Myth of the Amateur: A History of College Athletic Scholarships*. Austin: University of Texas Press, 2021.

Sorrenson, Maurice P. K. *Origins of European Settlement in Kenya*. Oxford: Oxford University Press, 1968.

Stevenson, John. *British Society, 1914–1945*. Harmondsworth: Penguin Books, 1984.

Stidwill, Howard F. "Motives Toward Track and Field Competition of Foreign and Domestic Grant-in-Aid Student-Athletes in NCAA Division I Colleges and Universities." PhD diss., Oregon State University, 1984.

Stimpson, Catharine R. "Dereliction, Due Process, and Decorum: The Crises of Title IX." *Signs* 47, no. 2 (2022): 261–93.

Stoddart, Brian. "Sport, Cultural Imperialism and Colonial Response in the British Empire." *Sport in Society* 9, no. 5 (2006): 809–35.

Suggs, Welch. *A Place on the Team: The Triumph and Tragedy of Title IX*. Princeton: Princeton University Press, 2005.

Sutton, J. E. G. "Denying History in Colonial Kenya: The Anthropology and Archeology of G. W. B. Huntingford and L. S. B. Leakey." *History in Africa* 33 (2006): 287–320.

Switzer, Kathrine. *Marathon Woman: Running the Race to Revolutionize Women's Sports*. New York: Carroll & Graf, 2007.

Tanser, Toby. *More Fire: How to Run the Kenyan Way*. Yardley, PA: Westholme Publishing, 2008.

———. *Train Hard, Win Easy: The Kenyan Way*, 2nd ed. Mountain View, CA: Tafnews Press, 2001.

Terret, Thierry. "From Alice Milliat to Marie-Thérèse Eyquem: Revisiting Women's Sport in France (1920s–1960s)." *The International Journal of the History of Sport* 27, no. 7 (2010): 1154–72.

Thomas, Damion. *Globetrotting: African American Athletes and Cold War Politics*. Urbana: University of Illinois Press, 2012.

Thomas, Lynn M. *Politics of the Womb: Women, Reproduction, and the State in Kenya*. Berkeley: University of California Press, 2003.

Thomson, Norman, and Jepkorir Rose Chepyator-Thomson. "Keiyo Cattle Raiding, Kechui Mathematics and Science Education: What Do They Have in Common?" *Interchange* 33, no. 1 (2002): 49–83.

Tricard, Louise Mead. *American Women's Track and Field, 1981–2000: A History*. Jefferson, NC: McFarland & Company, Inc., 2008.

Tripp, Aili Mari, Isabel Casimiro, Joy Kwesiga, and Alice Mungwa. *African Women's Movements: Transforming Political Landscapes*. New York: Cambridge University Press, 2009.

Tsikata, Dzodzi. *Lip-Service and Peanuts: The State and National Machinery for Women in Africa*.

Accra, Ghana: Third World Network-Africa, 2000.

Tucker, Ross, Vincent Onywera, and Jordan Santos-Concejero. "Analysis of the Kenyan Distance Running Phenomenon." *International Journal of Sports Physiology Performance* 10, no. 3 (2014): 285–91.

Turrini, Joseph. *The End of Amateurism in American Track and Field.* Urbana: University of Illinois Press, 2010.

———. "'It Was Communism Versus the Free World': The USA-USSR Dual Track Meet Series and the Development of Track and Field in the United States, 1958–1985." *Journal of Sport History* 28, no. 3 (2001): 427–71.

Tygiel, Jules. *Baseball's Great Experiment: Jackie Robinson and His Legacy.* New York: Oxford University Press, 1983.

Tyus, Wyomia, and Elizabeth Terzakis. *Tigerbelle: The Wyomia Tyus Story.* Brooklyn, NY: Akashic Books, 2018.

Vaios Gitersos, Terry. "The Sporting Scramble for Africa: GANEFO, the IOC and the 1965 African Games." *Sport in Society* 14, no. 5 (2011): 645–59.

Vamplew, Wray. "Playing with the Rules: Influences on the Development of Regulation in Sport." *The International Journal of the History of Sport* 24, no. 7 (2007): 843–71.

Verbrugge, Martha H. *Active Bodies: A History of Women's Physical Education in Twentieth-Century America.* New York: Oxford University Press, 2012.

Vertinsky, Patricia A. *The Eternally Wounded Woman: Woman, Doctors, and Exercise in the Late Nineteenth Century.* Manchester: Manchester University Press, 1990.

Vidacs, Bea. "Through the Prism of Sports: Why Should Africanists Study Sports?" *Afrika Spectrum* 41, no. 3 (2006): 331–49.

Vinnai, Volker. "The Creation of an African Civil Service in Kenya." *Verfassung und Recht in Übersee / Law and Politics in Africa, Asia and Latin America* 7, no. 2 (1974): 175–88.

Wacquant, Loïc. *Body & Soul: Notebooks of an Apprentice Boxer.* Oxford: Oxford University Press, 2006.

Waliaula, Solomon. "Envisioning and Visualizing English Football in East Africa: The Case of a Kenyan Radio Football Commentator." *Soccer & Society* 13, no. 2 (2012): 239–49.

Waliaula, Solomon, and Joseph Basil Okong'o. "Performing Luo Identity in Kenya: Songs of Gor Mahia." In *Identity and Nation in African Football Fans, Community, and Clubs,* edited by Chuka Onwumechili and Gerard Akindes, 83–98. London: Palgrave Macmillan, 2014.

Waller, Richard. "Pastoral Production in Colonial Kenya: Lessons from the Past?" *African Studies Review* 55, no. 2 (2012): 1–27.

Walton, Theresa. "Steve Prefontaine: From Rebel with a Cause to Hero with a Swoosh." *Sociology of Sport Journal* 21, no. 1 (2004): 61–83.

Ware, Susan. *Game, Set Match: Billie Jean King and the Revolution in Women's Sports.* Chapel Hill: University of North Carolina Press, 2011.

———. *Title IX: A Brief History with Documents.* Boston: Bedford/St. Martin's, 2007.

Weitzberg, Keren. *We Do Not Have Borders: Greater Somalia and the Predicaments of Belonging in Kenya.* Athens: Ohio University Press, 2017.

Welbourn, F. B. "Keyo Initiation." *Journal of Religion in Africa* 3, no. 2 (1968): 212–32.

White, Luise. *The Comforts of Home: Prostitution in Colonial Nairobi.* Chicago: University of Chicago Press, 1990.

Williams, Beth Ann. "'Call Us Ms.': *Viva* and Arguments for Kenyan Women's Respectable Citizenship 1975–80." *Women's History Review* 26, no. 3 (2017): 414–32.

Willis, Roderick. "A Historical Narrative of High School Athletics Amongst 'Coloured' Communities in Cape Town, South Africa, with Special Reference to the Western Province Senior Schools Sports Union, 1956–1972." *The International Journal of the History of Sport* 39, no. 2 (2022): 174–92.

Wilson, Wayne. "Wilma Rudolph: The Making of an Olympic Icon." In *Out of the Shadows: A Biographical History of African American Athletes,* edited by David K. Wiggins, 207–22. Fayetteville: University of Arkansas Press, 2006.

Witherspoon, Kevin B. *Before the Eyes of the World: Mexico and the 1968 Olympics.* DeKalb, IL: Northern Illinois University Press, 2008.

———. "'An Outstanding Representative of America:' Mal Whitfield and America's Black Sports Ambassadors in Africa." In *Defending the American Way of Life: Sport, Culture, and the Cold War,* edited by Toby C. Rider and Kevin B. Witherspoon, 129–40. Fayetteville: University of Arkansas Press, 2018.

World Bank. *Kenya: The Role of Women in Economic Development: A World Bank Country Study.* Washington, DC: World Bank, 1989.

Wushanley, Ying. *Playing Nice and Losing: The Struggle for Control of Women's Intercollegiate Athletics, 1960–2000.* Syracuse: Syracuse University Press, 2004.

Yamada, Shoko. "'Traditions' and Cultural Production: Character Training at the Achimota School in Colonial Ghana." *History of Education* 38, no. 1 (2009): 29–59.

Index